A HISTORY OF CHESS

JERZY GIŻYCKI

A HISTORY
OF CHESS

 **THE ABBEY LIBRARY, LONDON**

Original title Z SZACHAMI PRZEZ WIEKI I KRAJE
Copyright by "Sport i Turystyka" Warszawa
Chapter "Chess in Britain" by B. H. Wood
Translated from Polish by A. Wojciechowski, D. Ronowicz, W. Bartoszewski
Graphic design by T. Kowalski

First published in 1960 in Polish by
"Sport i Turystyka"

English text edited by B. H. Wood

I. S. B. N. 07196 0086 3

CONTENTS

I. A LITTLE HISTORY

The Polish "Wczele" coat of arms, dating back to the days of King Bolesław Krzywousty (12th century) has two chessboards and its genealogy can be traced back to a story connected with a game of chess.

10

Chess! Everybody has heard of this ancient game. How old is it? Does anybody know precisely? Archaeology and the study of ancient documents have brought to light many evidences of, and references to, chess as well as related games, but no definite date of origin has been established.

As far as can be ascertained, the game dates back to the middle of the sixth century. H.J.R. Murray, the eminent British orientalist and author of the classic History of Chess (1913), stated categorically that it originated in India about A.D. 570. (Later he became less categoric, conceding that the absence of earlier references to the game was only inferential indication of its non-existence — B.H. Wood). By chess we mean, of course, a game basically that of today. Many vaguely similar board games can be traced back much earlier. These games were based on other principles. Therefore, we should accept the year 570 as certain and at least proved, since proof can be found for it in ancient literature and history. Chess is mentioned in a Persian poem of the year 600 in which it is said to have come from India. A book in Persian of 650–750 describes its introduction into Persia during the reign of Chosroes I Anuschirvan (531–579). Chess terminology, the names of the pieces and the rules were described in considerable detail.

To support his date, Murray argues that there is no mention of chess earlier than 570. For instance, in 399–414 a Chinese traveller, Fa-Hien, wrote about India in detail without mentioning chess although he described various games and pastimes. Besides, we should remember that between 450 and 550 India was ruined by invading Huns who were only routed by Chosroes I.

The Persian poet Firdausi, living at the turn of the 10th century, often refers to chess. In one of his poems, he tells of the arrival of envoys of an Indian rajah at the Court of the Persian Shah Chosroes I bringing gifts which included a game depicting a battle of two armies.

Chess began to spread around the world when Persia was conquered by the Arabs.

Can the origin of chess be pushed further back?

Some historians maintain that a similar game was played in India as early as the 15th century B.C. and that the story about the chessboard and the grains of wheat or rice (see Chapter III), originated about 1000 B.C. The story based on the power of a geometrical progression to produce numbers of astronomical size could be based on any similar board: there is no necessary connection with chess.

Discoveries in Egypt, Iraq and India have from time to time given rise to rumours that chess was played 3000 years ago but these rumours have always proved to be without substance.

In the Archaeological Museum at Odessa there is a big photographic copy of a fresco of the 1st century A.D. from a Black Sea town. It shows figures of warriors on horseback and a large two-coloured chessboard. It is not known whether this depicts some game, or a military array.

Fanciful legends have been numerous. The game, said one, was devised by Palamedes, the Greek king, when he and his warriors became bored during the protracted siege of Troy. The Greeks did not seem to take to the game, and never played it until they re-learnt it from the Arabs centuries later. Chess in its origin in India was a four-sided game, its name *chaturanga* or *chatrang* being derived from the Indian word for "four." Though it has been established beyond doubt that there were four sets of pieces, theories of the origin of chess have been advanced quite recently which completely ignore the fact.

One eccentric, F. Villot, presented in Paris in 1825 a tract on the astronomical and cabalistic sources of the game of chess claiming that it had been invented by Egyptian priests. Magical set-ups of numbers and pieces on the chessboard were linked with astrological symbols of the Egyptian calendar.

It was not until 1951 that the Yugoslav scholar Professor Pavel Bidev presented an interesting

Ivory chessmen made in India in the 18th century after the style of ancient Hindu sets.

and diversely founded thesis tracing connections between chatrang and ideas of the mystics; these mystics were Indian, not Egyptian. The game was meant to illustrate the four elements: earth, air, fire and water, or the four seasons, or the four "humours" of man. Chatrang itself might be an allegory of the universe. The movements of the pieces on the board trace the outlines of geometrical symbols of various elements, taken from religious rituals: the queen was a symbol of fire or a triangle; the rook of earth or a square; the bishop of air or a six-pointed star; and the knight of water or a section of a circle. The king was the paramount symbol: ether or full circle. This theory of the genealogy of chatrang may possibly set its date of origin further back, but a lot more evidence is needed.

Chess was brought to the West, suffering slight changes on the way, by the Arabs. Migrating to the east, it took on other forms, the Korean, Burmese, Chinese and Japanese varieties all differing. Despite varying names, we are undoubtedly dealing with essentially the same game: the aim is uniformly to mate the principal enemy piece, and the moves of the men are similar.

Chinese historians do not fully accept the thesis of birth in India. They maintain that possibly Chinese and Indian chess originated from some common ancestor, so far unrevealed. That the earliest mention of chess in Chinese literature known so far, dates from the 8th century A. D. supports the theory of an Indian origin. It is hard to determine indisputably whether Chinese chess originated from India or *vice versa;* there are many legends in both countries, crediting the invention of the game to various mythical heroic figures and but few real people. It can, at any rate, quite safely be stated that chess was known in both countries by the 8th century.

The Soviet journalist G. Rokhlin wrote: "There is no doubt that chess was not invented by one man but is a result of collective, popular creation." Another Soviet author, B. Vainshtein,

Burmese chessmen in that country's traditional style. From the Pitt-Rivers collection.

extended this thought saying: "In its present form, chess is a result of popular creation, and not of one but of many nations." (H. J. R. Murray definitely thought otherwise; that it was probably substantially the invention of one man — B. H. Wood).

In tracing the history of chess much assistance has been furnished by philologists.

The Polish orientalist F. Machalski wrote: "... The origin (of chess) is Indian without doubt. In the Persian literature of the Sassanid period (A.D. 242–651) there was a work written in the Pahlavi language (Middle Persian) entitled Chatrang namakwor, A Manual of Chess. The word chatrang (in New Persian at first shatranj, and shatranj up to the present day) was taken by the Persians unchanged from the Sanskrit where chatur meant four, and anga meant a part or a detachment...

"Besides, we know from history that chess was brought to Iran from India together with the works of the famous fabulist Bidpai (or Pilpay)

at the time of the Sassanid ruler Chosroes I... From the Persians, the game of chess was borrowed by the Arabs in the 7th century, together with the name, spelt shitranj ... in present day chess nomenclature, we clearly discern three linguistic layers, representing three different cultural periods or even three distinct cultures: Indo-Persian, Arabian, and European. Here are the Arabian names: (1) al-shah ('king'); (2) al-firzan (literally 'sage', 'scientist'); (3) al-fil ('elephant'); (4) al-faras ('rider'); (5) al-rokh ('castle', 'tower') and (6) al-beizaq ('foot-soldier')... The name 'chess' was originally derived from the principal piece which the Persian called the Shah, i.e. king. 'Mate' comes from the word mat (literally 'dead'), an Arabian, not a Persian word."

The Arabs contributed a lot to the development of the game. Blindfold play was mentioned as early as 700 A.D. The first tournaments and qualifying contests were recorded in the second half of the 8th century, chess problems started

13

A 17th century Malayan chessman (king) carved in wood, painted in coloured lacquer and ornamented with precious and semi-precious stones. From the Hammond collection.

in 800, and 50 years later came the first book on chess written by Al-Adli.

The Moors brought chess to Spain, the first reference to chess in the Christian world being in the Catalonian Testament of 1010. The game was well known, however, much earlier than this. In France chess was patronized by Charlemagne (8th-9th centuries) who was even said to have received a fine set as a gift from the famous Harun-al-Rashid. Chess sets wrongly described as Charlemagne's in many museums are of later date, as the costumes of certain personalized pieces make evident.

Poetry, which does not necessarily give facts precisely, placed chess in France and Celtic lands in the reign of the legendary King Arthur and his knights of the Round Table.

France's first woman poet, Marie de France (12th century), described the following scene in her romance of Eliduc:

The King, rising from high table,
Went to his daughter's chambers
To play at his beloved chess
With an invited foreign guest.
His daughter, sitting next to him,
Was eager to learn chess, t'would seem.
Eliduc came, the King stopped play...

Another great poet, the Norman, Béroul, in his romance of Tristram and Yseult also mentioned chess as known in the period of King Arthur.

To Germany chess came in the 10th-11th centuries, the earliest reference in German literature being by a monk, Froumund von Tegernsee, in a Latin poem, "Ruodlieb," written in 1030–1050.

A chequerboard appears in the Croatian coat of arms. It is said that Svetoslav Surinj beat the Venetian Doge Peter II in a game for the right to rule the Dalmatian towns.

Several chessmen of a set reputed to have been Charlemagne's but which is from a later period; TOP: king, pawn, queen; BELOW: bishop (centre) and the back view of the king and queen.

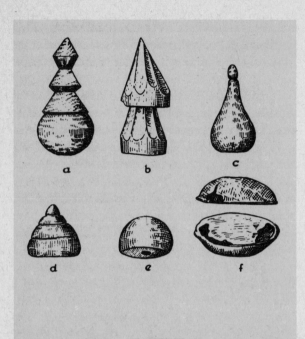

Early mediaeval chessmen found during excavation work in Polish Pomerania. Drawings (a and b) by M. Rulewicz after the originals, the rest taken from scientific publications.

a, b — wooden pawn and bishop (Szczecin, 10th century); c — wooden pawn (Gdańsk, 13th century); d — wooden pawn made on lathe (Kołobrzeg, 10th century); e — bone chess piece (Wolin); f — bronze chess piece (Wolin).

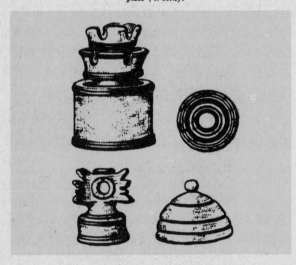

Chess and draughtsmen made of bone, Kiev (11th and 12th centuries).

Chess reached England from Italy through Germany, and from Spain through France. Its rapid spread and increase in popularity were witnessed by the fact that many old families in all four of these countries incorporated chess devices and mottoes in their coats of arms.

By the 10th–11th centuries, it was known in Scandinavia. A chess piece in the form of a man, of Scandinavian workmanship, was found in 1831 on the Isle of Lewis in the Hebrides.

It was in the 11th century that chess reached Bohemia too, brought from Italy by wandering Bohemian merchants.

To Russia chess came directly from the East, quite likely in the 8th–9th centuries, the names of the men to this day indicating Persian-Arabian origins. The queen, "fyerzh" in Russian is a derivative of "vizier." The bishop is slon ("elephant") and the rook ladia ("boat"), both derived from Persian-Arabic. There is one theory that chess was brought to Russia by the Tartars. There have been unproven suggestions that chess was independently brought in by the Teutonic Knights from the North later on. The present-day European game came to Russia from Italy, via Poland among other routes.

The old Russian epic poems in blank verse often mention chess as a really popular game. Chess was an esteemed accomplishment of the heroes whose praise they sang.

In the epic of Stavr Godinovich we find particularly interesting references. Praising his wife, he says:

Also, this young wife of mine
Plays well at both draughts and chess...

Later on, Stavr's wife, eager to wrest her husband from the Prince's dungeon, gathers her brave company:

Thirty brave master bowmen,
Thirty brave chess masters,
Thirty brave master singers...

FROM THE LEFT: 1. Arabian chess piece (king), 8th-9th centuries; 2. 12th century rook; 3. bishop of German make, 14th century; 4. Knight, Japanese sculpture of last century, after old artistic forms.

Disguised as a man, a Greek envoy, she enters the Prince's court, presenting an ultimatum. Delaying his reply, the Prince entertains the envoy and his company. At length, the Prince calls the envoy to a chess tournament:

> My dear guest and honourable envoy!
> Maybe you'd play with me at draughts or
> chess (...)

They both sat at an oaken table
And had a chessboard brought over (...)
So the young guest, the fierce envoy,
Won the will of Prince Vladimir...

In another epic, of Tsar Kalina and Prince Vladimir, there is a mention that "...they played at draughts and chess, a game from a foreign land."

Russian 16th century chessmen: the bishops are elephants.

Scandinavian chessmen (ca. 12th century) found on the Island of Lewis in the Hebrides.

Russian 16th century chessmen; the rooks are sailing boats.

18

Woodcut from an Italian treatise of 1493.

An epic of Nikitich related that Prince Vladimir sent his envoys to King Botyian of Lithuania. The King inquired whence they arrived and whether:

> *In your country they play at Chess*
> *Of this kind or the German one?...*

Archaeological excavations near Kiev produced draughts and chess pieces made of bone in the 11th and 12th centuries. The chess figures, the fyerzh (queen) and another unidentifiable piece, were delicately carved from one piece of bone, known as a "fish tooth," by local craftsmen. At Novgorod, several chess pieces have been found from sets dating back to the 12th-15th centuries. This discovery was of great importance historically for, being of characteristically Moslem abstract designs, they proved indisputably that the game of chess had arrived in Russia from Central Asia and the Middle East.

In many Christian countries in the Middle Ages chess was forbidden by ecclesiastical authorities because it was often abused for gambling. Saint Bernard, writing in 1128 his regulations for the Order of the Knights Templars, cautioned that they "should abhor chess as much as dice." The Synodal regulations of Odo, the Bishop of Paris of the 12th century, forbade the seminarists to have chessmen in their rooms. In 1208, the French Bishop de Sully forbade his clergy to play chess at all, and in 1254, under the influence of the Church, King Louis IX the Saint issued an edict totally forbidding the game (although he himself possessed a fine set received as a gift from Aladdin) as useless and boring. The game was also proscribed in Ruthenia and later in Russia by the Orthodox Church which even saw signs of paganism in it.

Still, nothing could hold back the spread of the game. Its growing prestige was proved by the fact it was the subject of numerous valuable manuscripts and first prints, most of them monuments of culture and fine writing as well. Al-Adli's Arabic treatise from the middle of the 9th century, unfortunately lost, contained openings and games, discussed the differences between the Persian and Hindu rules and contained the first chess problems called "mansubat."

A precious exhibit, discovered in a Yugoslav library, was exhibited in 1958 at the Congress of Problemists at Piran in Yugoslavia. It was an Arabian manuscript of the turn of the 9th century, hitherto unknown to chess historians, containing mansubat, some connected with legends. There is, for instance, one of the 10th century, called "the Dilaram mate." Dilaram was the wife of an Arab vizier, an ardent chess player who once lost in the game all he possessed and finally wagered his wife. The game went badly for the reckless vizier and, judging by the situation on the board, he should have lost. Yet, Dilaram noticed a possibility of winning by sacrificing two rooks, she

Beautifully illuminated page of a manuscript — the treatise on games by Alfonso the Wise, with a diagram of a chess problem (13th century).

Cover of a 15th century French book on chess.

Two wood engravings from Caxton's chess book (1474), one of the oldest prints in England: a monk is solving a chess problem (left); a king and a bishop sitting at the chessboard (right).

managed to whisper this to her husband and saved him for herself.

In 1167, the famous Spanish Rabbi, Abraham Aben Ezra, wrote a poem about chess in Hebrew which contained a description of a game between the pieces symbolizing the Ethiopians and the Edomites. The game was conducted according to the rules in force at the time in Arabian and Spanish lands. Several different manuscripts are ascribed to Ezra. In 1689, Thomas Hyde translated the poem into Latin; in the 19th century, it was translated into German by M. Steinshneider, who at the same time expressed doubts on the authenticity of Ezra's authorship. Here is a short extract of an English translation by Miss Nina Davis (Song of Exile, p. 131, 1901):

...And if by chance the King is caught
And ensnared pitilessly in the net
And there is no way out to save himself,
And no escape to a strong city of refuge,
He is doomed and removed by the foe;
There is no move to save him, and by death is he
                                              mate...

Another manuscript, by the Spanish king, Alfonso the Wise in 1283, was the greatest work on chess and other games in any European language the Middle Ages have left us. It is particularly important as a link between Arabian and European chess literature. It contains 150 miniatures in colour, based on Persian originals, providing a valuable picture of mediaeval customs, costume and interior design. Its chess includes a collection of end-games derived from Arabian literature, some varieties of ten- and twelve-square chess and astronomical chess. It is in the library at the Escorial.

This work existed in one copy only and was not reproduced in manuscript form, but the second famous chess work of the Middle Ages, an extensive Latin treatise by Jacobus de Cessolis, was a real best-seller for centuries. A Dominican monk from Rheims, de Cessolis wrote his book towards the end of the 13th century (the year usually quoted is 1275). The work is of a moralizing character, chess being used as a basis for ethical, moral, social, religious and political pre-

23

cepts. De Cessolis infused not only chess play but even the rules of the game with moral lessons. His text was interspersed with numerous quotations from the Bible, from ecclesiastical and lay writers and the classics. The result was quite an unusual book, and an odd one for the reader of today.

This treatise, "De moribus hominum et de officiis nobilium super ludo scaccorum" ("On the Customs of Men and Their Noble Actions with Reference to the Game of Chess"), circulated in many Latin copies and was translated into German, French, Czech, etc. There are, for instance, nine copies in the library of Prague and three in Cracow. It suffered from frequent adaptation and plagiarism. It also inspired original national versions in which the monk's old text was supplemented with new ideas and precepts. The first printed edition appeared in Latin in 1473. It was soon followed by numerous editions printed in other languages. "The Game and the Playe of Chesse," published in 1474, one of the first books ever printed in English, was a translation of the Cessolis's original Latin by William Caxton, as enthusiastic a chess player as he was famous a printer.

Other famous chess morality books of this kind included a manuscript by a German monk from the Rhine Palatinate, Konrad von Ammenhausen (1337), known from a printed edition of 1520, and a manuscript by Doctor Jacobus Mennel, an official scribe of Freiburg, printed in 1507 in Constance — a rare item nowadays. In the Vienna Library there is the only copy of a Czech manuscript by Tomáš of Štitné, a 14th century author, the father of national Czech literature. This was an adaptation of de Cessolis's work, introducing notes about the country then under the rule of Charles IV. Tomáš of Štitné's work also got into print.

In 1956, it was issued in Prague in a fine philological edition "Knížky o hře šachové a jiné" ("Books on Chess, and Other Works"). It ended, characteristically of morality books:

Permit us, Jesus Christ our King,
always to play this way
and later enter perpetual happiness.
Amen.

Morality texts were followed by books confined more logically to the game alone. The guide to

Copperplate by Jacob van der Heyden from Selenus's work, 1616.

the game of chess by the Spanish master Lucena which appeared in 1497 was the first book of true chess theory.

A book by the Portuguese, Damielano (or Damiano), published in 1512, won wide renown; it was rich in problems and opening analyses. Another work on chess theory, by Ruy López, a splendid Spanish chess master of the time, came out in 1561. In 1597 appeared a treatise by Gianutio (or Mantia), an Italian. This work surpassed its predecessors in analysis of games and endings. A manual of chess play, by Salvio, a fine Italian player, first published in 1604, went through a host of editions. To the second edition, in 1634, he added information on the history of chess. For a long time afterwards, authors inserted fragments of Salvio's books into their own works. A book of chess by Selenus published in Leipzig in 1616, was based almost wholly on the works of López and the Italians. Selenus was a pseudonym used by Augustus the Younger, Duke of Brunswick, a great enthusiast for chess play. A treatise by the Italian Carrera, published in 1617, comprised more than 500 pages and contain-

ed much analytical material. A manual by a noted player, Gioacchino Greco "Il Calabrese," printed in Rome in 1620, greatly influenced chess theory and practice. In 1625, Greco re-edited his manual, altering the laws of castling and enlarging the end-games and analyses sections. This new edition appeared in print several years later, after his death. He left in manuscript much other material on the theory of chess, some of which was later published. About thirty versions of Greco's manuscript are known, in a variety of editions and translations. Such abundant literature — we have mentioned only relatively few of the books which appeared in the Middle Ages — could only have originated from a flourishing chess activity in which most of these authors engaged. The end of the 16th and the beginning of the 17th centuries was a golden age for chess in France and Spain — renowned masters reigned, and some matches became news all over Europe.

Ruy López was a modest man in the small town of Zafra in Spain. He had unusual talent for chess, surpassing in his ability for combinations numer-

Chessmen of china covered with coloured glaze, made in Russia, mid-eighteenth century.

26

A Meissen china chessboard of the 18th century, purple-and-green with drawings of personified chessmen in Oriental style. (Cracow National Museum).

Set of chessmen made of ebony, tortoise-shell and mother-of-pearl, a gift from the Turkish sultan to the Polish hetman Adam Sieniawski in 1726 (Cracow National Museum).

Two-sided board for playing chess and mill, richly inlaid, which was in Baron Kronenberg's collection in Warsaw up to 1939. It was lost during the war.

Chess at an old Polish manor house. An engraving dated 1872, after a drawing by Kruger.

ous players who were invited to the Court of King Philip II from many lands. As a reward for defeating several eminent players in Rome in 1572, he was presented by the King with an award of several remunerative church livings and a fine golden chain with a golden rook pendant. He was an authority on problems of strategy and openings, and his work, "Libro de la invencion liberal y arte del juego del Axedrez" ("Book of the Liberal Invention and Art of Playing Chess") established his reputation as a theoretician.

He was rivalled by an Italian, Giovanni Leonardo da Cutri, an ambitious player, who showed great talent for chess. Defeated by López, he trained and prepared himself over a considerable period, then travelled to Spain to challenge his vanquisher again. In a tense match staged at the Royal Court in Madrid in 1575, which is depicted in a painting by L. Mussini, after losing twice (apparently so as to raise the temperature of the contest), he won three games in succession, to take the match and with it a big money stake. He also defeated other Spanish and Portuguese masters. After returning to Italy, he died from poison administered by an unknown person said to have been jealous of his fame.

On his journey to Spain, da Cutri was accompanied by another prominent Italian, G.C. Polerio. During the matches, Polerio wrote down the games; thus he became not only one of the first known "seconds" but also a forerunner of chess tournament reporters.

Another biographer of da Cutri was A. Salvio, LL.D., a theoretician and historian of chess, mas-

Chess players. French engraving of the late 19th century, after a painting from the Algerian cycle by E. Delacroix.

ter player and teacher of later famous chess players. His pupils included Gioacchino Greco "Il Calabrese" who defeated his master at the age of 14. Greco won fame as a chess genius in matches in France and England. Later on he visited Spain, where his successes continued. He agreed to accompany a certain Spanish grandee on a voyage to the West Indies, where he died.

These encounters, the personalities of the experts and the numerous books all no doubt fostered increasing interest in the game. There developed in southern Europe several strong centres of chess from which interest spread to areas where chess had been the pastime of restricted social groups or had not even spread beyond the precincts of the court.

The exact date when chess arrived in Poland is not known. Tradition has it that Polish knights returning from the Crusades during the reign of King Bolesław Krzywousty at the beginning of the 12th century, brought it back with them and taught it to their friends. The game — not an easy one to all — must have spread slowly and was known only among a few people for some time but achieved considerable prestige in the royal and ducal courts as a scope for intelligence and wit. Ability at chess was regarded as one of the accomplishments of a knight. Consequently, chess became a frequent theme in heraldry throughout the West.

A heraldic crest named *Wczele*, granted in 1103 during the reign of Bolesław Krzywousty,

The Arabs did a lot to popularize chess. Scene from the German film "Die Geschichte vom kleinen Muck" (1954).

Although Church authorities were often against playing chess, it was a favourite game in monasteries. Scene from the German film "Der Klosterjäger" (1953).

had a black and yellow chessboard on a shield and a crowned Moorish woman bearing a smaller chessboard. As explained in Polish books on heraldry, the design was based on a legend.

"... A Slovak named Holub visited the Moors in his travels. He was famed for knightly valour and a skillful chess player, too. When news of his arrival reached the royal court, the king's daughter who considered herself a fine player, challenged him to a game.

"Confident of victory, she proposed that the stake should be simply that the winner should hit the loser on the head with the chessboard. Though the Slovak refused for a long time to agree to such a condition, the other insisted; he won the game and exacted the penalty.

"The Moorish king quite approved, and placed both the board and the coloured princess on his (Holub's) crest."

A chessboard device was incorporated on the coat of arms of the Duchy of Legnica and Wrocław, on the pennons of the Duchy of Legnica and Brzeg in Silesia (13th century), and on the coats of arms of the House of the Silesian Piasts and the old city of Kalisz (Calisia).

A chess rook is quite common in heraldry.

"The Duke of Mazovia when gravely preoccupied with wars, asked a knight named Pierzchala to play chess with him to take his mind off his troubles. Pierzchala mated him with a rook.

The Duke magnanimously placed the rook on his crest and granted him an estate."

In India, the cradle of chess, the game retains its popularity to this day. Scene from the Indian film "Pardosi", (1939).

A game of chess in old Spain. Scene from the Spanish film "Locura de amor" (1953).

Chess scene from the German silhouette film "Abenteuer des Prinzen Achmed" (1926).

Interesting crests with a chess motif have resulted from mergers. For instance the crest named Wieruszowa (on a white shield — a goat half black and half chequered) perpetuates a union of two noble families, one of which had a goat on its crest, the other a chessboard.

A controversy on the origin of the crest named *Zabawa* (Play) has not been settled yet; one half of the crest itself bears a chequerboard with black and red squares. According to some opinions, it originated from a fact of playing (holding back) the enemy until the arrival of reinforcements. There is, however, a more probable version of this story, namely, that the name originated from the game (play) of chess, and in a metaphorical and symbolic way it recorded distinguished combat against an enemy, illustrated by a battle on the chessboard.

The Arcemberski crest which appeared in 1630, shows a stag on a chessboard. It was bestowed by the Duke of Pomerania on one of his courtiers. The Duke was playing chess at a hunt when a stag sprang hard by but was soon brought down with three arrows shot by the courtier.

More Polish crests with a chess motif are those of Wyszogota, Karega, Kizinek, Szachman and Pudwels.

Research by Polish archaeologists in connection with the thousandth anniversary of the Polish state — the crossroads of influence from East and West — brought to light chessmen from the 10th–13th centuries, excavated in Pomerania, which indicated that chess had been spread by sea trade routes as well as land.

Excavations in 1962 in Sandomierz, an old Polish town on the Orient to North-West trade routes — yielded a remarkable find of chessmen.

Chessmen are carved by hand (with no use of, for example, a lathe) in animal bone (presumably hartshorn). All are the same in colour —slightly yellowish — and not over 25 mm in size (kings — 25 and 23 mm., queens — 20 and 18 mm., rooks — 20 mm., bishops — 20 and 18 mm., knights — 18 mm., and pawns — 17 to 19 mm).

"Oh, my lady, answered Sharr-Khan, whoever plays with you must lose." Illustration to a tale
in the Arabian Nights. Drawing by Janina Petry-Przybylska

Individual pieces and pawns differ in detail of workmanship and ornamentation, shape and size, but they are easily distinguished into two opposite sets which, for reasons of convenience, will be referred to in the text as "White" and "Black." The forms of the chessmen are based on Arabic patterns with their characteristic abstract shapes avoiding representation of real things in compliance with the Islamic commands prohibiting the reproduction of images of live things. The purely geometrical shape of the chess pieces is but reminiscent of the symbolic features of figural chessmen of India and Persia (e. g. the two protrusions on the specimens of a bishop represent either elephant tusks or a couple of riders mounted on elephant; a single such protrusion on the knight is a remnant of a rider on horseback; the boss on the king piece is a monarch on an elephant, etc.).

The two opposite sets differ in the quality of workmanship. The "White" (all chessmen, including two knights slightly differing in design — one of them perhaps a later addition — and only five pawns, including a single unornamented one, clearly a substitute) are more carefully made, more lavishly ornamented and are less worn from usage. The "Black" — the full set — are plainer in design, shiny from wear, carved less accurately and less ornamented. This seems to indicate that in the game was used not a single combined unit of two opposite issues of chessmen, but two individual separate sets. Perhaps there was no observance by manufacturers and traders of the rule of making two separate 16-piece sets but the matter was left to their discretion, a fact motivated by the need to differentiate the chessmen, which were identical in colour.

Chess was a favourite game at the courts of the French aristocrats. Scene from the French film "Les visiteurs du Soir" (1942).

During the reign of Elizabeth I, chess was very popular in England. Scene from the American film "The Sea Hawk" (1942).

As early as the start of the 19th century chess was played in Warsaw cafés. Scene from the Polish film "Młodość Chopina" (Chopin's Youth) (1952).

In a French salon of the First Empire; a contemporary drawing.

The question remains open whether the chess sets of Sandomierz were manufactured locally or whether they were brought over from foreign lands. According to Mr and Mrs. Gąssowski, the discoverers of the sets, it can be assumed that the chessmen were a local product, with the addition that in producing them their maker closely imitated the Arabic chess pieces at that time popular in the region. The ornamentation of these sets which consists of linear cuttings and minute circles, resembling that on Arabic products, is not opposed to Slavonic decorative motifs. The local character of the chessmen seems to be also reinforced by the fact that they were made of hartshorn, while in the case of the Arabic East ivory would be more typical.

The answer to the pertinent question must be left for further research, but the affinity of the Sandomierz chessmen with those of the Middle Asia and Near East is, however, undoubted. The penetration of chess to Poland by way of mediaeval Russia seems unquestionable. This may have preceded even the Crusades which provided a secondary route — in addition to maritime trade centres — for propagation of the game.

The thesis of the Arabic origin of chess in Poland has been further confirmed by recent findings in Novgorod where archaeological excavations revealed a number of chess pieces of the Arabic type with many remarkable variants of shape, workmanship, material and period of production. The chessmen of Sandomierz are undoubtedly the oldest and most complete sets yet discovered. (Novgorod pieces represent a large span of time, and yet with the considerable number of pieces discovered they present no complete single set of chessmen).

Today it is even harder to surmise what conclusions a thorough analysis of findings at Sandomierz may lead to; and a great number of questions concerning them yet awaits solution. One thing is,

The French musician André Philidor was a leading chess player of the second half of the 18th century. Dozens of editions of his treatise "L'Analyse du jeu des échecs" appeared in many languages. Drawing by J. Skarżyński.

chess set from the early mediaeval times is a rarity among the European collections. This distinguishes the findings at Sandomierz among the unique European collections; they not only supply remarkable material evidence for the history of culture in Poland but also enrich considerably the record of proofs of the flourishing of a world civilization at the crossroads of Eastern and Western influences. Sandomierz, as mentioned, was an active commercial centre on the Orient-North--West route.

The town has been for some time the site of systematic archaeological investigations carried out by teams from the Institute of Material Culture of the Polish Academy of Sciences, which has a permanent scientific post established there. On October 9th, 1962, a team of archaeologists, under Dr Jerzy Gąssowski and Eligia Gąssowska, M. Sc., during excavation work at the settlement on St Jacob's Hill, discovered, in a large partly dug-out hut in a depression filled with dry earth, a collection of 29 primitive chess pieces. The age of the settlement is estimated to within a range of 180 years, with the later extreme falling to the 1259-1260, when it was completely destroyed by Tartar raiders. The ancient hut (still bearing traces of handicraft occupations of its inhabitants) is situated in the older part of the settlement, and on the basis of the arrangement of its subsequent strata, its origin may be traced back to the late eleventh or the early part of the twelfth century. The chess discovery is evidently of the same period. It should be borne in mind that the chess pieces, which bear traces of extensive usage (ornaments worn out), could have apparently been made in an earlier period, and the theory that they were used for play in Sandomierz in the eleventh century is highly plausible.

The research indicates that chess reached Poland in three ways: by sea routes, through the commercial ports; by knights returning from the crusades; and finally via Russia, as proved

however, certain that the 1962 Sandomierz Piast chessmen are the most sensational archaeological discovery in Poland ever recorded.

The chess sets of Sandomierz are a highly valuable museum piece as including an almost complete set of chessmen (only three pawns are lacking) with carefully established localization both in space and time. Such a fairly complete

A chess player. French lithograph of the mid-19th century.

The famous Café de la Régence in Paris, where chess playing flourished from the mid-18th century to the end of the 19th century.

A game of chess in a French 18th century salon. Gravure by Jules Noël, mid-19th century.

38

Chess players. One of the first daguerreotypes in England.
A photograph by W. H. Fox Talbot (1840).

Anderssen and Morphy playing chess in Paris (1858).
A contemporary engraving from an original photograph.

by similarities between men excavated in Sandomierz and Novgorod.

Janko of Czarnkow, writing in the 15th century,
told how chess in Poland a century earlier had
fallen foul of the law, being classed as a game of
chance.

During the Renaissance period, when Queen
Bona Sforza came to Poland with her numerous
courtiers from Italy, chess gained prestige and
popularity, and became a Palace game.

In a work by Łukasz Górnicki, "Dworzanin"
(The Courtier) of 1566, which was a free Polish
translation of an Italian work by Castiglione,
there were some thoughts on chess. The game was
also provided with a permanent and immortal
monument by Jan Kochanowski in his poem,
"Szachy" (Chess), c. 1654, unparalleled in world

literature for its blend of chess content
with poetic art of the highest order. The poem
was an important contribution to the history of
chess in Poland. It showed the great respect chess
enjoyed in the country by that time.

Poland's first chess manual was little known
outside. The compilation of Jan Ostroróg written in the 17th century was never actually published; the manuscript was to be found in the
Krasiński Library in Warsaw until it went up
in flames during the Nazi invasion. Though mainly based on works by foreign authors, it had
original features, notably the introduction of
algebraic notation.

Jan Bystroń said in his "Dzieje obyczajów w da-
wnej Polsce" (The History of Customs in Old
Poland) that later on, as the intellectual level of

the population declined, this game, requiring a mental effort, began to give ground to cards and draughts. If chess was played at all, this was done without any ambition and in a hazardous manner, for sums of money. T. K. Węgierski, a poet of the Polish Renaissance, wrote in one of his poems:

You also asked, how our young men in Warsaw fared?

Well, some of them now play at gambling chess...

Another Polish historian of customs, Ł. Gołębiowski wrote in his "Gry i zabawy różnych stanów" (The Games and Pastimes of Various Classes) of 1831, about the spreading of cards:

" ... the game was known to few but it began to spread, first in the Capital, from 1740, and soon throughout the country. Both chess and draughts were given up: they took to cards..."

Obviously, chess as a gambling game could not compete with cards.

As the intellectual level of Polish life declined, chess became less popular than cards or draughts and even what chess remained was often played as a game of chance with dice thrown to decide the piece to be played.

Good chess did not disappear from Poland entirely. A few dedicated enthusiasts kept it alive. One amusing story centres about a Jew in Warsaw. A superb player, a foreigner (in some versions, an Englishman) was invited to play chess at the court of King Stanisław August. The visitor defeated every opponent put up against him,

"Mr. and Mrs. Barry playing chess." Canvas by an unknown English painter (19th century).

The famous chess player Rosenthal giving a simultaneous display on 30 chessboards in Paris (1891).
Drawing by Louis Tinayre.

even Stanisław Trembecki, a distinguished writer and strong player. All felt the country's prestige was at stake.

Trembecki invited the Englishman to his house. Feigning indisposition, he asked his guest if he would not divert himself for a while at a game with a Polish Jew, 'quite an able player.' The proud foreigner cast a look of disdain, suggesting a high stake. The Jew agreed to pay it if he lost, but on the other hand declared that if he chanced to win he would not desire the Englishman's money but would like to cut off one of his buttons as a souvenir. The Englishman agreed, sat down to play, and lost.

"Well, I've won one button," said the Jew. He cut off a button from the other's trousers, as if loath to spoil his jacket.

The surprised and mortified Englishman played on and on with worse and worse results. Other guests drifted in, some of them from the royal court. The Englishman lost not only his buttons, one by one, but also his temper and, grasping garments now somewhat in need of support, ran out into the courtyard... and finally left Warsaw.

The King laughed and laughed at this occurrence and at the proud man's downfall. The winner, loaded with honours and gifts, came to stay with Trembecki as a bosom friend, playing him many a game of chess.

The names of the unfortunate English chess player and the Jew befriended by Trembecki are equally unknown. The story could have been based on some authentic incident but is probably fictitious.

*

* *

The mid 18th century began a period of splendour in chess. Two names became the corner-

stones of the modern era in the history of the game: Stamma and Philidor.

A French musician, André-François-Danican Philidor (1726–95), had an inborn talent for the game. At only 14 years of age he had beaten strong players at the famed Café de la Régence in Paris, a Mecca for leading French players and enthusiasts from abroad.

Soon Philidor had toured England with dazzling success. All the best English players went down before him. At the age of twenty he wrote "Analyse des échecs" ("An Analysis of Chess"), a manual which was soon to be found in almost every household of culture. It appeared in Lon-

don in 1749. It contained an introductory historical outline of the development of chess, some observations on the rules, descriptions of numerous openings with critical analyses and a selection of end-games. He employed a descriptive and rather cumbersome notation. About sixty editions are known. Its fame was abused by some dishonest publishers who continued to bring out pirated editions for many decades afterwards, even though the practical value of this pioneer work soon diminished as the theory of the game began to advance by leaps and bounds. Philidor himself as an author inspired fresh research. His visits to Berlin, Potsdam and London, as

Emanuel Lasker, world chess champion in 1894–1920.

stay in London he published another edition of his collection of problems and end-games with a supplement containing analyses of more than fifty new openings.

Philidor's teaching helped the Englishman Staunton to achieve mastery. In Russia there appeared Petrov, author of the first Russian manual of chess in 1824. In France, La Bourdonnais won considerable fame. In Germany, great success fell to Anderssen, a professor of mathematics in Breslau. It was he who gained first place in the first international chess tournament held in London in 1851, and for a long time he was regarded as the best chess player on the Continent.

The genius of Morphy, the American player,

José Raoul Capablanca, the "chess king" in 1921–1927.

well as his activities in Paris, confirmed his fame as the greatest player of his day. After defeating Légal, the leading French player, he was presented by his supporters with a chess sceptre as a symbol of grand mastership.

Philip Stamma, an Arab from Syria, was a professional chess player, yet there was nothing really to distinguish him as a practician. He was distinguished as a composer of problems, a hundred excellent ones being published in his book of 1737. He was the first to use the algebraic notation in print. In the preamble of his book he described the origin of chess in Arabian lands. He suggested that the contestants should treat chess as a real combat, hence military strategy was an example to be followed. During a longer

43

shone briefly. For three years (1857–1859) he toured, beating the best players of Europe and America; then he suddenly, unexpectedly, left the chess scene for good. He made a great contribution to the development of chess play, teaching the beauty of combinations and of subtle strategy. He was undoubtedly one of the more interesting figures in the history of the game, but became an example of the tragic fate of a talented genius plagued by intrigues. In his later years he suffered from delusions.

The title of "World Champion" was first assumed by a German player, Wilhelm Steinitz, when, in 1866, he defeated Anderssen in London. He retained it through a series of great matches with Zukertort (1886), Tchigorin (1889), Gunsberg (1890) and Tchigorin again (1892). Only in 1894 was he defeated by the German Emanuel Lasker, an eminent theoretician, mathematician and journalist. Lasker held his chess sceptre for many years, shaping the course of chess until the 1920's. He confirmed his championship in a return match with Steinitz in 1896 and successfully repelled attempts to unseat him by Marshall (1900), Schlechter (1907), Tarrasch (1908) and Janowski (1909).

Lasker's defeat in 1921 by J. R. Capablanca, a young Cuban, surprised the world. Capablanca introduced a new atmosphere into the game, dissipating many outdated views. A devotee of simplicity, he hardly ever lost. And yet... he was routed in 1927 by Alekhine, the Russian. Considering that he reigned only for six years, Capablanca gained an astonishing degree of fame. It has been said that no other chess champion has ever been so renowned in the world outside chess.

Alekhine raised the art of chess to the heights. He infused romance into the game whilst employing the most precise mathematical thought, an iron logic, and far-reaching analysis. Once and for all, he destroyed the idea, which had gained credence in Capablanca's day, that chess might perish through an excess of drawn games. Alekhine showed that chess was a wide-open field for creative thought yet.

He retained his world championship until his death in 1946, with the exception of a brief period, 1935–1937, when he was robbed of it by Max Euwe, the brilliant Dutch player, at a time of slight physical and mental breakdown.

Alekhine's death was followed by an interregnum which was ended in 1948 by Mikhail Botvinnik, a Soviet player who had taken over the mantle of Petrov, Tchigorin and Alekhine. In 1957, Botvinnik lost his title to another fine Soviet player, Vassily Smyslov but regained it in a return match in 1958. A new World Championship challenger was now coming forward every third year.

In 1960 Botvinnik was defeated in brilliant style by another Russian, Mikhail Tal.

The course of this match stirred the world. The building in Moscow in which it took place was mobbed daily. The play was reported by both press and radio. World interest was especially aroused by the contrast between the respective contestants' styles of play, their temperaments and tactics. Botvinnik, as a representative of the classical school, founded his play on precision and logic. An electrical engineer by profession,

his mind worked along mathematical lines. By contrast, the twenty-odd-year-old Tal was an adherent of the neo-romantic school. His play was keen, sometimes reckless, but full of originality, ingenuity and imagination. He constantly confronted his opponent with situation demanding unusual resource, often in situations little analyzed before. Tal was then a young scientist, a lecturer in philosophy at the University of Riga, and a comparative newcomer to the science of chess. His success confirmed the view that chess offered inexhaustible conceptual and tactical possibilities, and it could always provide new, relational creative achievements.

However, Botvinnik did not tolerate his defeat for long. A year later (1961), he won again in

Soviet chess champion David Bronstein. The picture taken by a staff photographer of "Der Spiegel."

45

A Soviet cartoon by B. Yefimov published in "Krokodil" in 1948 when Mikhail Botvinnik became world champion.

a return match, achieving the unparalleled feat of winning the world title for the third time.

Yet new attacks on the throne were constantly developing. In a tournament of world championship "candidates" held on the island of Curaçao in the Dutch West Indies, first place went to another Soviet arch-master, 33-year-old Tigran Petrosian, who thus won the right to challenge Botvinnik. The rules were changed. For the first time the champion, if deposed, was not to have the right to a return match. The new champion was to keep his title for three years in any event and only the winner of the next "candidates" tournament should challenge him. Botvinnik

accepted these conditions though it was seriously considered that he might have been justified in declining them, or retiring undefeated. The match between the now 52-year-old Mikhail Botvinnik and Tigran Petrosian, the Armenian journalist nearly twenty years his junior, consequently took place on the stage of the Moscow Revue Theatre in March 1963. It aroused even greater interest both among the Soviet public, who filled the theatre to capacity, and the outside world. After a dramatic struggle still undecided after seventeen games, Petrosian won.

The ninth official world champion, Tigran Petrosian was born in 1929. He has a positional style of play, does not seek for showy combinations but gradually strengthens his position, not yielding lightly any advantage once gained. His mastery of technique and quiet strategy is greatly reminiscent of Capablanca. In 1966, he retained his title against an assault by Boris Spassky.

Spassky was beaten, but emerged as a player worthy of competing for the highest position in the hierarchy of world's chess players. Before he secured the privilege to measure swords with Petrosian, he became Champion of the Soviet Union (in 1962), and much earlier, in 1955, as a 18-year-old youth, he had won the title of the world's junior champion.

At another match, however, held in Moscow in the spring of 1969, Petrosian was defeated by Spassky in a dramatic meeting. And thus a new king ascended to the chess throne — Boris Spassky, a journalist by profession (born in 1937) a dynamic player distinguished for his brilliant strategy and tactics.

In 1972, the American grand master Robert Fischer became the eleventh — one of the youngest in the history of chess — world chess champion, when at the exciting and dramatic "match of the century" held in Iceland's capital city, Reykjavik, he won a decisive victory over Spassky. A superb chess player, noted for his crisp style of play, boldness and resourcefulness as a tactician, his urge to innovate and high-precision playing, Robert Fischer (born in 1943) obtained the title of the United States champion as a fourteen-year-old boy, and the title of international master as a sixteen-year-old boy. He secured the right to confront Spassky in the trial heats when he scored a sensational advantage over his contestants and won 6 to 0 in the game he played against the Russian Taimanov, and again 6 to 0 over the Dane Larsen, and 6.5 to 2.5 in the game against the former world chess champion, the Russian Petrosian.

Robert Fischer has ascended the chess throne!

Mikhail Tal won the title of world champion in 1960, but had to hand it back to Botvinnik a year later.

47

TOP LEFT: Mikhail Botvinnik maintained his reputation as the world's best chess player from 1948 to 1963, losing the title of the world champion only twice: in 1957–58 and 1960-61.

TOP RIGHT: Tigran Petrosian became world champion in 1963 after an exciting match with Mikhail Botvinnik, and retained the title in 1966.

LEFT: In a match in 1969, Tigran Petrosian was defeated and Boris Spassky won the title of world champion. He was defeated by Robert Fischer in 1972.

Robert Fischer born in 1943, the United States grand master and the world chess champion after the "match of the century" played against Boris Spassky.

(Photo C. Fox and Co., Inc., the "Newsweek").

II. CHESS IN BRITAIN

Karel van Mander (1548—1606)
Ben Jonson and William Shakespeare at chess (1600).

At Nottingham 1936. A world famous picture of the strongest international tournament ever organized in Britain. Left to right, seated: Sir G. A. Thomas, Dr. Emanuel Lasker (Germany), J. R. Capablanca (Cuba), Alderman J. N. Derbyshire, patron of the tournament, and his wife, Dr. M. Euwe (Holland), Dr. A. A. Alekhine (France), W. Winter. Left to right, standing: Reuben Fine (U.S.A.), Dr. S. Tartakower (Poland), Dr. M. Vidmar (Yugoslavia), E. D. Bogolubov (Germany), T. H. Tylor, C. H. O'D. Alexander, S. Flohr (U.S.S.R.), S. Reshevsky (U.S.A.), M. M. Botvinnik (U.S.S.R.) and A. J. Mackenzie (Controller). Lasker, Euwe, Alekhine and Capablanca were past or present world champions and Botvinnik was to become one.

Nowadays, with an international chess tournament starting somewhere in the world every few days, it is difficult to realise that such an event had, prior to that date, never been known. It was entirely Howard Staunton's idea and inspiration.

A mighty man. Where is his biography? There is none, though about Paul Morphy, who played chess brilliantly for six years, but contributed nothing else to the game at all, maybe a dozen absorbing books have been written.

The truth is that Howard Staunton was a most unlikeable man. He had a few good friends but countless enemies.

In his "Illustrated London News" column, enthusiastic admirers writing in to send their games or suggestions received replies like "Your games are disfigured by errors." "You are signally wrong"; "Your problem is defective"; "Inferior"; "Much too simple" were typical observations.

Once he wrote: "A player may have two or more pawns on the board at the same time." Simply that. A puzzling statement in view of the fact that each player starts with eight pawns and rarely ends with fewer than three. One mystified reader plaintively seeking enlightenment received the broadside: " 'Pawns' was an obvious misprint for 'Queened Pawns' or 'Queen'." No apology; just (in effect) "You fool!"

He once published an unsound problem; over a hundred readers remonstrated but he verbally mowed down the lot.

Paul Morphy came over to Europe in 1858, bent on challenging Staunton, as the world's acknowledged best player, to a match. He never got even a game. It was 15 years since Staunton had beaten Saint-Amant. His powers were declining, he had for months been devoting most of his time to a huge commentary on Shakespeare, and knew Morphy would beat him. He equivocated and gibed at the young American through his column, earning general odium. Freud's biographer Ernest Jones has seriously maintained that Staunton's attitude fostered Morphy's mad-

ness. Morphy himself was over-sensitive and provocative. Anyway, the two of them provided a ready-made Oedipus theme for the armchair psycho-analyst of today.

Howard Staunton will never be forgotten but, could he only have tempered his arrogance, our respect for his extraordinary achievements would have been greater.

England has certainly produced no such colossus of chess before or since.

THE TIMING OF PLAY

Among other campaigns, Staunton constantly pressed for some sort of control over the time spent per move.

The La Bourdonnais-MacDonnell match games sometimes went on all night, though there was a stipulation in the terms that they should be adjourned at 4 a.m. Two hours or more were often spent on one move: either player could take as long as he liked.

Staunton's own great tournament of 1851 had been sadly marred by slow play. His campaign for some sort of timing in chess was to succeed, but only after his death.

For one match, it was stipulated that no move should take more than twenty minutes; even so, one game took fifteen hours. Obviously a player's time allowance must be spread over a number of moves. For instance, three minutes per move might be a fair average; but for the first move of the game, three seconds might suffice; on the other hand, three quarters of an hour might be justified, or even insufficient, at a crucial stage.

Sand-glasses were tried. One was allocated to each player, running only whilst he pondered; if an hour's sand had run out before his twentieth move had been made, he had lost. The drawbacks of sand-glasses were many and obvious.

Next came a double pendulum clock arrangement: the clock of the player thinking out his move ticked merrily whilst his opponent's was stopped by being tipped well over.

There has, just once in history, been a British Commonwealth Championship. This was at Oxford in 1951, when advantage was taken of the adventitious presence of several strong Commonwealth players. Left to right are A. Yanofsky (Canada), G. Berryman (Australia), the Master of Balliol College and his wife, W. A. Fairburst (Scotland), Leonard Barden (England), R. G. Wade (New Zealand), Sir Robert Robinson F.R.S. (a keen and gifted amateur player) and W. Heidenfeld (South Africa). W. A. Fairburst won. One of the greatest bridge designers this country has ever produced, he has been British Chess Champion once and Scottish ten times.

Finally, about 1880, came chess clocks as we know them today; the modern chess clock is a British invention.

The great tournament of 1851 was followed by a series of matches involving British players and the continentals it had brought to London, and a tremendous boost this must have given the game. London became for thirty to forty years the Mecca of chess, drawing and adopting many of the world's greatest players. Steinitz from Vienna assumed the title of world champion as a resident of London. Polish-born Zukertort, his main challenger, lived in London, too. A German, Harrwitz, followed Steinitz into the editorship of "The Field." The similarly named Horwitz also came from Germany; Lowe from what is now Czechoslovakia; Löwenthal, Hoffer and Gunsberg from Hungary; Falkbeer, like Steinitz, from Austria; Janssens from Belgium, Mason from America.

In spite of the presence of this powerful group of visitors, the most gifted player of all for at least a decade was the English historian Henry Buckle. A determined amateur, he put his "History of Civilisation," which earned him world fame, before his chess, though how he loved the game!

Asked "Why don't you play a match with Staunton?" "I was always careful to maintain friendly relations with him," Buckle replied!

LONDON PLAYERS DOMINATE

About 1880, international chess tournaments began to be organized on the Continent. Not unnaturally in view of the city's intense chess activity, Londoners repeatedly took the honours.

To Vienna in 1873, for instance, went Steinitz, Blackburne and Bird. Against opposition from Anderssen, Rosenthal, Paulsen, Meitner, Schwartz and others, Steinitz and Blackburne finished first and second, Bird fifth.

G. H. Mackenzie, the strongest player Scotland produced in centuries, three times won the U. S. Championship; at Cleveland in 1871, Chicago in 1874 and New York in 1880.

In 1882 Vienna organized a still greater tournament than 1873's. Steinitz, Zukertort, Blackburne, Mason and Bird went from London with Mackenzie now representing the U.S.A. Winawer, Tchigorin, L. Paulsen, Englisch and Weiss headed the opposition. Steinitz tied first; Mason finished third; Mackenzie and Zukertort equal fourth-fifth; Blackburne sixth. Of the 8,800 francs prize money, 4,800 fell to four London players and another 350 to Ross-shire-born Mackenzie. But from now on the Germans began to take the lead in both organization and play.

Steinitz's stamping-ground for years, and virtually the centre of world chess, was Simpson's restaurant in the Strand where you could get a coffee, a cigar and an afternoon's chess for a shilling. Though chess long ago left this great restaurant, there is still preserved, in a showcase in the foyer, a World Championship chessboard nearly a century old.

Chess columns in newspapers and magazines have played a tremendous rôle in fostering British chess, but throughout the second half of the 19th century, whether through Staunton's influence or not it is hard to say, they were persistently misused as organs of vituperation and hate. Scurrilous invective was the rule. If two clubs became rivals, the columnist, ever eager to pour oil on the troubled flames, converted dislike into hatred. Perhaps this was why so many decades went by before a national governing body came into existence. Löwenthal, a pleasant-natured man, toiled hard and long to establish a "British Association for the Promotion of Chess" which did a certain amount of good work but it lapsed with his death in 1876, nobody being sufficiently enterprising to continue his work.

Yet there was enthusiasm and power in British chess at the time. In 1884 the City of London Chess Club had 225 members. In 1885 the British

Chess Association had Lord Tennyson, the Poet Laureate, as its President, with Lord Randolph Churchill, Sir Robert Peel and John Ruskin as Vice-Presidents; apparently, however, more than distinguished patronage was needed, for the Association petered out in little more than a decade.

It is piquant that the Scottish Chess Association of today was founded in 1884, decades before the British Chess Federation which now rules, and even a year before the British Chess Association from which the B.C.F. grew. Older that any is the British Chess Magazine which started in 1881, gestating in quaint fashion from, of all things, the Huddersfield College Magazine which, in the course of eight or nine years, had itself developed from a typical college magazine with a reasonably sized chess section to one in which the chess had, like a cuckoo in the nest, displaced almost everything else. Today, only one existing chess magazine, the Deutsche Schachzeitung, can claim a greater age than the "B.C.M." and whereas the English magazine has had an uninterrupted existence, the German ceased publication from 1940 to 1950.

J. H. BLACKBURNE

Comparable almost with Staunton's fame was that of J. H. Blackburne who, born in 1842, virtually lived chess, from the age of eighteen when (already a fine draughts player) he learnt the moves, to his death in 1923. Throughout half a century or more, if he was not taking on all and sundry in some chess café or engaged in some tournament abroad, he was travelling around giving simultaneous displays the length and breadth of the country, often getting through 4,000 games or more in a season. Though the son of an earnest temperance reformer, he enjoyed whisky as much as chess, in spite of which and of his strenuous life (travel itself demanded stamina in those days), he maintained his powers for an extraordinary length of time. At the age

of 72, he opened with the ridiculous move 1.P-K.3 against Nimzowitsch at St. Petersburg — and won!

HASTINGS ENTERS THE PICTURE

1895 was noteworthy for the great International Tournament at Hastings, precursor of — up to now — 45 other great tournaments there, a series which has made that little Sussex seaside town the most famous chess venue in the world. Hastings 1895 was a tremendous event with sad echoes. The writing on the wall became depressingly clear. The young American Harry Nelson Pillsbury won. A Russian, Tchigorin, finished second; four Germans, another Russian and an Austrian took the remaining six prizes and only two places later came the best of the Englishmen, Blackburne. British leadership of world chess had departed, not to return.

Chess languished a little in the early years of this century, in England as elsewhere. But the present-day British Chess Federation came into being, and provided the country with, at any rate, one reliable annual event, a British Championship and a British Ladies' Championship. The pattern was at once set which has continued to this date, of a congress with a different venue each year — Hastings in 1904, then Southport, Shrewsbury, Sydenham, Tunbridge Wells, Scarborough, Oxford, Glasgow, Richmond, Cheltenham, Chester in turn. Apart from the championships, the main events were the famous cable matches between Great Britain and the U.S.A. for the Newnes trophy, annually from 1896 to 1903 and 1908 to 1911. With three successive wins in 1909–11, Britain won the trophy outright. This proved to be the kiss of death, for the event then lapsed.

H. E. ATKINS

H. E. Atkins was the dominant figure of this epoch. A product of the same Huddersfield

The English editor of this book (centre) has been President of the British Universities Chess Association for the last 26 years. 1954 when this photograph of the annual congress was taken, was a vintage year for the Association. In the picture are, among others, B. Cafferty, P. C. Gibbs, G. J. Martin, L. Edelstein, V. G. Jenson, J. R. Nicolson, D. E. Lloyd, J. H. Watts, all of whom became very well known in British chess competition in the ensuing decade.

58

College which had gestated the British Chess Magazine, he modelled his style on that of Steinitz, with such success that he won the British Championship from 1905 to 1911 without a break, and again in 1924 and 1925. His record of nine titles was broken only by Jonathan Penrose in 1969.

At Hanover in 1902 Atkins finished third to Janowski and Pillsbury ahead of Mieses, Napier, Tchigorin, Marshall and others, but he took his duties as a schoolmaster seriously and hardly went abroad again.

England's main torch-bearers now became Sir George Thomas and F. D. Yates. Two curiously contrasted figures. Sir George, the son of a diplomat, a courteous dilettante, a badminton international and excellent at tennis, serving games as administrator, for years on the committee at Wimbledon. Always immaculate, always taking care of himself.

F. D. Yates, blessed with perhaps a spark more genius, was eventually ruined by the lack of the private means to which Sir George must have owed a lot. Blackburne had been hardly less humble of origin than Yates but possessed a business sense that the latter conspicuously lacked. Yates died a sloven, a drunkard, in pathetic circumstances; but he was British Champion six times — once above the ephemeral Indian wonder Sultan Khan — and he twice defeated Alekhine when Alekhine was at his best.

Sir George Thomas's halcyon day was to come when, at Hastings in 1934-5, he crowned decades of steady effort by tying for first place with Euwe and Flohr, ahead of Capablanca (!), Botvinnik and Lilienthal.

Each of two world wars in turn gave organised chess a noteworthy boost. Chess seems to flourish in service conditions; war nowadays seems to station numbers of people in bleak surroundings with time on their hands.

J. H. van Meurs emerged as an outstanding figure. This irascible, domineering, loveable Dutchman made the secretaryship of the London Chess League his own for about forty years. He started the annual England-Holland matches. Probably his most permanently valuable work came in the provinces. Pushing, prodding, persuading, he brought into existence about half the County Chess Associations we have today, welding them into the British Chess Federation to make that body really nationally representative at last. Four devoted secretaries served the B. C. F. well in turn: L. P. Rees, R. H. S. Stevenson, H. Meek and A. F. Stammwitz. Among devoted workers outside London, the name of J. T. Boyd cannot be passed over. Rees excelled himself above all in the inauguration of the International Team Tournaments. The first of these, London, 1927, drew sixteen teams. Hungary won, with Denmark second and England, led by Atkins, Yates and Thomas, third. The "Chess Olympiads" became the outstanding events of the entire world chess calendar. Havana's in 1966 attracted 52 teams, the USSR, the U.S.A., Hungary and Yugoslavia taking the first four places with the B.C.F. team now a lowly 21st, Scotland 28th and Ireland 40th.

Throughout the between-war years, London had the world's greatest chess coffee house, the Gambit rooms in Budge Row. Miss Edith Price, a dear soul and strong player who, curiously, barred others of her sex from the place entirely (apart from waitresses) held court.

Not even Simpsons' in its day challenged the Gambit for world fame. Any world master of renown finding himself within a hundred miles of it would unfailingly head there. Yates and Winter became resident professionals, taking on all comers, but at a miserable sixpence or shilling a game. In 1947 the entire building was demolished, to be replaced by a huge block of offices.

Incidentally Kriegspiel, not ordinary chess, was the first game you encountered as you walked into the Gambit, the set of three boards in the front window being manned from morning till night, often by near-millionaire business men from the City nearby. The game, then and since, has had considerable popularity in England. Each player toils away in ignorance of the disposition of his opponent's pieces, except what he can deduce from bumping into them with his own. G. F. Anderson wrote an entertaining book entitled "Are there any?" from the question repeatedly asked of the umpire during the game "Are there any pawn captures?"

In 1935 the writer founded a new magazine CHESS; livelier and in popular style, it soon outstripped the "B.C.M." in circulation but the old magazine, in its 90th year as we write, goes happily on. The CHESS offices at Sutton Coldfield soon became a sort of clearing house for chess goods, literature and even thought, serving some 120 different countries throughout the world.

In 1936, Alderman Derbyshire in Nottingham brought about single-handed the greatest tournament in England since 1895. He had won a minor event in an earlier congress there. This had to be celebrated, though it was to cost him well over £1,000. To four world champions, Alekhine, Capablanca, Lasker and Euwe, went appearance fees of £200 each. Botvinnik — soon to become another — finished in first place, tied with Capablanca. The home contingent, comprised of Tylor, Alexander, Thomas and Winter, collapsed neatly into the last four places.

After the Second World War came a spate of radio matches. England held the U.S.S.R. to a score of 6–14 (the U.S.A. had been beaten 7½–12½ in a similar event just before). Australia beat France over the ether soon after but as air travel developed these affairs became unnecessary.

Cork-born C. H. O'D. Alexander, the strongest player Ireland ever produced, beat Botvinnik in one of their 1946 radio match games. He finished first at Hastings in 1946–7 above Tartakover and Janowski and again in 1953–4, equal with Bronstein above O'Kelly, Matanowic, Olafsson, Teschner, Tolush and Tartakower. He was a leading figure in the British Chess Federation's consolidation through four decades.

Lacking Alexander's fire though more dependable at his own level, H. Golombek (b. 1910) earned world fame as a prolific author with 30 fine books on chess to his credit, and gained the first O.B.E. awarded for services to the game.

BRITISH CHESS FEDERATION STIRS

The British Chess Federation had limped along hampered by inadequate finance (its leading figures were possibly a little too remote from the man in the street). Its prizes were being exceeded by congresses of lesser status. Suddenly, from a South African as unknown before as since, came a bequest which expanded the prize fund annually by £180 at a stroke. Jonathan Penrose, student son of a world-famous professor of genetics, won the title seven times in succession and thrice more later. He fared less well in international tournaments in Madrid and Buenos Aires, but defeated Tal in one fine match game. Sadly, like Atkins, in bygone days, he rates his profession as a lecturer above chess and has even declined more than one invitation to the short ten days contest at Hastings. He too was awarded the O. B. E., in 1971.

The British Chess Federation's National Club Championship has produced some worthy tussles but suffers from the adjudication of games infinished after one session, a practice rife among the Leagues until its drawbacks were recognised, which has played havoc with British players' ability in the end-game.

1951 was marked by two events of importance. The "Staunton Centenary Tournament," in memory of 1851, was held in Cheltenham, Leamington and Birmingham. It attracted Gligoric, Trifunovic, Pirc and Matanovic from Yugoslavia, Stahlberg from Sweden, Donner and Van Scheltinga from Holland, Rossolimo and Tartakover from France and Unzicker and Bogolubov from Germany.

Scene at start of a day's play in one of the Chess Festivals organised by the English editor in Eastbourne Town Hall.

Chess takes over in a typical English public house.

The other was the first-ever World Junior Championship, with entries from Yugoslavia, Argentina, Denmark, Finland, Switzerland, France, Germany, Austria, Australia, Iceland, Canada, Norway, Eire, Scotland, Sweden and Belgium. Ivkov won, with Malcolm Barker second. Barker's rare promise was matched only by his insouciance: within a few weeks, he had given up chess for good. Competitors destined to become famous were B. Larsen (fifth) and F. Olafsson (12th!).

This was W. Ritson Morry's heyday as an organizer; he played the major part in each event. The Junior World Championship immediately became an irreplaceable item in the world's chess calendar.

1953 saw the start of the writer's "Chess Festivals" which have continued annually at Cheltenham, Skegness, Southend, Whitby, Eastbourne and Southport in turn, big prizes and an easy-going atmosphere attracting 250–300 entries a time.

SCOTLAND AND IRELAND

If 1851's was the first, Dundee's in 1867 was the fifth international chess congress ever held, with Steinitz as invitee. Its centenary was celebrated by a five-nation affair sponsored by W. A. Fairhurst, an adopted Sassenach who, in the intervals between designing some of the finest bridges in Scotland (or, indeed the world) annexed the Scottish Championship ten times. J. M. Aitken was his main rival. As we write, a new star seems to be rising in lanky A. M. Davie.

We have mentioned how G. H. Mackenzie and C. H. O'D. Alexander, the best players Scotland and Ireland ever produced, went abroad for their fame. J. J. O'Hanlon was Ireland's next best player, as well as a generous promoter of the game. Enda Rohan brought a World Championship Zonal Tournament to Dublin in 1956 and another international tournament to Cork but vanished from the chess scene as suddenly as he had appeared. Ireland's greatest contribution to recent chess has come from C. Parker Glorney of Dublin, who donated a fine cup for a competition between teams of juniors which has enticed not only England, Scotland and Wales but France and Holland as well into the ring.

A MEDLEY OF CONGRESSES

In 1935 we could rely on just two chess congresses per year, the British Chess Federation's in the summer and Hastings in its already traditional date just after Christmas. Then H. G. T. Matchett organized three big gatherings at Margate. Though these came to an end with the outbreak of war, the attraction of the end-of-season Easter date had become very apparent. A positive explosion was to follow, when the war ended.

By 1968, there were Easter congresses at Wolverhampton, Birmingham, Leicester and Dundee, Weymouth, Swansea, Aberystwyth, Folkestone, Penzance, Richmond, Southend, Liverpool, Manchester, Wallasey and Bognor Regis. Each drew at least 50 competitors; Wallasey's junior congress drew 880. At Liverpool, T. J. Beach, G. A. M. Boswell and their co-workers regularly break all world records with attendances of 1,400 juniors or more.

Around May and June 1968 there were congresses at Birmingham again; Rhyl, Scunthorpe, Ilford, Dorchester.

The summer saw a seven weeks' unbroken run, Whitby being followed by the B.C.F.'s congress, the Chess Festival and Paignton's in turn.

Llandrindod Wells, Marlow, Ayr, Dublin, Newcastle-upon-Tyne, Edinburgh, Glasgow, Hull, Brighouse, Plymouth, Hatfield were other venues for chess congresses in this one year, 1968.

It is difficult to convey a true picture of the proliferation of chess congresses in this country without our recital degenerating into a catalogue.

There may be over a thousand players engaged in a dozen different towns the same day.

THE UNIVERSITIES

The Universities have been for a century the backbone of British Chess. The annual Oxford-Cambridge match started in 1873 and it is hardly an exaggeration to say that the two teams have supplied since that date about one third of the keenest and best chess players of the land.

In 1945, the other British Universities came to life with the formation of the British Universities' Chess Association, which, under the writer's almost permanent presidency, has sent a team to every Students' Chess Olympiad and organised annually an individual championship which has rather languished, but a team championship which has prospered beyond belief; on Swansea in April 1968 there converged enthusiastically 23 teams of ten. Only London has challenged Oxbridge with any consistency in this later event. British students had their greatest moment when a team comprising M. J. Basman,

British problem composers have throughout decades been among world's best. Here, Comius Mansfield, universally recognised as the greatest composer of mate in two move problems, enjoys a joke with Dr. K. Fabel (Germany, right) who is as distinguished in the realm of Fairy chess as in orthodox problemdom.

R. W. Bonham (right centre) is Britain's leading blind player, though T. H. Tylor in his day was greater. A chess olympiad for blind players drew teams from the U.S.S.R., Yugoslavia, Rumania, Germany (GDR and FRG), Czechoslovakia, the U.S.A., Austria, Hungary, Spain, Israel and some other countries to Weymouth in 1968.

W. R. Hartston, R. D. Keene and A. N. Whiteley beat the Soviet Union in Czechoslovakia in 1967 by three games to one.

CHESS BY POST

Correspondence chess has been developing in Britain more intensively than perhaps in any other country except Germany. The pioneer body, the British Correspondence Chess Association, founded in 1906, organised the British Correspondence Chess Championship under the B.C.F. from 1921 on. Other groups of correspondence players came into being and keen rivalries developed but a British Postal Chess Federation united all in an atmosphere of extraordinary harmony, fostered by T. Vaughan Williams and R. J. Potter as president and secretary, and exemplified by the grace with which the B.C.C.A. gave up the right to control the championship to the new Federation. In 1944 the writer founded the Postal Chess League, a competition for teams of ten which draws 60 to 70 teams per year and took over control of the British Postal Chess Team Championship in 1967.

A PROUD RECORD

So Britain organized the first modern type International Chess Tournament and introduced the code of laws in use everywhere today. Britain started the Chess Olympiads and the World Championship for Juniors. Britain brought in the chessmen and chess clock all chess-players use and can boast the oldest chess column and the oldest chess magazine with a continuous history. British chess literature is unsurpassed.

There are 3,500 senior clubs and as many school and junior clubs. 8,800 players are affiliated to the B.C.F. but some 100,000 others are not.

Yet, for a century, no Briton has attained the topmost rank. The intensive organization is starting to produce young players of great promise. Shall we see a British World Champion in our lifetime? I doubt it. There are still serious obstacles, particularly the lack of financial incentive. Even a Jonathan Penrose cannot risk his fortunes on chess. The government hands out £100,000 to opera, not a farthing to chess. Nor is there any group of dedicated enthusiasts, polishing their skills against each other, such as London's in the 1870's, or those of Moscow, New York or Yugoslavia today.

III. RAMIFICATIONS OF CHESS

Lucas van Leyden (1508): "A game of chess." A version of chess known as "Courier's Game," played on a 12 × 8 board; very popular in the Netherlands, France and Germany in the 14th-16th centuries (The Berlin National Gallery).

We have become accustomed to playing chess on a black and white chequered board of 64 squares with sixteen men on each side; but it has mutated during the centuries through a fantastic variety of forms, some so eccentric as to be hardly recognisable as chess at all.

Its family tree has been painstakingly compiled by researchers in history, art, literature, philology and other branches of learning. Archaeologists have made useful contributions. Though much remains obscure, a reasonable certificate of origin can be drawn up.

Firstly, we have to ask: what is chess, and what is not?

(1) It is a board game played between opposing forces;

(2) Opponents each make one move in turn;

(3) The aim is to checkmate your opponent's principal piece, i.e. to bring about a situation in which it is doomed.

So — an important point — victory is not gained, necessarily, by either reaching any particular part on the board or purely by captures.

Can we define chess without describing the pieces or the board...? Yes; our definition covers a variety of games but curiously, and perhaps not by chance, they are all recognisable as forms of chess. Sometimes the moves of the men are familiar but their names are strange; sometimes the reverse.

On the other hand, games may resemble chess in some respects but fall outside our definition. Draughts (chequers), for example, uses the same board but is certainly not chess.

Chess as we play it today has remained substantially unchanged since the turn of the 15th century. Previously, however, it had gone through considerable alteration.

For instance, among the Arabs up to 1200, the queens were weak; they could move only one square diagonally. In the Middle Ages they became the strongest pieces on the board. Up till about 1200, a bishop was limited to a three

square jump diagonally (it could jump over another piece on the way). A rook could at one time move two squares only. That the other pieces were so much weaker greatly increased the kings' powers of resistance, and slowed down the game. To make it more exciting, its attackers were given greater and greater powers. These increases in the powers of the attack were felt by the Polish writer Karol Irzykowski (1873–1944) to have had an explosive effect on the game comparable to that of the invention of gunpowder on the history of mankind.

In some places, innovators went to extremes. In Russia, for instance, an "absolute queen" was tried out which combined the powers of a queen with those of a knight. For a long time, whenever they started a game, players had to agree whether their queens were to be ordinary or absolute.

Castling has varied a lot.

About 1560, in Spain, an unmoved king, not in check, could leap two squares in any direction, provided he did not cross an enemy line of fire. In France it was the same but in addition, if the squares between the king and one of his rooks, previously unmoved, were unoccupied, he could be moved up to the rook and the rook brought on to the square thus vacated. In Italy, some players followed the Spanish method; others gave the king a longer leap and some allowed a pawn to move in front of the newly castled king, all this counting as one move only! Some players simply interchanged king and rook; others admitted no "castling" move at all; yet others castled as we do today.

"Free castling" had a long vogue. In this, the rook was placed on any square up to and including the king's and the king moved to any square beyond the rook. This method persisted in parts of Italy up to the end of the 19th century.

Finally, in Iceland and some other countries the king was allowed to move, once only during the game, as a knight!

Castling was in many places given a name wit-

tily based on the idea that the king fled from his foes into the kitchen.

In the early days of chess, "bared king" was often counted as a loss, victory going to a player who captured all his opponent's men except the uncapturable king. This rule did not persist beyond Arabic times. Warfare itself has, of course, developed similarly. Whereas victory commonly implied massacre, it has come to be accepted when one side has the enemy leader completely in its power.

In the battle of Brenneville (1119) in which the French were defeated, Louis VI's bridle was seized by an English soldier who shouted "I've captured the king!" Louis cried: "The king cannot be captured!" and in a moment the non-plussed attacker was felled by the King's sword.

Emanuel Lasker devised, in "Fress-Schach," a game in which the king was not inviolate; the game could go on after he had been taken. Chess? No!

Experimentation involved not only the men and their moves; the board has taken many shapes and sizes, too. Until about 1300, the squares were not black and white at all: for half its history to date, chess has been played on a plain board with ruled lines only. Difficult as we might find it to imagine chessboards without contrasting colours, they are common even yet throughout the East.

In many countries today the opposing men may be distinguished apart, not by colour, but merely by marks or notches or by being kept throughout facing the enemy — or even by memory alone.

The German explorer H. Geist describes chess among the Bataks in Sumatra, played in a native hut with the floor as the board. The squares were marked out by thinly cut lines with no contrast in colour. The men were random objects of various shapes and colour; bits of wood, shells, stones, etc. The players and the keenly interested spectators remembered without difficulty which pieces were which, and which were "black," which "white." The game was being played largely in the mind, the "pieces" being little more than a reminder of the situation in the game.

The Bataks did not promote a pawn; on reaching the eighth rank it went back to its original square and started again.

68

Allegoric drawing showing four-handed chess, known as "The royal game," on the title page of a chess treatise by G. Weickhmann published at Ulm in 1664.

The Bataks of Sumatra have been great chess enthusiasts from time immemorial. Drawing by M. Majewski.

Among the Chinese, the board needs no contrasting colours anyway, as the game is played on the lines, not on the squares, the pieces being posted at intersections.

Chess is not necessarily a game for two persons. Several players can battle on the board, each with a full set of his own.

In fact, chess started as a game for four, as its old Indian name *Chatrang* reveals. As in modern bridge, partners sat opposite each other, playing against opponents at their sides. The Sanskrit word *chatrang* indicates a military formation of four units (chatur: four; anga: part), so implies a quadruple four-fold contest. There were four kinds of arms (elephants, horses, war chariots and infantry), and four armies. Each army was of a different colour: yellow and

red fought against black and green. An army consisted of four pawns and four pieces, starting in one corner. Dice were cast to decide which player should move, and what piece he should move (!). If a player managed to place his Rajah in his opponent's royal space, he took over the other army as well as his own. The aim of the game was to capture both enemy Rajahs, this being an important development from an earlier, relatively short, period when victory could be gained by capturing other men.

Though card games were known in the Egypt of the Pharaons, the division into four suits in a modern pack almost certainly originated from chess. In early card games, the aim was to defend the king, just as in chess. As if to repay the debt, about 1890 two Germans patented a card game called Schachett, with cards which were of two suits, black and white; court cards were chess pieces, others pawns, and the rules were a blend of cards with chess.

The Indian Chatrang soon became a game for two, and remained so. Perhaps four players could not always readily be found. The use of dice persisted, on and off, for centuries but the improvement when chance was eliminated and only skill told was too obvious to gainsay.

Yet the quadruple game did not die without a struggle. More in the East than in Europe, it lingered on sporadically throughout the Middle Ages.

Catherine II of Russia liked the quadruple game. Old books and manuscripts describe and illustrate it. Chessboards were sometimes in the shape of a cross, with lines crossing diagonally as well as at right angles. Although the departures from ordinary chess might be pronounced, the aim of the contest, to mate the enemy king, and the resemblances of the pieces to those of today identified the game, clearly, as chess. Four-handed chess was called "The Royal Game" for centuries but later this name was adopted by ordinary chess.

"Great Chess" is another variant which originated in India and enjoyed considerable favour over great areas for awhile. On a 144-square board (12 × 12) stood 48 men. Each player had 12 pieces and 12 pawns. Sometimes dice were cast, sometimes players exercised their own initiative. Each strove to checkmate his opponent's Rajah. The pieces were named after real or legendary creatures: the Aanca Bird (Phoenix?); the Crocodile, the Giraffe, the Unicorn, the Lion; also two more normal to us, rooks. For Tamerlane too, the famous 16th century Mongolian conqueror and a passionate devotee of the game, an 8 by 8 board was not big enough. He devised his own "Great Chess" on a board of 110 squares (10 × 11) with one additional square in the middle of each edge adjacent to the player. Eleven kinds of chessmen were drawn up in three ranks. He

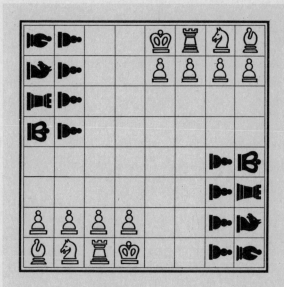

Old Indian Four-a-side chess, "chaturanga." The drawing shows the chessmen set out for the start of a game. The yellow and red chessmen (in the drawing — the light ones) play against the "green" and "black" (the dark ones).

The chessboard for "The Royal Game" as described by C. Weickhmann in 1664. The board was in the shape of a cross, with lines crossing diagonally as well as at right angles.

71

invented rules to suit his own military tastes. Beside the king, there were a General, a Vizier, a Camel, an Elephant, a Giraffe, a War Machine (chariot?), a Knight, a Rook and so on.

A 15th century Uzbek poet, Alisher Navoi, described "Great Chess" as played in Central Asia in the 13th and 14th centuries. Each side's men started in three ranks on a 100 square board. The king had the assistance of two Viziers, an Elephant, a Giraffe, a Bear, a Camel, a Ruhbird, Horses and Pawns.

Another kind of "Great Chess," called the "Courier Game," played on 96 squares (12×8), spread widely during the 14th and 16th centuries throughout the Netherlands, France and Germany. Apart from the men named above, each player had four more pawns and two Couriers, a Counsellor and a Jester. The pieces being weak-

er in those days as we have seen, the new Couriers, moving like the bishops of today, at once became popular for their speed and range. It is the "Courier Game" which the eminent Dutch painter Lucas van Leyden depicted in his famous 1520 oil painting "The Chess Players." A set of "Great Chess" pieces was presented by the Elector, Prince Frederic of Brandenburg, to the German village of Ströbeck, in 1651, but vanished about a century later.

"Astronomical Chess" was the most complicated offshoot of all. Seven players took part. The "men" were the planets and the stars. The board represented Heaven and was divided into twelve zones marked by the signs of the zodiac. There were seven concentric circles, representing the orbits of the Moon, Mercury, Venus, the Sun, Mars, Jupiter, and Saturn, each the field of ac-

An attempt to combine chess and cards, a German invention of the late 19th century, called Schachett. The cards had only two suits, black and white, corresponding to chessmen: the "honours" — to the rook, knight, bishop, king and queen and the remaining cards from 1 to 8 — to "pawns." In the drawing: a black rook, white king and white knight.

tion of one of the players. The pieces moved according to mathematical calculations.

One variety of "Astronomical Chess" used ordinary chessmen, moving on 64 spaces on, again, a circular board. This was Zatrikion, or Byzantine chess. The board was divided into four concentric circles each divided into 16 segments by radii from the centre. Anna Comnena, daughter of the Byzantine Emperor Alexius I (1081–1118) told in a biography of her father how Zatrikion had been brought to Byzantium by the Arabs.

Chinese chess, called Hsiang-chi, developed from Chatrang along different lines from European chess. It is played on a rectangular board of 9 by 10 points, divided in the middle by a blank neutral belt, the "river," which separates the opposing forces. The pieces move along the lines and stand at their intersections. They take the form of small discs, marked on top with symbols which indicate what they are. The chief piece is the General, who stands with two Chancellors (there is no corresponding piece in European chess) in a reserved part of the board apart — the headquarters as it were — which they may not leave. Next, there are Counsellors, rather like bishops, to reinforce the General's defence but they cannot attack; they cannot cross the river. There are Chariots like our rooks, and Horses like our knights except that they cannot leap over other men.

The pawns can move one point forward and, after crossing the river, one point sideways as well. Last come pieces unknown to us: Cannons. These move like rooks but can check or capture an enemy man only when separated from him by another.

Games of Chinese chess are generally short. It is more like the original chess of India than might be thought.

In an article entitled "Chess in China" by George F. Cooks and I-Chang which appeared in Lasker's Chess Magazine in December 1905 and January 1906, is given an extensive description of Chinese Chess, also called the

"Big chess" played on a board of 144 squares. Apart from kings, the chessmen included exotic animals. A miniature dated 1283, from the manuscript of Alfonso the Wise.

Elephant Game. The analysis of the game is accompanied by a considerable number of interesting observations on local customs and manners. Among other things the article reads:

"The natives are very fond of the game, and one rarely finds a village which does not contain some who both understand and love it. But I have never heard of a Chinese chess club. Professional players abound, and are often to be seen on the streets with the board set up for a middle or end game and offering the passer-by the option of playing either side, the loser to pay a forfeit. For John Chinaman is so made that he would not really enjoy the game unless it brought with it the chance of making a few sach. They play as a rule very rapidly and there is no call for

73

such a control as a timing clock. 'Touch and move' are unknown, to 'tap a chessman' being a common phrase for pondering and meditating. There are no penalties for illegal moves. It is more or less understood that on removing the hand from a piece the move is completed, and usually on the 'river' is written a short rhyming couplet which roughly translated reads:

The Yellow River who can wade?
When your hand is off your move is made.

But your opponent will make no remark if you repent of your move before he has made his, and probably only a mild protest will be made if after his move you replace the pieces to reconsider a move your opponent's answer has shown to be unsound. Some players I have met do not call 'check' and should you fail to notice it, will take off your king and claim the game. Chess 'sans voir' is practically unknown, although one of my teachers told me the following story:

A famous warrior had come disguised to spy out the land he wished to conquer. Sleeping one night at an inn, he heard two women talking behind the thin partition of his room. Peering through a crack he could see nothing for they had lit no lamp. So he listened to their conversation and found they were playing together a game of chess in the dark and with no boards. This great wonder astounded him, and he went away to seek other fields to conquer, reasoning that if the women of that country were so powerful, what would the men be.

Books on end-games for the use of professional player abound, but I have not been able to obtain any on the openings though such do exist. The problem art is not popular and compared with the perfection reached by our home artists may be said not to exist. Chinese poems and proverbs contain some references to chess and I append a few rough translations, and it will be seen that some of the ideas expressed can doubtless be applied to the game as played in our own land. One says: 'Chess playing is like being put in charge of a bank, it fills one with such anxiety.' Another 'The affairs of this world resemble chess, where every combination is a new one, and things get very mixed.' And lastly this ditty seems to hint that love of chess in China is dying out:

Of old rich men did but desire
To play at chess, and touch the lyre,
But modern men are growing rude
Their one desire is lots of food.

The concluding passage of the article carries an interesting note of a historical nature:

"The Chinese scholars in this place say that their classics prove that the 'elephant game' was invented by Wu-Wang of the Chou Dynasty B. C. 1122. This Emperor wrote the following in one of his edicts:

We invent music to resemble scholarship,
We invent chess to resemble warfare.

Now the Chinese words 'resemble' and 'elephant' are practically indistinguishable, and these scholars affirm that in the good old times chess was always known as 'Resemble war game,' that the word war was afterwards dropped for the sake of brevity; and that 'Resemble game' and 'Elephant game' became synonimous in Chinese."

Chess travelled via Korea in due course to Japan where it became further transformed and re-named Shogi or "The Generals' Game." This is played on the squares (not lines now) of a singly coloured board 9 by 9. The pieces all have the same colour and shape — an irregular pentagon — and are marked on top with symbols. The direction in which a piece is playing is indicated by

one of its corners being kept pointed towards the opponent. Each player has 20 pieces of eight kinds placed in three ranks. The main pieces "Generals of precious stones," face each other across the central belt. On either side, are generals of lower rank, one of gold, the other of silver. Of pieces familiar to us, there are Shogi (knights), bishops, rooks, and pawns — with, of course, different names in the Japanese. The pieces not like ours are the Chariots. As in Chinese chess, there is no piece corresponding to our queen.

We now stray a little farther afield. Egyptian "chess," of which traces have been found in excavations dating back thousands of years B. C., is really not chess at all. The most carefully investigated among the relics have proved to be of Senet, a board-game akin to draughts. Its similarity to chess is superficial, lying possibly in the shapes of the stone pieces which are built up, not small discs.

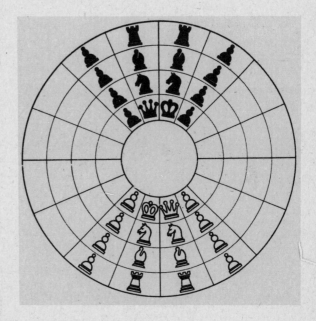

Byzantine chess, "Zatrikion," played on a round board, the chessmen and their moves being similar to those in Arabian chess of the same period.

75

Hsiang-chi, or Chinese chess. The chessmen move along the lines. The chessboard is divided in two by a neutral belt known as the "river." Green men play the red ones.

Men set out for the Japanese version of chess known as shogi, or "the generals' game."

That board games and card-games were popular at the Egyptian Court and among the priests, numerous paintings in the tombs make clear. There are 30-space boards with 12 men as well as 144-space boards with 48 men. Some boards are narrow and oblong. Contrasting colours are absent.

Then there is draughts. A distant relative os chess; shall we say a half-brother? Both games use the same board. They have been with us for a long time, sometimes competing, at other times peacefully co-existing. The origins of draughts can be traced in various types of board games, from the most ancient of all, yet in the form generally known it is none too old, in fact is about six centuries younger than chess. It may have developed as a cross between chess and a Spanish game, "The Mill," in which one captures a piece by leaping over it.

A Polish author Bystroń, writing on the history of customs in old Poland, describes how chess was found too difficult. "Draughts ... an easier game ... was incomparably more popular. It was played at courts and in camps, to relieve days of waiting and boredom."

Draughts played on a board of 100 squares, though early named Polish draughts was, in contrast to the 64-square variety, never played in Poland. It was devised in the 1820's by a French officer, together with a Polish lieutenant from the retinue of Princess Maria Leszczyńska, at the court of the French Prince Regent Philip II of Orleans. The Frenchman courteously gave the full credit for the invention to his friend. "Polish draughts" gave an impetus to the invention of other types of draughts of which a number of countries throughout the world have different national varieties.

Not everybody has considered draughts inferior to chess. The Polish poet Adam Mickiewicz wrote a highly complimentary poem about draughts, as a counter-blast to Bishop Vida's famous Latin poem on chess. Here are a few lines:

Know, then, this is an image of array;
Ground is wanted to bring troops to play.
First, then, accoutre well the list for Draughts,
Marked on each side with seven equal shafts;
Next, fashion all the Black and the White squares,
Place the alternate on the thoroughfares
When the lot is marked, writ and bound,
Do not be slow to call the knights to ground.
Twelve men has one side, so does the other;
With pawns they fight, as Pawns they are gathered.
So as to shun an error in the crowd,
Some wear the Black, and others the White Shroud.

In Nicholas Gogol's "Dead Souls," winning at a game of draughts decided the conditions for the purchase of "dead souls" — that is, of dead serfs still figuring in the records. Nozdryov wished to sell his dead to Chichikov but in order to avoid the form of a commercial deal he suggested they settle the deal by a game of cards:

'Well,' said Nozdryov after a short pause, 'what about it? Won't you play for my dead souls?'

'I've told you, my dear fellow, that I don't play. I'll buy them if you like.'

'I don't want to sell them. It wouldn't be acting like a friend. I don't want to make a profit out of any damn thing. Now, a game of cards is a different matter. Let's have just one game, anyway!'

'I've told you already I won't.'

'And you won't exchange them for anything?'

'No.'

'Well, look here, let's have a game of draughts. If you win, they're all yours. You see, I've got lots who should have been struck off the census register. Hey, Porfiry, bring the draught board here.'

'You needn't trouble, I'm not going to play.'

'But this is not cards: there's no question of luck or cheating here. It's all a matter of skill, you know. In fact I must warn you that I can't play at all. You really should give me a piece or two.'

'Well,' Chichikov thought to himself, 'why not sit down and have a game of draughts with him?

Egyptian caricature (13th century B.C.) showing a lion and an antelope playing a board game. The lion symbolizes the Pharaoh Rameses III, who used to strip court dignitaries of their money.

Ancient Egyptian interior. In the foreground, a table serving to play senet, a precursor of draughts. Drawing by S. Siennicki.

Egyptian board-game (senet) found in Tutankhamen's tomb. In the background an ancient Egyptian wall-painting showing two people at play.

I used to play draughts quite well and it will be difficult for him to get up to any tricks at draughts.'

'All right, so be it. I'll have a game of draughts with you.'

'The souls against a hundred roubles!'

'Why a hundred? Fifty's enough.'

'No, what sort of stake is fifty? I'd better throw in a middling puppy or a gold seal for your watch chain.'

'Oh, very well,' said Chichikov.

'How many pieces will you give me?' asked Nozdryov.

'Whatever for? I won't give you anything.'

'You might at least let me have the first two moves.'

'I won't. I'm a poor player myself.'

'We know you', said Nozdryov, moving a piece.

'We know what sort of a poor player you are.'

'Haven't touched a draughtsman for I don't know how long,' said Chichikov, also moving a piece.

'We know you, we know what sort of a poor player you are,' said Nozdryov, moving another piece and at the same time pushing forward another with the cuff of his sleeve.

'Haven't touched a draughtsman for ages,' said Chichikov. 'Hullo, hullo! What's that, my dear fellow? Put it back.'

'Put back what?'

'Why, that piece there,' said Chichikov, and, at the same time, saw almost under his very nose another which seemed to have got almost far enough to become king; where it had come from goodness only knows. 'No, sir,' said Chichikov, getting up from the table, 'it's quite impossible to play with you. One doesn't play like that with three pieces all at once?'

'Why with three? I'm sorry, I made a mistake. One was moved accidentally. I'll put it back if you like.'

'And where did the other one come from?'

'What other one?'

'Why, the one which is going to be a king.'

'Good Lord, don't you remember?'

'No, my dear fellow, I don't. I've counted every move and I remember them all. You've only just placed it there. That's where it should be!'

'What? There?' said Nozdryov, reddening. 'I can see, my dear fellow, you like to imagine things.'

'No, my dear fellow, it's you who seem to be imagining things, only not very successfully.'

Napoleon Bonaparte preferred draughts, basing on it his military tactics of lightning-quick regrouping of forces for attack.

Edgar Allan Poe wrote in "The Murders in

Louis XIV playing draughts. A cartoon with political overtones, from a late 18th century calendar.

Satirical drawing by Honore Daumier from the Paris periodical "Le Charivari" in 1847 with an ironic caption: "Parisians who will never be under observation by the secret police."

Draughts enthusiasts at a Paris café in the 19th century. Contemporary lithograph by de Boilly.

"The queen is captured" — *a satire on enthusiasm for draughts. Early 19th century French caricature.*

the Rue Morgue": "To calculate is not in itself to analyse. A chessplayer, for example, does the one without effort at the other. It follows that the game of chess, in its effects upon mental character, is greatly misunderstood. I am not now writing a treatise, but simply prefacing a somewhat peculiar narrative by observations very much at random; I will therefore take occasion to assert that the higher powers of the reflective intellect are more decidedly and more usefully tasked by the unostentatious game of draughts than by all the elaborate frivolity of chess. In this latter where the pieces have different and bizarre motions, with various and variable values, what is only complex is mistaken (a not unusual error) for what is profound. The attention is here called powerfully into play. If it flags for an instant, an oversight is committed, resulting in injury or defeat. The possible

moves being not only manifold but involute, the chances of such oversights are multiplied; and in nine cases out of ten it is the more concentrative rather than the more acute player who conquers. In draughts, on the contrary, where the moves are unique and have but little variation, the probabilities of inadvertence are diminished, and the mere attention being left comparatively unemployed, what advantages are obtained by either party are obtained by superior acumen. To be less abstract — let us suppose a game of draughts where the pieces are reduced to four kings, and where, of course, no oversight is to be expected. It is obvious that here the victory can be decided (the players being at all equal) only by some recherché movement, the result of some strong exertion of the intellect. Deprived of ordinary resources, the analyst throws himself into the spirit of his opponent, identifies

81

A game of draughts in the Warsaw flat of Frederic Chopin's parents. Scene from the Polish film "Chopin's Youth" (1952).

Draughts on a hotel terrace, 1929. An original variety of the game demanding physical as well as mental effort.

himself therewith, and not unfrequently sees thus at a glance, the sole methods (sometimes indeed absurdly simple ones) by which he may seduce into error or hurry into miscalculation."

In China, for some thousands of years, a game has been played called "Wei-chi," i.e. "The Siege Game." It is a peculiar form of draughts on a board marked with 19 horizontal and 19 vertical intersecting lines. Each opponent has 180 stones. The aim of the game is to seize territory and trap opposing pieces. Play starts with only a few men on each side; further pieces are gradually brought in from the players' reserves. The men are posted on intersections. Chinese draughts has a rich tradition and an extensive literature, and is advancing steadily in popularity in Europe and America.

Ludus Latrunculorum, "the game of soldiers" or Latrunculi for short, was very popular in the ancient Roman Empire. It had certain resemblances to both draughts and chess. It was played on a tablet like a chessboard. Each player set out two rows of men; a rank of "great" soldiers moving like the queen in chess, and a rank of "small' soldiers corresponding to draughtsmen. The game was played all over the board and whoever captured or trapped all his opponent's men won. Owing to the double meaning of the word latro, which means "a soldier" — also a "brigand" — the name was often wrongly translated as a "game of little brigands." The word latrunculus is a diminutive of latro and definitely means "a little soldier." But this was not the end of errors: later on Latrunculi was repeatedly confused with chess. In Poland for instance, one author, in translating Jan Kochanowski's poem "Chess" into Latin, rendered the title as Latrunculi, whilst another, translating Seneca into Polish, made a similar mistake in reverse by calling latrunculi chess. To make things worse, he wrote in his preface: "It is obvious that chess was often played among the Romans." Chess was, however, definitely unknown in either ancient Rome or Greece.

"A Game of Draughts." Lithograph by Edouard Vuillard, French impressionist.

Yet another game, "Arithmetical Chess," though outwardly bearing little relation to chess, was in practice very close to it as a result of the fact that the aim was to trap the main piece.

The board was divided into 128 black and white squares (8×16). Each player had 24 pieces marked with numbers. There were three kinds of pieces — round, triangular, and square — moving in different ways. Capturing and mating were based on numerical combinations. The rules were fantastically complicated. An interesting game but one demanding great mathematical skill. Its complexity put amateurs off whilst mathematicians preferred to employ their talents in other

Henri Matisse's "Family evening," in oil. From the Eremitage collections, Leningrad.

directions so that, though it had a certain vogue in the Renaissance period, it faded out soon after.

War games of various kinds allied to chess have been devised in some variety and new kinds are still being invented today. One's opponent's forces may be invisible, so that their dispositions have to be found by trial. "Sea Warfare" is one quite well-known game of this type.

Another which appeared in England in 1770 was described in a book "The Game of War, an Improvement on Chess." The board, divided into black and white squares, served as a battle-field for a number of pieces — more than in chess. The king had to be checkmated by new pieces called Cannons. In 1782, Helwig presented a similar game, Estralography or Military Chess, in which each player stormed an enemy fort. The pieces represented not only Infantry, Cavalry, Artillery, and Transport but also Fortified Camps, Stores, etc.

About 1850, another type of "war game" was suggested in book form. It was based on a plan of the battlefield of Ostrołęka, 1831, in which Polish insurgents fought the troops of the Tsar, this plan of the battlefield being divided up like a chessboard. We fear war has diverged very far from chess these days.

Innumerable modifications of chess such as changing the shape and size of the board, introducing new pieces etc., have been suggested to reduce the value of book knowledge. A lot of people have felt that study of the openings has gone too far and they try to foil the "swot".

Of the hundreds of suggestions put forward, we can quote only a few.

The pawns are usually left unaltered but many changes in the pieces have been proposed. In one game, the players start with an empty board. White places one of his men on any square he likes; Black places a similar man wherever he likes, then places a second on the board wherever he chooses. White places a second and third piece, then Black a third and fourth and so on, until the whole array is out. It has been calculated that the game could start from any of at least ten thousand different positions, so that all established theory becomes useless.

A long way down the scale, more than one innovator has asked "Why not simply interchange White's king and queen?"

Another simple idea: we start play in normal fashion until Black has made his tenth move. Now we turn the board round so that the player originally Black makes his eleventh move with the white men. After move 20, another half-turn again reverses the players' roles. This variety of chess, called "Rotational" (England, 1913) testifies to its designer's sense of humour, but to little else.

In the group of games based on chess may be included, as specific individual variants, those in which one contestant plays merely with pieces the other merely with pawns. Described below is a variant which may, after J. Boyer, be termed "one-move pieces against two-move pawns." The game, invented by Verney in 1884, has recently been recalled by an Englishman named Vesselo in his pamphlet "Chess in Schools." The

"Wei-chi Players." Drawing from the period of the Sung dynasty (960–1279).

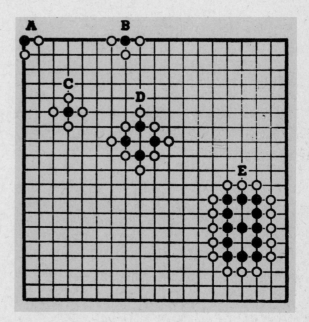

Chinese draughts "wei-chi" derives its name from a word meaning "siege." The drawing shows the 19-line board with some examples of men besieged by adversary forces.

85

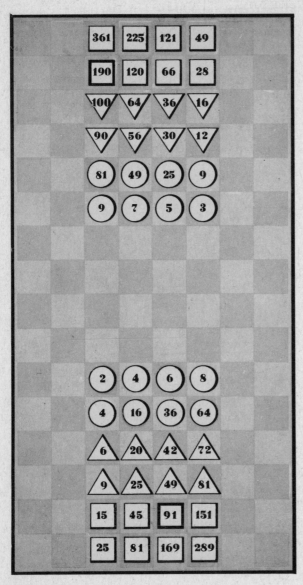

The men and board set out for "rhythmomachy," or arithmetical chess. The men move according to their shape. Capturing is governed by numerical combinations and position. The game was practised in the 16th century.

his opponent's king. The black pieces move and capture in accordance with conventional procedures, making one move at a time, but when White makes a Capture on his first move, he forfeits his second move. Moreover, the black king may be checked only on the second move. In the case of the white king being checked by Black, the first move has to be made by the king to escape the check, and the second is — at the player's option — made either again by the king or by any individual pawn. It has been found out in practice that the odds are in favour of White especially since an individual white pawn, upon reaching the eighth rank and being promoted to a piece, rapidly concludes the game having two moves at its command. The game creates amusing situations.

In 1942, another variant of the pawn-versus--piece game was proposed by Lord Dunsany. Black pawns, thirty-two in number, occupy the upper half of the chessboard and have no king. White chessmen on the other hand include no pawns. The Black are defeated when all their pawns are captured by white pieces, whereas the white king is to be checkmated in accordance with the rules of the conventional chess. On reaching the eighth rank a black pawn is promoted to a bishop or other piece. Despite appearances the game requires unyielding attention, and will punish any nonchalant playing by ending in the rapid defeat of any player who is contemptuous of his adversary.

Four-a-side chess has also been modified with four teams of sixteen chessmen each. White and red play against black and blue, on two ordinary chessboards placed side by side. Partners sit side by side facing opponents. The game can end with the checkmating of one king or both one side's kings, at choice.

Capablanca once played Maroczy in a public exhibition on a 12 × 16 chessboard consisting of two normal boards side by side with an additional four rank wide belt in the middle.

Byzantine chess with its circular board was

opening position of chessmen is that like in the ordinary chess, the difference being that White has only pawns and a king, all alone and deprived of other pieces, whereas Black has no pawns whatsoever. Each contestant strives to check-mate once taken down from its cupboard and dusted and rules drawn up for playing it by three or four combatants. Normal chess has also been ingeniously adapted to make it a game for three.

Among a host of new chessmen proposed for use on an expanded board have been Grenadiers, Engineers and, after the first World War, Tanks and Aeroplanes.

A notable Polish lawyer, Stanisław Hofmokl-Ostrowski, devised a system which he called "Mephisto." Two teams of 20 battled on a 10 by 10 board. The normal chess set was expanded by two extra pawns and by two Devils with a move like a knight's but continued one jump further. Whereas a knight always moves a square

of different colour, a Devil ends up on a square of the colour it left.

Many inventors strived to develop a hexagonal chess, experimenting with various forms of chessboard, varying the number of pieces and adapting the rules of the game to new geometrical conditions. In 1926, the rules for Hexagonal and Three-coloured Chess were published by Lord H. D. Baskerville. His chessboard consisted of eighty-three hexagonal fields arranged in the form of a rectangle with a zig-zag border line. The hexagons were white, blue or red. Each contestant had — as in the traditional game of chess — sixteen pieces, however, differently arranged on the chessboard, their moves adapted to the possibility of travelling in six

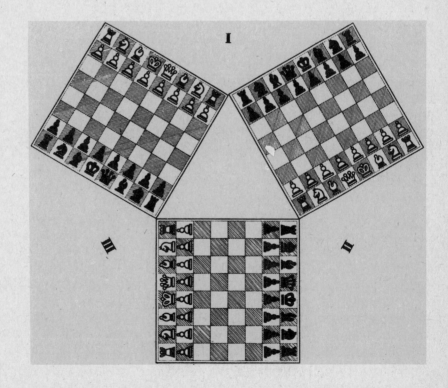

Three chessboards placed with their corners touching, so that three people can play at once. Each has white men on one board and black on another. This is not so much a variety of chess, as a small-scale simultaneous display.

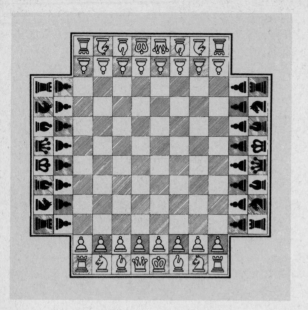

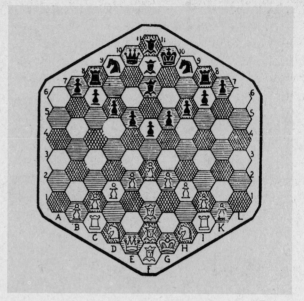

In modern, four-handed chess, as in bridge, two pairs of players compete with each other. White and red chessmen play against black and blue.

Hexagonal chess is played on a board of 91 squares — black, white and brown. Each player has a set of 18 pieces, including three bishops and nine pawns.

directions. Baskerville's system failed to be adopted as being a compromise between the traditional game of chess and its new variant which opened far greater prospects of radical changes in the rules of the game that was the case with the system proposed.

The system invented by Gliński, a Pole living in London, proved more of a success. His version of hexagonal chess, introduced in 1949, was further modified in 1953 and was patented in that form. Gliński's chessboard consists of ninety-one three-coloured hexagonal fields arranged in the form of a large regular hexahedron. The position of the pieces at the opening of the game is shown in the diagram. Pawns, to the number of nine, move and take like those in the ordinary chess. The chessmen, consequent on the possibility of moving in six

directions, are subject to modified rules which may easily be deduced from the geometrical analysis of the chessboard. Since squares of the same colour are not adjacent to one another, bishops (to the number of three) travel diagonally along the rows of hexagons of different colours. The movements of rooks in perpendicular lines are obvious, while their horizontal movements are made by leaping over to hexagons of the same colour. Gliński's variant makes for an exciting game and creates original situations.

For "Atomic Chess," which was patented in France in 1949, the board was of 12 squares by 12, and Tanks and Aeroplanes reinforced the normal set. When a pawn reached the twelfth rank, it became an Atom Bomb. This could be used only once but then destroyed every piece, friend or foe, in a certain area around it. The atomic explosion did not necessarily end the game. If the king perished, his functions were taken over by the strongest remaining piece. Mate had been abolished. The aim was destruction.

Why not combine chess with football? It has been tried!

In the late 1940's, we were offered "Football Chess" devised by the French author Henri Boissier. On a board of 9 by 9 squares stood the normal pieces with a second queen on each side instead of the king. No pawns. The middle squares in each player's back rank were empty, and represented the goals. The "ball," a special piece, was placed in mid-board. You could use a starting whistle if you liked. Each player attacked the "ball" with his pieces trying to push it on before them into the goal.

Our survey would not be complete without three-dimensional chess. Play can be conducted over the surface of a globe, the pieces being pegged into holes in ruled-out "squares." Or the "board" can be a cylinder. Perhaps the most frequently tested type of three-dimensional chess is that in which the men move inside a framework of eight squares erected one above the other to form a cube. Transparent plastic is a highly suitable material for this. Nearly a century ago, the famous chess player Kieseritzky had hit upon this idea, that chess might be played on (in?) a "board" of 512 cubes 8 by 8 by 8.

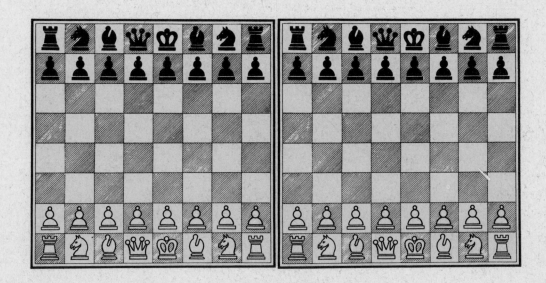

Another way to play four-handed chess: two chessboards placed side-by-side forming the field of battle. Light-coloured armies play the dark ones. The "allied armies" differ in colour only slightly.

One can smile at some of these extravagancies. None has seriously challenged chess. Anyway, why should not people enjoy themselves like this if they choose? One group in Paris has set up a "Centre d'Études des Jeux de Combinaison" which publishes booklets, organizes matches and tournaments and initiates investigation of unorthodox varieties of chess and draughts, on an international scale.

"Alcoholic Chess" has given birth to a host of anecdotes. This is played on a large board on which, stand instead of pieces, glasses or bottles of strong drink. If you capture a piece, you must drink up its contents. It is said that in one game in Hungary in 1898, played on a billiard-table appropriately marked out, the king was represented by a bottle of champagne, the queen by liebfraumilch, other pieces by tokay and the pawns by vin rouge. The game beat the players, for they both finished up under the table with quite an interesting middle-game position on the board.

(Lasker is said to have won a game of "Alcoholic Chess" by sacrificing his queen in ridiculous fashion at the very outset of the game. The queen contained about a quarter litre of cognac; quaffing this seriously incapacitated his opponent in the ensuing complications — B. H. Wood).

Thus traditional chess, though it has accepted a few slight changes, has withstood one assault after another. Some suggestions were too simple,

Shortly before the last war, an Austrian player invented a new version of chess, using a 100-square board and introducing extra men: aircrafts (a combination of a rook and knight) and banks (a combination of a bishop and knight).

Alec Guinness with an extraordinary set of draughts in the American film "Our Man in Havana" (1960), based on Graham Greene's novel.

91

"If you want to win, you must move the queen."
Cartoon from "Perec", 1959.

"This is my new invention."
Cartoon by J. Hegen ("Frischer Wind").

No comments.
Cartoon by E. Lipiński ("Przekrój").

"And now the black piece moves to QKt 5."
Cartoon by L. Werner ("Neue Berliner Illustrierte").

No comments.
Cartoon by K. Baraniecki in "Szpilki."

"They have been playing for four weeks without any result."
Cartoon by J. Hegen ("Frischer Wind").

others too complex. In some forms, the game became too slow.

It may be that chess has achieved a most delicate balance in its present form. It is not easy. It could never bore; yet its essentials can be mastered by any reasonably intelligent person in an evening. It is even not so cut-and-dried as to rule out the possibility of a little luck, or scope for intuition.

It may suffer a few slight amendments yet but any modification of its essential characteristics seems unlikely for as long as it continues to be played.

IV. CHESS AND MATHEMATICS

"Wait a moment, please, till we've finished the game."
("Zeit im Bild").

"On a desert island."
Cartoon by K. Baraniecki ("Karuzela").

"They agreed to a draw."
Cartoon by I. Zubov ("Ogonyok").

"The king is in check!"
Cartoon by J. Kosieradzki ("Szpilki").

"We wonder what kind of game to buy.'
Cartoon by J. Hegen ("Frischer Wind").

"Agitation."
Cartoon by A. François ("Przekrój").

"It's not fair, all of you against one!"
Cartoon by K. Klamann ("Eulenspiegel").

Some fifteen hundred years ago, a Hindu ruler called Shehram brought his state, by poor government, to the verge of ruin. One of the Brahmins, the sage Sessa, son of Daher, stirred up his courage to draw his ruler's attention to the unwisdom of his actions, by a tactful method which avoided any provocation to Shehram's anger. He devised a game in which the most important piece, the Rajah, could achieve nothing without the assistance of his fellow men. It was chess. Shehram perceived the lesson and mended his ways.

Eager to repay the sage who had provided him not only with a valuable lesson in the conduct of affairs, but also a fine new game, he offered the sage any reward he chose. Sessa named an apparently modest reward. He asked for a grain of wheat on the first square of a chessboard; two grains on the second. On the third again twice as many, i.e. four grains, and so on, to the 64th square, the number of grains being doubled each time. Shehram agreed, glad that the sage's demand was so moderate. Grain was brought from the granary. But soon it became evident that there was not enough grain in the world to satisfy the sage's demand. Centuries later, it was computed that the 64th square alone would demand 9,223,372,036,854,775,808 grains. The total number of grains required, being the sum of the series composed of the figure 2 with all the powers in numerical order from 0 to 63, i.e. $1+2^1+2^2+2^3+2^4$, etc. would amount to:

18,446,744,073,709,551,615 grains,

i.e. 18 trillion, 446,744 billion, 73 milliard, 709 million, 551 thousand and 615 grains. If 20 grains fill a cubic centimetre, 20 million are required for a cubic metre. So the number of cubic metres would be more than 922,337,203,685.

It was subsequently computed that, in order to obtain this amount of corn, it would be necessary to sow the whole of the Earth's surface and harvest the lot eight times over.

In this way, Sessa taught his ruler a further lesson: not to make rash promises.

Though these computations are only incidentally connected with chess, they provide a glimpse of the fantastic mathematical possibilities of the apparently simple little 64-square board.

Arabic manuscripts reveal that the chessboard was occasionally used as a sort of auxiliary abacus for purposes of calculating. It became quite important for this purpose in England from the 12th century onwards. The French name "l'échiquier" became the "Exchequer," the main financial department of the State, nowadays the Treasury. The state budget was portioned out on a special chequered board, each square of which represented a different kind of expenditure. The final fiscal allocations were decided by transferring definite sums of money from one square to another. In Ireland there were once two families whose representatives played a game of chess once a year. The winning party was entitled to receive the income from the loser's estates for the ensuing twelve months.

Most published mathematical monographs on chess have concerned themselves with the numerical mysteries of the chessboard and of the movements of various pieces on it, not with the theory of the game itself. Efforts to create a mathematical theory of chess have not so far produced any sensible results as obvious as, for instance, the application of geometry to billiards. Probably the largest of known works was a big, three-volume treatise by the Russian mathematician and theoretician C. F. von Jaenisch, published in 1862, in French, under the title "Traité des applications de l'analyse mathematique au jeu des échecs" ("A Treatise on the Applications of Mathematical Analysis to the Game of Chess").

This started by defining the powers of the pieces in various situations, the relative effect of exchanges, etc. The principal works in this respect, by the Belgian scientist M. Kraitschik, a contemporary of ours, have not taken us much further. Kraitschik has, however, gone with particular thoroughness into problems with many queens on the board, knights' tours etc.

The Brahman, sultan and chess, as seen by the cartoonist G. Miklaszewski.

The same subject, the birth of chess, as seen by another cartoonist, M. Pokora.

The problem of finding a general method of moving a knight around the board in such a way as to move over every square without stopping twice on any one, has attracted mathematicians through two centuries. The first to examine and describe the "knight's tour" in detail was the great Swiss mathematician Leonard Euler. In the second half of the 18th century, he presented works analysing the movement of the knight in what is known as the closed cycles, i.e. those in which, after of a series of moves, it returns to the starting point. This type of knight's tour has been named the Buler.

The Polish author Szczepan Jeleński in his book about mathematical games, "Lilavati," described four knights' tour methods: Euler's; Moon's, a "frame" method of 1843; Moivre's, from the beginning of the 18th century, another frame method, i.e. depending on the setting apart of the centre squares of the board and of a "frame" around; and, finally, Roget's, from the middle of the 19th century, which is based on dividing the chessboard into quarters.

The possibilities for knights' tours are greater than it would seem. It has been calculated that the number of different solutions on a 64-square board exceeds 31 million.

Tours for other pieces have been investigated, mainly for the rook, but also for combinations of knights with other pieces. The theme attracted interest among the Indians, Persians and Arabs as early as a thousand years ago.

Sometimes the piece had to return to its original square, sometimes it had to describe a magic square.

The mention of "magic" squares recalls a discussion by the Polish poet Julian Tuwim in his collection of literary curiosities named "Pegasus head-over-heels." This was a famous mediaeval lettered square made up of five mysterious cabalistic words, in which by using (in general), a knight's move (a move several times with another piece according to a hitherto unrevealed key pattern is to be made), we obtain an

An Arabian chessboard used for counting: the horizontal rows of white or black squares range according to arithmetical progression; the diagonal ones, according to geometrical progression.

8	4 mil.	6	6 mil.	4	8 mil.	2	10 mil.
400 tys.	60	600 tys.	40	800 tys.	20	1 mil.	9
600	60 tys.	400	80 tys.	200	100 tys.	90	300 tys.
6 tys.	4 tys.	8 tys.	2 tys.	10 tys.	900	30 tys.	700
40 tys.	800	20 tys.	1 tys.	9 tys.	3 tys.	7 tys.	5 tys.
80	200 tys.	100	90 tys.	300	70 tys.	500	50 tys.
2 mil.	10	900 tys.	30	700 tys.	50	500 tys.	70
1	9 mil.	3	7 mil.	5	5 mil.	7	3 mil.

additional solution beyond the basic meaning of the words themselves, of a "mystic" character:

```
S A T O R
A R E P O
T E N E T
O P E R A
R O T A S
```

Going over the letters in knights' moves, we read twice PATER NOSTER AO, where A and O stand for the Greek letters Alpha and Omega, or metaphorically the beginning and the end.

The knight's peculiar move has been the key to many a mental puzzle. His moves would spell out some phrase through the letters on the squares he traversed. Or the squares might bear pictures which, grouped in the order of the knight's move, themselves conveyed a message.

The Soviet film "Blue routes" (1947) in a story set after the Second World War, showed the Soviet Navy disarming minefields laid by the Nazis. Three minefields, lying in the route of transports, were causing great trouble. Out of 36 heavy magneto-sonar mines laid on each field, the engineers had disarmed 32 only. The remaining four could not be traced and threatened every ship passing over. Captain Ratanov decided

The knight and his relations.
Cartoon by L. Mintycz ("Przekrój").

amusing scene: a casualty of a bicycle accident, all in bandages, is driving his one-cylinder engined invalid chair. Rattling past a couple of chess players at a game he catches up some of their knights. The knights, thrown into the engine skip around like fleas, adding to the engine's power and revolutions. On the car goes! Such is the power of the chess knights!

Many scientists have been attracted by the mathematical aspects, not only of the movements of pieces about the board but of situations in which a number of pieces have to be placed according to specified conditions. For example, that they should cover the maximum number of squares, or the minimum number of squares; that they should not attack each other and so on.

It is possible to place five queens on a chessboard, so that they cover every square, in 4,860 different ways.

The problem of placing eight queens on the board, so that none attacks any other, has attracted tremendous attention. The German mathematician Karl Gauss calculated that there are 92 positions in all. Of these, only twelve are essentially different; the others can all be obtained by rotating the board or reflecting one of the essential twelve as if in a mirror.

The same problem with eight rooks has no fewer than 40,320 solutions. Eight bishops or eight knights give rise to even greater numbers which nobody has been able to compute exactly — at least, nobody has tried.

On the other hand, much time and effort has gone to trying to find how many different positions are possible in chess as a whole. This problem is more of the essence of chess than mere pastimes such as knights' tours or the puzzles of the queens.

Two kings can be placed on a board in 3,612 different ways. Add one pawn and the number of different positions rises to 167,248. Naturally illegal situations are not included, for instance those with a white pawn on White's back rank.

to unravel the scheme of their lay-out at all costs. Examining all the circumstances connected with their lay-out, he learned that it was designed by a German engineer who chanced to be deeply interested in chess. Captain Ratanov was also a keen chessplayer, and had recently been interested in knights' tours. He arrived at an unexpected conclusion that the mines had been laid as if on a chessboard, following a plan based on knights' moves from the centre. He was right; the remaining mines were traced and rendered harmless.

Lasker is said to have had one casual game with an unknown opponent, who lost quickly then asked, "what do you think of my play?" "It is curious," replied the champion, "why, for example, haven't you moved your knights even once?" "Why? Because, dear sir, I haven't the faintest idea how they do move!"

The short puppet film "Desire" produced in Czechoslovakia in 1962 by Jiři Trnka features an

With two kings and two pawns, we can have about 7,400,000 legal positions. We are already among the millions! Two kings and two pieces can be placed in thirteen million ways; two kings, twelve pieces and a pawn in a number of different ways which contains 27 figures.

If you start to set up all 32 men on a 64-square board, you have at your disposal at least 7,534, 686, 312, 361, 225, 327 × 10³³ different ways of doing it.

Even these astronomical figures give only a small idea of the variety of possibilities in an actual game.

White can make his first move in any of twenty different ways (sixteen moves with pawns, four with the knights). Black has as many possibilities in reply.

For his second move, White has the choice among 28; for his second, Black among 29.

For his third move, White has 30 possibilities; for his third, Black has 31. For his fourth White has 32, Black 33.

After one move by each player, we have 400 (20 times 20) different possible positions. To simplify further computation, let us assume that for his first five moves, each player can choose from 20 alternatives each time, and among 30 each time after that. We can also assume that the average game lasts 40 moves a-side. Games can, of course, be longer or shorter. It is only a rough estimate anyway, but the result is interesting. We get:

$$(20 \times 20)^5 \times (30 \times 30)^{35} = 2^{10} \times 3^{70} \times 10^{80} =$$
$$= 25 \times 10^{115}$$

This is a number of 117 figures.

It is many times higher than the number of various combinations of all the 32 chessmen, which is understandable, since every move by

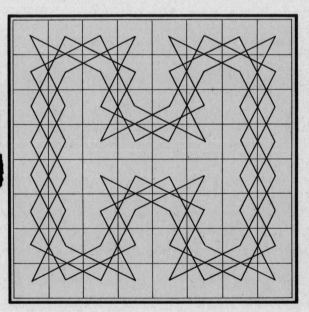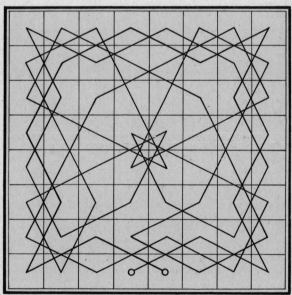

Diagrams showing knights' tours of the board, no square being visited twice, and the tour ending where it began.

either player brings about a new situation, and the number of men alters repeatedly as a result of exchanges.

Somebody might complain that the total number obtained is an exaggeration, including many moves that nobody in his senses would make. Let us make a more conservative calculation then. Suppose, after three or four moves have been played, there are only a couple of plausible moves to choose from each time; then, after seven moves by each player, any of 16,000 different positions could have been reached. If there were three good moves to choose from at each turn, then after seven moves by each player more than five million different situations could have arisen — all this, of course, from only one particular opening.

Under somewhat different initial assumptions the calculations yield still higher numerical results determining the number of all chess games possible. In the Polish mathematician's "Wstęp do teorii gier" ("Introduction to the Theory of Games"), by Edward Kofler (1963) we come across the following analytical considerations contained in the chapter devoted to multi-step games:

"On his first move, player I has twenty possible moves. To each of these, player II, on the second move, can reciprocate with twenty moves. Thus the original apex of a dendrite* separates into

---

* Dendrite — a geometrical figure composed of a finite number of segments separating from a certain original apex (starting point of the game) and branching off in such a manner that each end apex is directly connected with only one apex of the immediate lower level.

49	42	40	51	9	34	36	11
47	52	52	45	39	12	14	33
41	50	48	43	37	10	8	35
55	44	46	53	15	32	38	13
61	22	16	63	5	26	28	7
19	56	58	21	31	64	2	25
17	62	60	23	29	6	4	27
59	20	18	57	3	24	30	1

Solution of an old Arab problem: a tour of the chessboard, knight and bishop moving alternately (the latter making the move of those days, just two squares diagonally).

37	14	16	35	33	18	24	31
15	36	34	17	19	32	30	25
13	38	48	11	21	26	28	23
39	12	10	49	27	20	22	29
9	42	40	47	61	50	52	63
43	8	46	41	51	60	62	53
45	6	4	59	57	2	64	55
7	44	58	5	3	56	54	1

A problem showing a tour of the chessboard with alternate moves of knight and queen — the latter making its old move, one square only.

twenty branches with each branch further divided into another twenty branches. On subsequent moves, the number of possible moves by each player is further increased.

We can also roughly define the upper limit of the number of all possible branches of an entire dendrite and that of the number of segments on individual branches. It may be assumed — as has been shown in practice — that the number of moves in any individual game is not in excess of 300 (150 moves by each player). It may also be assumed that the number of all possible moves by one contestant in any individual situation on the chessboard is not in excess of 100. Now we consider the number of all possible combinations of moves by player I on the first move with all possible moves by player II on the second move — with all possible moves by player I on the third move, etc. The number in question is equal to that of all possible games of chess. However, on the other hand, that number is — in accordance with the above assumptions — undoubtedly lower than

A letter puzzle based on the move of a knight, common in mediaeval times. Starting from the bold "R," by making a knight's move each time, the solver spells out a message. Syllable, picture and rebus puzzles using a knight's move have been common.

$$\frac{\overbrace{100 \times 100 \times 100 \times \ldots \times 100}^{300 \text{ times}}}{300 \text{ times}} = 100^{300}$$

This enormous quantity, expressed by 601 digits, is just the upper limit of the total branches of the dendrite. As regards the upper limit of the number of segments on individual branches, this is of course equal to 300.

Since the assumptions of the principal theorem are fulfilled; it may be considered that the value of the game of chess is unambiguously determined and that each contestant has at least one optimum strategy to follow to achieve the value of the game. In view of the enormity of the dendrite it is at the present time impossible, even with the aid of most powerful computers, to determine precisely the value and the optimum strategy of the game. Thus, with the value of the game precisely determined, we are not yet in a posi-

tion to establish whether player I entering the contest — and following an optimum strategy, which is of course an unknown to us — is going to win, draw or lose the game."

The possibilities of chess are thus, for all practical purposes, virtually unlimited. All the tournaments we could organise in a hundred thousand years would not exhaust them.

A geometrical puzzle. The knight is to be placed on an empty square so as to capture all the black pawns in the least number of moves ("Mathematical Puzzles" by B. Kordemsky).

Mathematics can to a certain extent help to crystallise the theory of the game, but a comprehensive mathematical theory of chess is impossible of attainment. The famous French mathematician Henri Poincaré conceded this, among other things, in his treatise on scientific hypotheses. He pointed out that moves on a chessboard do not fall into any sequence capable of mathematical analysis. It is impossible to work out any generalising theses simply on the basis of moves played. An embracing science of chess is out of the question. A player thinks several moves ahead but the figures we have seen make it clear that his analysis can never be complete. He is guided by intuition to a large extent. To be able to calculate out to the end mathematically is possible only on the rarest occasions.

If we could analyse all the variations (each right to the end of the game) which could occur at any particular moment of a game, we could formulate certain laws. In some end-games,

we can work out how to play so as to win, or what the result will be, depending on the choice of move. Rarely is our analysis accurate enough to be reliable. We may decide that one particular first move ensures eventual victory. Later we discover a move by our opponent that completely wrecks our whole plan. The difficulties, even in an apparently simple situation, may be colossal.

If we were to ignore the practical aspect of the game — that we are faced with almost unlimited possibilities of choice and method of play, which makes it a human impossibility to arrive at a mathematical theory — then chess could be expressed in some fairly simple mathematical terms. Let us not delude ourselves. Even though the essence of chess became completely defined, this would not influence the game itself in the least degree. This sounds almost paradoxical but it is the truth.

Chess, then, contains an enormous but finite number of combinations. Because of a certain limitation imposed by the laws, that a threefold repetition of any position leads to a draw, the idea that any one game might go on for ever is an unreality. This could have happened if the rule about the draw were not binding. Then, for instance, perpetual check would really be a perpetual check and not a draw. (Here the author errs. The laws allow either player to claim a draw on three-fold repetition but do not compel him to do so; two sufficiently obstinate players could go on repeating moves for ever — B. H. Wood).

Moreover, it can be proved that chess is a game in which the result could be foretold in advance. Only, we cannot yet say what result, whether a win for White, a win for Black or a draw, if the play on each side were 100% correct.

The problem was discussed by Grzegorz Krochmalny in the Polish weekly "Przekrój": "... No one doubts that chess is a rational game. The initial position is always the same and White always starts. The players move alternately.

Draughts, 'Fox and Geese,' 'Noughts and Crosses' and other games are of this type... The outcome of a game of 'Fox and Geese' cannot be a draw. It could be classified as a 'categorical' game. Chess could be made 'categorical' if we were to amend its laws slightly and say that anybody who repeated the same move in the same position had lost. The question now is what would happen if contestants played 'categorical' chess faultlessly. It might be asked 'Can you define strictly what is a game without fault?' Modern logic has overcome this objection. It is possible to define correct, victorious or faulty moves, won or lost positions, and winning, effective or faulty methods. Having done this, we arrive at a peculiar result. All 'categorical' games are unjust, i.e. they provide an assured victory for one player, irrespective of his opponent's play. In other words, they are all like 'Fox and Geese.' Non-categorical games, such as ordinary Chess, are not necessarily unjust but as long as they are just, they lead to no particular result if both the opponents play correctly. Ordinary chess play is so complicated

that we do not know whether it is just or not. The rule that White should move first produces a privileged colour: whether this colour is Black or White we do not know — or whether the privilege sways the balance sufficiently to eliminate draws. If a hundred demons, each capable of perfect chess, sat down to play in a tournament, the same colour would win on all fifty boards..."

It clearly follows from this that if in ideal, i.e. faultless play, the result were pre-determined for one opponent, one player would be as privileged as in "Fox and Geese," where the geese should always win.

To show how closely related is the concept of games, and therefore of the game of chess, with certain branches of modern mathematics, let us quote some excerpts from "Introduction to Probability Theory and its Applications" (1950), an American university textbook by William Feller. Explaining various aspects of the probability theory, and considering its "formal logical contents," the American mathematician writes:

Cartoon by J. Flisak ("Szpilki").

A Belgian chemist G. D. Hooghe with an electric machine of his own construction for making knights' tours. After receiving appropriate "instructions" on a small chessboard, the machine automatically solves the problem, successively lighting up the squares to be visited by the knight. The machine was exhibited at the 14th Chess Olympiad in Leipzig, 1960. The lower photograph shows the complex construction of the apparatus, with thousands of electric wires.

"Axiomatically, mathematics is concerned solely with relations among undefined things. This property is well illustrated by the game of chess. It is impossible to 'define' chess otherwise than by stating a set of rules. The conventional pieces may be described to some extent, but it will not always be obvious which piece is intended for 'king.' The chessboard and the pieces are helpful, but they can be dispensed with. The essential thing is to know how the pieces move and act.

"It is meaningless to talk about the 'definition' of the 'true nature' of a pawn or a king. Similarly, geometry does not care what a point or a straight line 'really are.' They remain undefined notions, and the axioms of geometry specify relations among them: two points determine a line, etc."

In the passage on "intuitive background," we read:

"In contrast to chess, the axioms of geometry and mechanics have an intuitive background. In fact, geometrical intuition is so strong that it is prone to run ahead of logical reasoning. The extent to which logics, intuition and physical experience are interdependent is a problem into which we need not enter. Certainly intuition can be trained and developed. The bewildered novice in chess moves cautiously, recalling individual rules, whereas the experienced player absorbs a complicated situation at a glance and is unable to account rationally for his intuition. In like manner mathematical intuition grows with experience, and it is possible to develop a natural feeling for concepts such as four-dimensional space."

Many chess players have tried to assess how a perfect game of chess should end from experience of actual master play.

Philidor thought, for instance, that whoever made first move and made no mistake would win. Lasker and the majority of the masters of his day thought that the developing knowledge of technique tended to make the perfect game a draw.

Many "experts" (in the 1920's and 1930's) announced a belief that chess was a dying game, because chess skill had reached such a level that neither opponent could win unless his opponent blundered. An anecdote based on Eastern fables which circulated freely about that time, provides good evidence that there were many to ridicule this view:

"At the time of the Caliph Harun-al-Rashid, chess flourished in Baghdad. Everybody played; old and young, men and women, rich and poor. There appeared a sage, who announced that he had discovered a way to work out the very best move in any position. He published his method — and what happened? Everybody made use of it. Soon nobody wished to sit down to a game of chess any more. The excited group of spectators who used to watch the games melted away.

"The wise Caliph saved the situation by having the sage's treatise burnt. Masters in the schools undertook not to teach his method any more and everybody was happy again."

"Too much learning...!" We are far indeed, however, from the point where we need to start suppressing study of chess technique.

The Cuban genius, J. R. Capablanca thought that chess was approaching its demise; that the human mind was achieving the ability to choose the best move among the multitude of combinations and variations to such an extent that two equally gifted in this respect, must always draw. When in 1927 he came to defend his world title against Alekhine, indeed 25 out of the 34 games were drawn — but Alekhine won six. Alekhine proved convincingly that the combinational possibilities of chess are far indeed from exhaustion.

Soviet chess players have probably abolished for good the idea that the "ideal game" must be drawn. The successes in the international arena of Botvinnik, Bronstein, Smyslov, Tal and others, have shown how dynamic chess can be. Their enterprises have thrilled their fellows and the public alike.

Chess problem with the knight — a magic square: the sum of the figures indicating the knight's position is always the same: 260.

There does exist one guaranteed way by which a weak player can draw with, or even beat, a master. Here again, we wander into anecdote. The method is to play simultaneously against two opponents, having the white men in one game, the black in the other. Our opponent makes his first move with white — we then make the same move on the other board and await the reply. We repeat the black move in turn on the first board, wait for the reply, and in the same vein continue the sequence against the second opponent, and soon we shall either draw both games or win one and lose the other. In effect, of course, our two opponents are playing each other, we acting merely as a go-between.

This witty idea of a double game has supplied the basis for many a fanciful story. There is a short story by the Russian writer V. Azov, describing a sad thing which is supposed to have happened to Emanuel Lasker. We summarise:

During an international tournament, Lasker, then world champion, was approached by an individual who said that his little son was a pro-

Five queens placed so as to check on every square of the board: one solution to a well-known problem.

One of the many ways of placing eight queens on the chessboard in such a way that none attacks any other.

digy who would probably grow up to be a chess genius. He proposed that the master should play one game only with his son and, so as to cause the least trouble, by correspondence. Appreciating the value of the master's time, he was prepared to pay $500 for the game his son was of course bound to lose. He was prepared to forfeit this for the benefit his son would gain from a game with such an accomplished player. However, should his son win — a contingency not, of course, to be seriously considered — then Lasker would pay $2500. Unable to shake off the intruder, who kept calling on him at his hotel daily, Lasker agreed. At first, he took his opponent lightly, but when the game began to become very difficult, he concentrated on it with all his might and finally managed to win, though only with the greatest difficulty. The prodigy's father paid the $500 without demur.

Some time later, talking to Capablanca, Lasker recalled the incident. The puzzle was then cleared

up. Lasker had really been playing Capablanca, who had agreed similar conditions; the "prodigy" was only an intermediary in a game which had cost Capablanca $2500. Net profit for the "prodigy's" father: $2000.

Other versions ascribe to Alekhine the playing of such a "double" game. The master is supposed to have agreed to play two unknown opponents for a high stake under similar conditions. In this situation, even a drawn game could have cost him dearly. The position seemed desperate. Unnerved, Alekhine made a very bad move on one board. Scenting easy victory, his opponent cast caution aside and decided he could win the game by himself, and thus pick up the entire stake by winning on both boards instead of only one. This thoughtless departure from the scheme of closely following the master's moves proved fatal. Having separated the games, as it were, from each other, Alekhine soon outplayed his opponents on both.

108

This is not meant to imply that nowadays — in the period of cybernetics, electronics and, therefore, of computers, and also the period of the steady development of the theory of games approached in terms of philosophy and mathematics — no unforeseen developments are likely to occur in future to form new links between the theory and practice of chess playing and purely mathematical and geometrical questions and also those of calculus. We cannot possibly know what results will emerge from studies along these lines.

As early as 1905, R. W. Martin wrote in an article entitled "The Mathematics of Chess Playing" which appeared in Lasker's Chess Magazine (April 1906):

"... Mathematics as a factor of chessplay, will appear, I think, as a truism to the player of even very moderate skill and experience. This phase of the game I believe has never been developed apart from the concrete problems with which it has to deal, and these at the best are usually investigated by very empirical methods.

Chess has never occupied a place as a sub-science, assuming a name under the form of applied mathematics.

I am, however, led to believe through my own efforts and those of others, that a true inductive science of chess is capable of being formulated, which will constitute an exact mathematical theory of the game in its entirety, thus forming a critique to which all empirical observations must be made to conform.

Such a science must necessarily be an evolution from the simplest mathematical truths to the more complex, and involve a series of propositions, each becoming more heterogeneous in its construction until the whole process culminates in a final grand law, if the series converges; but will be incapable of any finite limit, if the series diverges or continues in the same straight line..."

This opinion remains feasible and — a point of importance — it seems to take on appearances of sound forecast if we consider it in the light of recent scientific results.

V. SPORT, SCIENCE OR ART?

The giant Gargantua, hero of Rabelais's famous novel, learns to play chess. Drawing by L. Morin in a French edition of "Gargantua et Pantagruel."

Many have wondered why chess has attracted so many devoted followers throughout the centuries; people of the most varied temperaments, outlooks and ways of life.

Why do millions of people in all parts of the world today battle away on the chessboard, study books on chess or spend solitary hours solving chess problems or end-games? Why has chess conquered whole continents and occupied so many of the leisure hours in which people customarily satisfy their desire for arts or sciences or sport?

The answer is not simple. It is probably that chess is of so many-sided a character that almost anybody can find in it something to his own taste. Sometimes it does more than satisfy; it absorbs, consumes. It can be just a game, a mental pastime, a relief from work, anxiety or pain, or a stubborn intellectual struggle, engaging emotions as tense and endurance as severe in its way as any competitive contest known. On the other hand, it is a sphere of artistic and scientific creation; a game of chess can have the same attraction as mathematics or please like a work of art. An enormous amount of inner satisfaction can be derived from your own achievements on the chessboard, from your own analysis with its undertones of logic, geometry and even psychology; the overcoming of difficulties, the cultivation of foresight, the shaping and schooling of habit; the sheer struggle, not always with your opponent but sometimes with yourself.

As one early chess master put it, "A perfect chess player is an artist, a scientist, an engineer, and a conqueror in one."

Naturally, not every lover of the game attains a stature like this. Yet the possibilities of beauty, artistry, and creativeness are always there and few of us fail to get an occasional glimpse of them in our games. Just as in music, literature or drama, there exists, apart from the virtuosos, a huge public comprised of their admirers on the one hand and enraptured imitators on the other.

As one American observed: "Chess has elements of culture and art, and has formed a part of culture throughout the whole history of civilization."

This idea has been elaborated by the Soviet chess historian Y. G. Rokhlin:

"We would not maintain that chess is of practical use. As in any sphere of art, however, chess activity creates real cultural values which make a precious contribution to the treasury of culture as a whole. It is not without reason that the greatest national libraries and museums carefully preserve the works of chess authors, ancient manuscripts, prints and other materials connected with the game. Relics like these reveal much about other aspects of man's life in particular periods... It is not by accident that encyclopedias, which catalogue every branch of knowledge, give chess an honourable place..."

Many people have tried to establish the precise place of chess in world culture. Some of the earliest literature on the game busies itself with this problem. Pseudo-scientific exaggerations have been common. Research in other fields has often cast incidental light on the question. Famous artists and philosophers, writers and statesmen have contributed brilliant opinions. The bibliography of the "Philosophy of Chess" is rich indeed but, unfortunately, no book on it has escaped severe devaluation in the course of time. Old works abounded in faulty metaphysics, confusion or unscientific thought, or they worked from premises so false as to be useless. Even today haphazard theorising is too common. A really scientific evaluation of chess is badly needed.

The theory of games, which has been developed a lot during the last fifty years, is largely relevant to chess, and has a lot to contribute. The word "game" took on a new meaning when scientists started on a methodical evaluation. The theory of games is becoming an increasingly important field of research, linking up with economics,

Teacher becomes pupil. The young Swedish chess champion Ove Kinnmark teaches his swimming master to play chess.

sociology, cybernetics and other branches of science.

Much importance is attached to chess in the Soviet Union, where its essential character has been under discussion for years, so far without reaching any definite conclusion.

Y. Bykov stated: "Chess is an intellectual sport which permits the creation of aesthetic values and which may help man to shape his traits necessary for creative activity…"

This was opposed by Rokhlin who wrote: "On account of its specifically creative character, chess cannot be limited to the scope of a 'sporting game'; in our times this is too narrow a definition… Chess is a historically complex, cultural phenomenon which is organically bound with the spiritual life of the community and is a state of continuous change and renewal…"

B. Vainshtein suggested that we might well start by trying to define what we are talking about. He found that "chess" had more meanings than one might expect; it can be

(1) a game played on a board; or
(2) a game conducted by correspondence (by letter, telephone or radio); or
(3) a game which can take the form of research (e.g. analysis to find an improvement in the opening) or aesthetic experience (e.g. search for a more beautiful way of setting up a problem); or
(4) a mental exercise, e.g. the solving of some set problem; or
(5) "theory," the body of knowledge and technique which exists about chess; or
(6) its origin and history.

"… If we say that chess is an art," he concluded, "it is not any one of these manifestations but only all of them taken together that provide a picture of peculiar creation. If, however, someone maintains that chess is just a game, then he is limiting himself to only the first of the connotations above."

"Smokers." A photo-composition by H. Braun-Chotard, 1955.

"The chess problem." Cartoon by I. Grinstein ("Ogonyok").

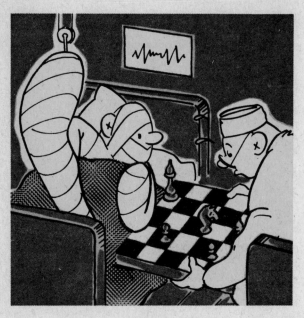

"You're in a difficult position, doctor."
("Krokodil").

Chess enthusiasm knows no obstacles.
Cartoon by Chaval ("Sie und Er").

The discussion goes on. Perhaps this book, by unfolding the story of chess in various countries and periods, may contribute a little to the discussion.

Not to be too solemn, I might quote the Polish author Jan Sztaudynger:

You want to catch the essence of chess?
It's a game where you prefer your queen to someone else's.
Yet, much as in life, here too, insincerely,
Whilst preferring your own you may take someone else's instead.

It was Stefan Zweig who wrote:

"...In chess, as in love, someone else has to be there."

Zweig also wrote: "...Is chess not also a science, an art...? Thought which leads nowhere; mathematics which does not compute anything, art without work, architecture without substance, and yet nevertheless, something more enduring than many books and works? Is it not unique among games, belonging to all peoples and to all times; a game of which nobody knows what god sent down to Earth to kill boredom, sharpen the senses and tensen the spirit? Where is its beginning, where its end? Every child can learn its basic rules, and yet, within the confines of this narrow square, masters can arise who cannot be compared with any others; men with one sole talent, specialist geniuses in whom vision, patience and technique function along strictly defined lines, just as in mathematicians, poets or musicians..."

Benjamin Franklin, the eminent American scientist, politician and educationist of the 18th century, was noted as a pioneer of writing on chess, treating it from an educational, ethical and moral point of view. In his work "Morals of Chess," the first book on chess published in the United States, Franklin saw in it such character-shaping properties as the creation of an ability to plan and foresee, of a sense of reflection, prudence and carefulness, and finally, of responsible decision.

"The Game of Chess is not merely an idle amusement; several very valuable qualities of the mind, useful in the course of human life, are to be acquired and strengthened by it, so as to become habits ready on all occasions; for life is a kind of Chess, in which we have often points to gain, and competitors or adversaries to contend with, and in which there is a vast variety of good and ill events, that are, in some degree, the effect of prudence, or the want of it. By playing at Chess then, we may learn:

"1st, Foresight, which looks a little into futurity, and considers the consequence that may attend an action; for it is continually occurring to the player, 'If I move this Piece, what will be the advantage or disadvantage of my new situation? What use can my adversary make of it to annoy me? What other moves can I make to support it, and to defend myself from his attacks?'

"2nd, Circumspection, which surveys the whole Chessboard, or scene of action: — the relation of the several Pieces, and their situations; the dangers they are repeatedly exposed to; the several possibilities of their aiding each other; the probabilites that the adversary may make this or that move, and attack this or that Piece; and what different means can be used to avoid his stroke, or turn its consequences against him.

"3rd, Caution, not to make our moves too hastily. This habit is best acquired by observing strictly the laws of the game; such as, if you touch a piece, you must move it somewhere; if you set it down, you must let it stand.

"Therefore, it would be the better way to observe these rules, as the game becomes thereby more the image of human life, and particularly of war; in which, if you have incautiously put yourself into a bad and dangerous position, you cannot obtain your enemy's leave to withdraw your troops, and place them more securely; but

you must abide all the consequences of your rashness.

"And, lastly, We learn by Chess the habit of not being discouraged by present bad appearances in the state of our affairs; the habit of hoping for a favourable chance, and that of persevering in the search of resources. The game is so full of events, there is such a variety of turns in it, the fortune of it is so subject to vicissitudes, and one so frequently, after contemplation, discovers the means of extricating one's self from a supposed insurmountable difficulty, that one is encouraged to continue the contest to the last, in hopes of victory from our skill; or, at least, from the negligence of our adversary; and whoever considers,

Waiting for the guests ("Münchner Illustrierte").

what in Chess he often sees instances of, that success is apt to produce presumption and its consequent inattention, by which more is afterwards lost than was gained by the preceding advantage, while misfortunes produce more care and attention, by which the loss may be recovered, will learn not to be too much discouraged by any present successes of his adversary, nor to despair of final good fortune upon every little check he receives in the pursuit of it.

"1st, Therefore, if it is agreed to play according to the strict rules, then those rules are to be strictly observed by both parties; and should not be insisted upon for one side, while deviated from by the other: for this is not equitable.

"2nd, If it is agreed not to observe the rules exactly, but one party demands indulgences, he should then be as willing to allow them to the other.

"3rd, No false moves should even be made to extricate yourself out of a difficulty, or to gain an advantage; for there can be no pleasure in playing with a man once detected in such unfair practice.

"4th, If your adversary is long in playing, you ought not to hurry him, or express an uneasiness at his delay; not even by looking at your watch, or taking up a book to read: you should not sing, nor whistle, nor make a tapping with your feet on the floor, or with your fingers on the table, nor do any thing that may distract his attention: for all these things displease, and they do not prove your skill in playing, but your craftiness and your rudeness.

"5th, You ought not to endeavour to amuse and deceive your adversary by pretending to have made bad moves; and saying you have now lost the game, in order to make him secure and careless, and inattentive to your schemes; for this is fraud and deceit, not skill in the Game of Chess.

"6th, You must not, when you have gained a victory, use any triumphing or insulting expressions, nor show too much of the pleasure you feel; but endeavour to console your adversary, and make him less dissatisfied with himself by every kind and civil expression that may be used with truth; such as, you understand the

In the dentist's waiting-room: chess is an excellent anaesthetic. Cartoon by Y. Cherepanov ("Ogonyok").

"Try some water!" Cartoon by Z. Lengren.

"The writers' club." Cartoon by Y. Semyonov.

"Only 4 minutes left before we knock off, and there are still a good 20 moves to make." Cartoon by I. Gench.

"When you have nobody to play with." Cartoon by Tetsu.

game better than I, but you are a little inattentive, or you play too fast; or you had the best of the game, but something happened to divert your thoughts, and that turned it in my favour.

"7th, If you are a spectator, while others play, observe the most perfect silence; for if you give advice, you offend both the parties; him against whom you give it, because it may cause him to lose the game; him in whose favour you give it, because, though it be good, and he follows it, he loses the pleasure he might have had, if you had permitted him to think till it occurred to himself. Even after a move or moves, you must not, by replacing the Pieces, show how they might have been placed better; for that displeases, and might occasion disputes or doubts about their true situation.

"All talking to the players lessens or diverts their attention; and is, therefore, unpleasing: nor should you give the least hint to either party, by any kind of noise or motion; if you do, you are unworthy to be a spectator.

"If you desire to exercise or show your judgment, do it in playing your own game, when you have an opportunity, not in criticising or meddling with, or counselling the play of others.

"Lastly, If the game is not to be played rigorously, according to the rules before mentioned, then moderate your desire of victory over your adversary, and be pleased with one over yourself.

"Snatch not eagerly at every advantage offered by his unskilfullness or inattention; but point out to him kindly, that by such a move he places or leaves a Piece en prise unsupported; that by another, he will put his King into a dangerous situation, etc.

"By this generous civility (so opposite to the unfairness before forbidden) you may happen indeed to lose the game; but you will win what is better, his esteem, his respect, and his affection; together with the silent approbation and the goodwill of the spectators.

"When a vanquished player is guilty of an un-

Room-mates: "Mrs. Brown, please move my knight over there." Cartoon by E. Shcheglov ("Krokodil").

In the harem. Cartoon by Kovarsky ("The New Yorker").

The organizers are in a panic — the champion is losing every game. Cartoon by B. Tabey ("Noir et Blanc").

A new year card printed in London from a cartoon by F. Themerson.

"The game seems to be warming up." ("L'Echiquier de Paris").

truth to cover his disgrace, as 'I have not played so long — his method of opening the game confused me, — the men were of an unsual size', etc., all such apologies (to call them no worse) must lower him in a wise person's eyes, both as a man and as a Chess player; and who will not suspect that he who shelters himself under such untruths in trifling matters, is no very sturdy moralist in things of greater consequences, where his fame and honour are at stake? A man of proper pride would scorn to account for his being beaten by one of these excuses, even were it true; because they all have so much the appearance, at the moment, of being untrue."

Benjamin Franklin certainly esteemed chess!

Though the psychology of chess and its players has been touched on by countless writers, this does not imply that investigation has been pursued to any real depth.

About 1938, however, a Polish school teacher, K. Kozłowski, contributed to the periodical Szachista a thoughtful article going into the influence of psychological factors on quality of play. He assumed that the final result of a game is a vector of a certain set-up of circumstances and facts related to the players' relative intelligences.

"In chess, we know neither all of the facts nor their mutual interplay. We are adrift in a sea of uncertainty. Some of the elements may be partly known: combinational ability, intuition, state of nerves, physical health, ambition, skill in rationing of time or application of energy, etc. These elements may in turn be affected by the time of day, state of nourishment, etc. Finally, there are unforeseeable factors of the type that produce complete upsets of form and sensational tournament results."

As long ago as 1835, the author of a Polish chess manual Karol Krupski wrote: "From men's actions we may come to know their character, mental ability, emotions... If we cannot see enough of their actions to judge, some of us think to judge their character from their faces, or even from their writing. I believe you can

In a chess champion's home. Cartoon by K. Klamann ("Eulenspiegel").

"Are they still playing, or have they dropped off to sleep?" Cartoon by K. Klamann ("Eulenspiegel").

estimate a man's attributes more accurately from the way he plays chess than from any anthropological or graphological examination. Every game is a telling revelation of the player, chess above all."

Chess as a possible instrument of psychological investigation has produced some amusing aphorisms.

"Your opponent leaves you to set the pieces out — he is already considering himself your superior."

"He's a poor player but won't accept odds. He is an egotist thinking only of his own enjoyment."

"Plays quickly and even in critical moments still moves without reflection — he is successful in life only when things go his way: he is fundamentally uncertain of himself."

"Chess is a struggle; mainly against one's own imperfections."

"Playing chess does you good because it confronts you with repeated disappointments."

We have leapt to and fro in time. Let us see how chess was regarded in 1868, a century ago. A press report on a chess tournament held in Warsaw read:

"It's my lucky day: checkmate!" Cartoon by K. Klamann ("Eulenspiegel").

"In the course of the tournament now completed, we heard voices, quite serious ones, speaking against chess, as a useless and time-consuming game, only good for idlers. It seems to us that this opinion is only partly justified. Of all the games in the world, chess without doubt demands most ability; it shapes and develops the mind, instructs in deeper thinking and for this reason, even in many educational establishments, is being applied as a means of education."

Few people today would consider it necessary to defend chess like this (though in Moscow of all places an engineer once described chess masters to us as useless people who "could do nothing with their hands" — B. H. Wood).

In Russia and other Socialist lands, chess falls under the aegis of the Ministry of Sport, only marginally separate from football, athletics etc.

In this particular atmosphere, chess may tend to be confined to tournaments, classification contests and so on. The development of refined play, the idea of producing a game with the attraction of a work of art or the attainment of scientific precision — these may be discounted.

To class chess as a sport, merely mental as distinct from physical, is to over-simplify.

As a noted journalist Tomasz Domaniewski argued in a Polish weekly: "we have read for years about the 'sport' of chess... but sitting at a chessboard, moving bits of wood about cannot possibly be classified as physical action...

"Stringy muscles and a hollow chest are a disadvantage to a runner or thrower, but they may be no obstacle in reaching the highest level in chess. One can be a Titan of the chequered board

"A difficult problem with a second solution." ("L'Echiquier de Paris").

"Yes, I must admit the end-game is very interesting." ("La Marseillaise").

"I suggest we call it a draw."
Cartoon by J. Kosieradzki ("Szpilki").

In check!!!
Cartoon by J. Hegen ("Frischer Wind").

without having ever stepped on to a playing field. At the peak in chess, nothing counts but mind."

Maybe there are faint analogies? There are matches. There are elimination bouts; tournaments; even Olympiads. There are master players. Points are scored...

All this, however, hardly goes beyond mere nomenclature.

Musicians have contests, poets read in competitions at Eisteddfods, but these do not make music or poetry into sports, or poets into sportsmen.

Sport must inescapably remain associated with physical culture alone. On the other hand, football, racing, polo, etc., in all their manifestations have resemblances on the physical plane to those of chess in the mental. As a rule the combat is between opponents with, in principle, equal possibilities of winning. The winner is the better, the cleverer, the more attentive contestant but, ideally, not the luckier.

Through the intrinsic nature of conflict itself, the contestants go through similar emotions. You may class a spectator at a football match as

a sportsman but a keen chess enthusiast in play is closer than that spectator to the tensions and exertions of a footballer on the field. Football spectators and spectators at a chess championship, on the other hand, may be in very similar emotional states.

A leading Polish chess master in the thirties told a journalist in an interview:

"... an active chess player works mentally, nervously and physicially for several hours a day."

"Physically?"

"Yes, sir. Physically."

"I don't understand you."

"We were talking about the analogy between a boxer and a chessplayer."

"It seems to me there is no analogy as far as the physical effort is concerned."

The master smiled and said:

"There is one. The boxer loses weight before his bout and a chess player after. For instance, in the course of a hard tournament I lose several pounds weight."

(Stahlberg remarked the same to us. Leading masters and grand masters keep fit by walking, tennis, swimming etc., but it must be confessed that others do as well with no exercise whatever. Keres's no-smoking or Lasker's sedentary life and endless cigars? Take your choice! — B. H. Wood.)

Of course, we've all heard about the fellow who tells a friend "I've won a double world title: in boxing and chess."

"How?"

"I knocked out Alekhine in two rounds and beat Cassius Clay at chess."

Then there has been satire... "Chess develops the thigh muscles, thumb and forefinger."

Or this parody of sport reporting in a Polish weekly:

"In the three-nation chess tournament in Budapest, Poland managed to secure third place, immediately after Hungary and Czechoslovakia.

"... If we had taken our own equipment there — our captain told us — the result would have been better still. Unfortunately, our competitors could not get accustomed to the Hungarian design of knight. We had trained under different conditions and it was not easy to handle these Hungarian horses..."

To say that chess is not a sport in any sense whatever is to err. There are connections with sport which nobody would wish to sever.

The chess player, for instance, must accept the ethics of sport. He must learn to accept defeat with grace: has sport anything greater to teach than this?

"Chess adversaries are not enemies. They are rivals in noble combat, shaking each other's hands both before and after the contest." These words, spoken more than a hundred years ago

"If you'd captured the king at the very beginning, it would be easier for you now."

"The champion is making a splendid effort, he's getting nearer to a checkmate."

"Gentlemen, it's time to go home. The tournament ended on Sunday, three days ago."

Cartoons by G. Miklaszewski ("Express Wieczorny").

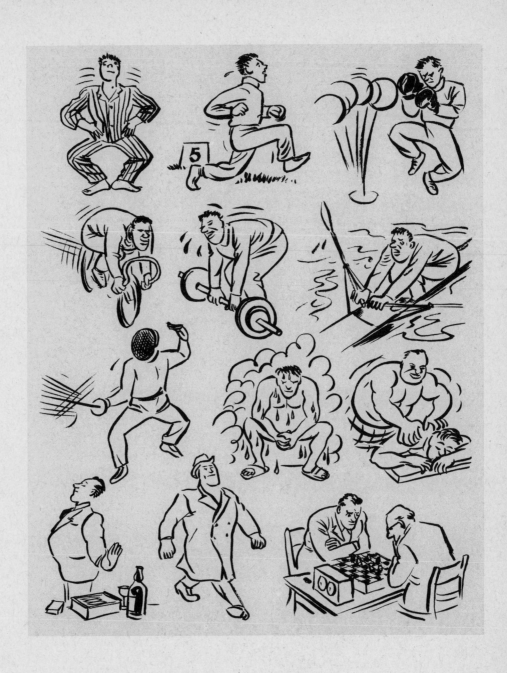

Training for the championships. Cartoon by H. Bidstrup.

"One feels much better now that chess has been included among the sports." Cartoon by S. Kobyliński ("Szpilki").

The start. Cartoon by Müller ("Lilliput").

by a French chess player, Doazan, set up a timeless ideal.

Alekhine maintained that there are no shortcomings or faults in a chess player's make-up from which he could not free himself, providing he himself fought sufficiently stubbornly to rid himself of them and that in doing so, he shaped his own character for the better.

"I have shaped my own character with the help of chess," he wrote. "Chess, first of all, teaches objectivity. In chess, you can become a great master only by facing up to your own errors and deficiencies, just as in life."

Those people who are enthusiastic only about the creative side of chess and decry the competitive aspect he called "chess's tragic actors."

Not that chess has been free from bad sportmanship.

In the last round of an important tournament, a master once became very nervous about his position. Banking on the fact that his opponent had an unusual reputation for chivalry, he suddenly complained of severe pain which was making it difficult for him to concentrate.

Suggesting that the position was more or less even and that if he were to lose, it could only be through a blunder induced by his sufferings, he proposed that the game should be agreed a draw. His gentlemanly opponent sympathetically acquiesced and as a result, only won the second prize. The "invalid," who was, of course, in excellent health, thus saved a valuable half-point.

It was Alekhine who said: "I regard three factors as indispensable to success: first, an understanding of one's strengths and weaknesses; second, an exact realization of your opponent's strengths and weaknesses; and thirdly, a higher aim than mere momentary satisfaction. I observe this aim in scientific and artistic achievements which place the game of chess in the rank of other arts."

VI. CHESS AND MACHINES

An automatic chess player in the form of a Turk, found in Vienna and brought to Paris where it was exhibited as Kempelen's.

The idea of constructing an artificial man fascinated many people in olden days, though few considered it as feasible as the quest for the philosopher's stone which could transmute metals into gold, the elixir of life which would ward off death and "perpetuum mobile," the machine which would run for ever. The transmutation of metals, albeit at great cost, is well within the bounds of science today. The conquest of death is just a little nearer today, with the new understanding of cell mechanisms, whilst perpetual motion is now recognised as an impossibility (after all, even the earth will not go round the sun for ever), though watches, self-wound through slight movements by the wearer and clocks perpetually re-activated by the fluctuations of temperature between day and night, have lives limited only by the wearing of their parts.

Inventors did produce, some centuries ago, a number of machines in human form which wrote a few phrases, danced, played musical instruments, and — long before Edison and his phonograph — even talked. A metal duck clucked and laid eggs. Could such an automaton be made to play chess?

This task was tackled about 1760 by one Wolfgang Kempelen, a 49-year-old Hungarian inventor and engineer, an adviser at the Court of the Austrian Empress Maria Theresa. He had already won renown and favour with an ingenious fountain in the palace park, a steam lift, a device for writing for the blind, a talking doll, etc. His mechanical chess player, however, was to earn him almost legendary fame. It defeated even players of international renown. The secret of its working was strictly guarded.

Though the whole apparatus was in essence a fraud, its construction called for unusual ingenuity. Of course, the machine did not think for itself. There was a man inside. The man who had to be virtually a dwarf and an extremely good chess player.

A figure in imitation of a Turk sat behind a big box on the top of which were a chessboard and men. Inside the figure was the dwarf who directed the intricate mechanism. By a cunning arrangement of mirrors, the box underneath the chessboard could be opened to "prove" that there was nobody inside.

That the machine was a fraud in a sense, does not detract entirely from the cleverness of the mechanism which enabled the player, confined in an extremely restricted space, to "see" his opponent's moves and make his own.

He could not see the course of play directly. The pieces standing on the chessboard had strong magnets placed in their bases. Inside the box, beneath each square of the chessboard, was a metal ball with a thread running loosely but freely through it. When a piece was raised, the ball underneath it would drop, indicating the square from which the piece had been taken. When the piece was placed on another square the magnet raised the ball under that square. In spite of the cleverness of the mechanism, it must have been a trying task to play a game from inside the apparatus, and far from pleasant physically.

The automaton was actually equipped with two mechanical systems. One was secret, one actuated by the hidden player. The one shown to the public was over-complicated and aimed at visual effect: cog-wheels and gears of various dimensions turned, levers shifted, and cylinders revolved — all aimed to produce the illusion that the machine was thinking for itself. Every twelve moves, the showman exhibiting the machine wound it up with a huge key, incidentally providing the hidden player with a little spare time for analysing the position in the game.

A check to his king was acknowledged by the Turk with three nods. Whenever his opponent made a false move, he would stop playing and sit motionless.

Kempelen, who had ambitions as a serious engineer, did not originally intend to keep up the farce for long, and referred to his mechanical chess player in off-hand terms. The public, however, did not allow him to treat it as a joke. Kempelen became a slave to his own fraud; not only the man in the street but distinguished men of science showered him with flattery. They insisted on recognising the automaton as the first manifestation of the "machine man" which so many hoped would be designed. So he refrained from explaining the mystery yet, all the same, he was reluctant to allow himself to be persuaded to take part in the automaton's performances. At the end of his first grand tour, he dismantled the Turk, obviously hoping that the memory of it would die.

It was not to be. When the Empress Maria Theresa died, and her successor, the Emperor Joseph II was entertaining the Grand Duke Paul, son of Empress Catherine II of Russia in Vienna in 1780, he remembered the automaton and ordered the mechanical chess player to give another demonstration at the court. So Kempelen had willy-nilly to put it together again.

In tackling the job, he was carried away by his enthusiasm as an engineer; he improved several details in the machinery, fitting it with a speaking device so that the Turk could say "Check!" This revised version of the automaton completely enchanted the Duke, and Kempelen was solemnly invited to take his invention to St. Petersburg.

There followed a lengthy tour of the "chess player" through the Courts of Europe, the chief towns of Germany, Russia, France and England. On the way to St. Petersburg, the automaton was shown in Warsaw. As before, there was endless speculation on the secret of its working. Apart from the most common supposition that there was a dwarf hidden inside — which was undermined by the ingenuity with which the box was apparently shown to be full of works — there was considerable speculation as to the possibilities of remote control.

After Kempelen died in 1804, his chess player was purchased by the impresario, Maelzel, who soon took it on a tour of German towns. In

An automatic "Turk" chess player constructed by Kempelen in 1769. Drawing from the late 18th century.

The back view of the same automaton with the clothes lifted to reveal the wooden back.

1809, the automaton was privileged to play against Napoleon Bonaparte at the Schoenbrunn Palace in Vienna. According to one account, the game became quite a ceremony with many guests invited. At one stage, Napoleon deliberately made an illegal move. The Turk corrected it and made his reply. Again, Napoleon made a wrong move. The automaton again corrected him. When Napoleon did it again, however, the Turk lost his temper and, with his hand, brushed the pieces to the floor. Napoleon was delighted, in fact, quite pleased with himself for managing to unnerve a machine. When he played another game properly, he was badly beaten. No wonder, for inside it was Johann Allgaier, one of the greatest Viennese chess players of all time whose name is commemorated in one of the variations of the King's Gambit.

In the period of almost seventy years during which the automaton was publicly exhibited, the "brain" of the automaton was supplied by more than fifteen eminent chess players in succession. The success of the demonstrator's quest for occupants for the apparatus — and the attractiveness of the money the machine earned — is attested by the fact that, of three hundred games played by the automaton, only six were lost.

The mechanical Turk was shipped by Maelzel to New York in 1826, where he made a lot of money by widely publicised sessions. After his death in 1837, it passed from hand to hand until, after reconstruction by Professor J. Mitchell, it found its way to the Chinese Museum in Philadelphia, where it was destroyed by fire in June 1854. So ended its astounding career.

It was thought for a long time that Kempelen's construction was lost irretrievably. Yet, in Vienna, in 1945, a French soldier of the Allied Forces of Occupation found by chance, in the cellar of an old house, a figure of the Turkish chess player together with a box and machinery. The origin of the figure was never strictly established but, in all probability, it was one of the variants of

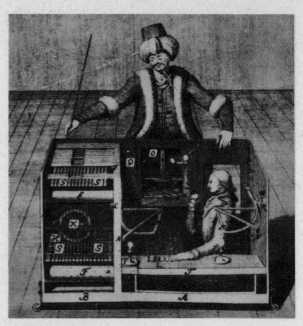

Kempelen's automatic chess player shown in a drawing made after the secret of its operation had been discovered. Left: the effect of empty depth obtained through appropriate use of partitions and mirrors. Next, the means of hiding a chess player in the box.

Kempelen's automaton. The finder brought the construction to Paris and had it repaired and restored.

Let us return, however, to the past. The secret of the machine's working was not revealed until 1834 by a French periodical. A better--known exposure was effected by Edgar Allan Poe in a long article "Maelzel's Chess Player" (1834).

Poe, as a frequent visitor to Maelzel's exhibitions, could not have failed to observe that certain routines were strictly observed and that there were certain incongruities. This set him on the trail to investigate the probability of "a man in the box."

The routine of apparently disclosing the interior of the box for inspection by the public was therefore analysed with the exacting precision of a detective-story teller.

"In the first place, the exhibitor opens door No. 1. Leaving this open, he goes round to the rear of the box, and opens a door precisely at the back of door No. 1. To this back door he holds a lighted candle. He then closes the back door, locks it, and coming round to the front, opens the drawer to its full extent. This done, he opens doors No. 2 and No. 3 (the folding doors), and displays the interior of the main compartment. Leaving open the main compartment, the drawer, and the front door of cupboard No. 1, he now goes to the rear again, and throws open the back door of the main compartment. In shutting up the box no particular order is observed, except that the folding-doors are always closed before the drawer.

"Now, let us suppose that when the machine is first rolled into the presence of the spectators, a man is already within it. His body is situated behind the dense machinery in cupboard No. 1, and his legs lie at full length in the main compartment. When Maelzel opens the door No. 1, the man within is not in any danger of discovery,

Napoleon playing the Automaton. Drawing by Antoni Uniechowski.

for the keenest eye cannot penetrate more than about two inches into the darkness within. But the case is otherwise when the back door of the cupboard No. 1 is opened. A bright light then pervades the cupboard, and the body of the man would be discovered if it were there. But it is not. The putting of the key in the lock of the back door was the signal. On hearing this the person concealed brought his body forward to an angle as acute as possible — throwing it altogether, or nearly so, into the main compartment. This, however, is a painful position, and cannot be long maintained. Accordingly we find that Maelzel closes the back door. This being done, there is no reason why the body of the man may not resume its former situation — for the cupboard is again so dark as to defy scrutiny. The drawer is now opened, and the legs of the person within drop down behind it in the space it formerly occupied.

"There is, consequently, now no longer any part of the man in the main compartment — his body being behind the machinery in cupboard No. 1, and his legs in the space occupied by the drawer. The exhibitor, therefore, finds himself at liberty to display the main compartment. This he does — opening its back and front doors — and no person is discovered. The spectators are now satisfied that the whole of the box is exposed to view — and exposed too, all portions of it at one and the same time. But of course this is not the case."

"... Maelzel, having now rolled the machine around, lifted up the drapery of the Turk, opened the doors in its back and thigh, and shown his trunk to be full of machinery, brings the whole back into its original position, and closes the doors." The man within, now at liberty to move about, gets up into the body of the Turk just so high as to see the chessboard through the bosom of the Turk, which is of gauze. With his right arm across his breast he now easily reaches the little machinery beneath the Turk's left shoulder to guide its arm and fingers.

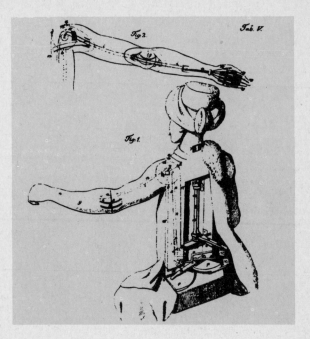

Although the automatic chess player was a spoof, the mechanism demanded extraordinary inventiveness and precision. A mid-eighteenth century drawing.

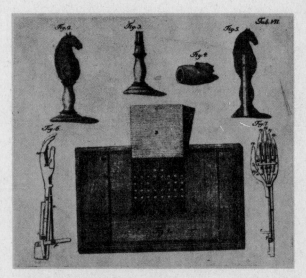

Certain details of the construction of the automatic player as imagined by the artist of the mid-19th century: the knight with a magnet inside; the "Turk's" hand and the chessboard as seen from below with metal balls for indicating what squares had been played to and from.

The arguments collected by Poe to prove his hypothesis that the machine was directly controlled by human mind amounted to 17.

Some of the more interesting among these said for instance, that a true automaton would observe the regularity of moves, instead of accommodating itself to the moves of the antagonist player, as it did when, on the sudden withdrawal of an opponent, it would stop of itself and wait till the opponent reappeared.

A true automatic player should invariably win, which was not the case with Maelzel's mechanism.

Also that the antagonist was not allowed to play at the board of the automaton, but was seated at some distance from the machine, since were it otherwise, he would be able, with the aid of a quick ear, to detect the breathing of the man concealed inside the box.

Six candles, each different in height from the other, were most obviously intended to give a sufficiently strong light to enable the man within to see through the transparent material composing the breast of the figure; this also greatly increased, by the dazzling effect of the complicated crossing of the rays, the difficulty of ascertaining the specific property of the fabric.

"The Turk plays with his left arm. A circumstance so remarkable cannot be accidental."

"... The automaton plays with his left arm, because under no other circumstances could the man within play with his right — a desideratum of course... The right arm of the man within is brought across his breast, and his right fingers act, without any constraint, upon the machinery in the shoulder of the figure."

"We do not believe that any reasonable objection can be urged against this solution of the automaton Chess Player."

The mechanical Turk's long succession of triumphal performances gave rise to a flood of legends and rumours. About 1801 the subject began to invade fiction and drama. In a Paris play of that year "Le Joueur d'Echecs," by Marseillier and Charet, an elderly chess enthusiast who declined to give his daughter's hand to a young officer was fooled by the latter who entered his house inside an automaton chess player presented by some anonymous friend. The daughter apparently inherited her father's passion

Two scenes from the French film "The Chess Player" (1926). LEFT: Kempelen's automatic chess player is being presented at the court of the Polish King Stanisław Poniatowski. RIGHT: In the night, Kempelen, mortally wounded, crawls out from inside the "Turk's" body: the automaton has been shot on the Empress Catherine's orders.

for the game, as she now started to spend many hours at play with the automaton. Unfortunately, the idyll did not last long, since the suspicious father surprised the young couple at a game bearing little resemblance to chess. However, all ended well. Father agreed to the marriage, especially as his future son-in-law proved to be a fair chess player and promised to play with him from time to time.

This facetious little comedy showed that at least some of Kempelen's contemporaries had grave doubts about the exclusively mechanical functioning of the automaton, and it must be supposed that they were as fascinated by the question of who was hidden inside the machine, as how the machinery worked. The enigmatic chess player inhabiting the automaton was rumoured to be a real dwarf; an invalid who had lost both his legs; a political rebel who had found a new way of hiding from authority.

One persistent rumour identified him as a Polish officer, Lieutenant Woroński who had taken part in Kościuszko's Uprising in 1794. Though the story gained widespread credence

139

and persisted for decades, it seems to have been pure fiction.

The Grande Encyclopédie Larousse gives this version: In 1776, four years after the first partition of Poland, a Russian regiment in Riga containing many Poles had revolted. The rebels had to flee. The leader of the revolt, an officer named Woroński, was injured in both legs. A doctor named Oslov came to his aid but had to amputate them. Baron Kempelen was a friend of the doctor and, knowing that Woroński had a price on his head, decided to take him out of the country.

For this purpose, he conceived the idea of constructing an automaton for playing chess and hiding Woroński inside. The automaton was ready in three months' time. To avoid suspicion, Kempelen exhibited his "chess player" on the way. Soon they were near the Prussian frontier, at Vitebsk. Suddenly there came an order from the Empress Catherine II that the automaton should be exhibited at the Imperial Court in St. Petersburg. A good chess player, the Empress wished to compare its skill with hers. The automaton played like a true sportsman and, ignoring the demands of diplomacy, won.

The offended Catherine, guessing that she had been defeated by a live opponent, offered to buy the automaton but Kempelen, pretending that he had always to accompany the machine, declined.

Lieutenant Woroński's story was taken up into a novel, "Le Joueur d'échecs" by the French writer H. Dupuy-Mazuel. A film based on this novel, and using the same title, directed by Raymond Bernard, was made in France in 1926, though many scenes such as wintry landscapes and a cavalry charge were filmed in Poland.

The film itself received much publicity as an early example of co-operation in production between France and Poland.

Both the novel and the film handled history in carefree style.

The story now told that in Riga (Vilna, in the film) lived a constructor of automata known as "Androids," whose name was Kempelen. He was joined by Bronisław Wnorowski (or Bolesław Worowski, in the film), a Polish revolutionary who fell in love with his ward, a young lady called Zofia. When the long-prepared insurrection broke out, the Poles captured the city; but only to be soon defeated. Wnorowski, badly wounded, took shelter with Kempelen who decided to try to save him by taking him away to Germany, hidden inside a chess automaton. The fame of the splendid Android reached the Polish king Stanisław Poniatowski who ordered that it be presented at his Court. The invention was demonstrated at the Warsaw Castle. The King appreciated the excellent construction of the automaton and symbolically awarded it with an order of merit, expressing at the same time a wish that the artificial Turk also perform before the Empress Catherine. Against Kempelen's recommendation,

Automatic chess playing "Turk" in the sound version of the film "The Chess Player," produced by film director Jean Dréville in 1938.

140

the highly-patriotic Wnorowski did not allow Catherine to win, and when she had made a false move on purpose he brushed the pieces away. As a punishment for the lèse-majesté, the Empress ordered the "chess player" to be shot. Kempelen, to save his friend, took him out of the automaton and took his place. The execution was arranged during a carnival ball. The idea was really to punish the proud Android only in jest, but the volley of shots wounded Kempelen mortally.

A short summary can hardly, of course, bring out all the "subtleties" of the drama or the spicy "historic realities." The part of the heroic Polish insurgent was played in the film by the actor Pierre Blanchard, the figure of Kempelen by Charles Dullin. The novel was not only filmed but dramatized by the playwright Marcel Achard. In 1938, the film director Jean Dréville made a sound version of the "Joueur d'échecs" in which Kempelen was played by the famous actor Conrad Veidt and Empress Catherine by Françoise Rosay.

One offshoot of the history of the chess automaton, is of fascinating interest: the more so for being absolutely authentic. It was Kempelen's "chess player" which inspired the English poet and inventor Edmund Cartwright to construct a power-loom. Cartwright felt he wanted to match the ingenuity of a mere toy without practical value, with an automaton useful to man. He was impressed by the precise action of the artificial chess player, and probably he was not aware then that it was a clever mystification. Ambitious to equal the mechanical efficiency of the "chess player," he finally completed in 1803 a model loom, the prototype of the machine which has become universal in the textile industry.

Returning to literature, it is impossible not to mention a short story by a Polish writer of the 19th century, Ludwik Niemojowski, "Szach

An imaginative science fiction idea of the chess game of the future. Illustration from the cover of a German youth magazine "Die Schulpost" (1957).

i mat" ("Checkmate") which was largely concerned with an artificial player.

The scene was set in Italy, and later in Marseilles, in 1855–56. Bartolomeo, a chess genius who lived in poverty as a result of his obsession for the game, was promised a big fee for a series of exhibition games. On arrival at Marseilles, he found he had been duped by a clever impresario, a merchant from England, who restricted his movements and tried to draw him into an illegal adventure, taking advantage of his parlous financial situation.

"With my inseparable companion, I entered a small square room, quite empty. In the middle stood a chessboard. To the right of this was a piano keyboard with each key inscribed with a chess piece. The pawns were numbered. A mass of fine wires issued from the keyboard, their ends disappearing in the opposite wall.

"I could not conceive to what use this intricate mechanism might be put, until the person whom fate had offered me as a guardian said, 'Lie down and look through the hole in the floor.'

"I did as I was asked.

"Putting my eye to the chink (which, being cunningly concealed in the stucco work of the ceiling, was virtually invisible from below) I saw a chessboard at which a player was sitting, engrossed in the game.

" 'Just touch this blank note on the keyboard,' commanded the Englishman.

"As I did so, how marvellous! The chess player, hitherto motionless, nodded and his hand rose high as if he sought which pawn he should move.

" 'Now touch any numbered key on the keyboard.'

"With my index finger I pressed the key marked 3. Obedient to my will, the imitation player slowly brought down his hand on the third pawn and moved it.

"I repeated the experiment several times, and each time the youthful figure below me executed the indicated move with mathematical precision.

" 'Do you understand now what I expect of you?' cried the Englishman. 'Do you understand why I have to cloak my actions with secrecy? If you are the best chess player in the world, I consider myself the best engineer. This automaton, the work of my hands, the result of many sleepless nights, and innumerable combinations, though it has wheels instead of a heart and springs instead of nerves; although it does not live — it's a masterpiece. What am I saying?' he added with increasing enthusiasm, 'It lives! It has no soul but you will impart yours to it; it has no feeling but you will warm it up with your breath. Under your influence, it will move, act, and almost think. ...Tell me, isn't it the summit of triumph and delight — to infuse an object with life?' "

Having no alternative, Bartolomeo accepted the unusual proposition. An aggresively publicised performance of the mechanical chess player attracted many curious spectators. The automaton defeated every opponent. Money poured into the impostor's pocket.

The automaton's fame grew. High class players were worsted. Exhibitions were organised with increasing frequency, every one a sell-out. Bartolomeo, compelled to play day and night, became physically and mentally exhausted. A slave to the public and the complicated machinery. Deprived of his own personality, he began to go mad. His play deteriorated.

"...Then came the fatal day: I blundered and lost. My opponent, delighted by this first victory over the hitherto unconquered automaton, doubled his stake. I lost again.

"A dull murmur rose from the hall below. The public shifted in their seats; they dipped into their pockets and a substantial sum of money was pooled. The double winner challenged me again, at tremendous stakes. I summoned up all the skill I could, drew on all the poor reserves of will-power left me — and lost again. Whistles and cat-calls crescendoed. The Englishman burst in on me, 'You treacherous villain, you're ruining me. You traitor; you've been paid by the crowd...!'

"He did not finish. He saw me crying like a child. Downstairs the uproar increased; stamping, whistling, breaking of chairs and benches... The crowd demanded another game.

"With difficulty, the Englishman asked for the session to be adjourned until the morrow, giving as an excuse that some internal piece of machinery had come loose. He could not withdraw altogether, nor could he decrease the stakes: the posters had advertised unconditional and unlimited return matches. I was laid in bed, a doctor was secretly sent for, I was dosed with medicine...

"Nothing helped. My temperature rose and rose."

The era of automatic chess playing machines for home use: "According to the rules he should win the game in 17 moves at most." Cartoon by H. Parschau ("Eulenspiegel").

Kempelen standing in front of a completely automatic factory: Can it really be operated by one man hidden inside? ("Ludas Matyi").

'Don't be so sure of yourself!'　　　*... I can always push a button...*　　　*... and you will lose. ("Świat").*

The next day, long before the advertised hour, the hall was full of spectators eager for fresh sensations. The marvellous chess player's failure attracted many more curious spectators than his previous triumphs.

"I was dragged out of bed and laid on the floor; my head was put to the chink in the floor and I was told to play. I do not know how I managed it — I was almost unconscious. I heard only an infernal din of mingled voices roaring underneath me. To this day, I could not say whether they were sounds of displeasure or a morbid illusion caused by the racing rhythm of my own pulse. I do not remember what happened next.

"I was ill for a long long time, finally regaining consciousness to find myself in hospital. The Englishman, I learned, had lost his entire fortune through the automaton's collapse and had disappeared from Marseilles."

A novel "The Collapse of Chess" by the Soviet writer Abramov, published in 1926, ends very differently. Here the automaton was always successful, defeating even the strongest masters. The unusual machine caused a world sensation. Unfortunately, the designer of the machine became mad and died. A friend of the designer explained in a letter to a newspaper the secret of the mechanism but an essential key to the mathematical formula was not to be found. And so chess was saved!

There is a lot of fantasy in the foregoing.

But recent times have brought us an even more fantastic development based on the most exact of sciences. Even before the First World War, the Spanish scientist Leonardo Torres y Quevedo, President of the Academy of Sciences in Madrid, had constructed an electro-magnetic automaton in which the white king and a rook mated the black king from any position. This end-game is, of course, a simple one, but the construction of an apparatus to effect it by classical mechanics was a great achievement. From the theoretical point of view, the construction of a machine to mate by means, for instance, of two bishops, would be only a slight further advance. Even the simple end-games, however, demand complex technical design. Even though the Torres y Quevedo apparatus employed only two men against one, it was exceedingly complex.

In a book "La pensée artificielle, sur l'introduction au cybernétique" ("Artificial Thought, an Introduction to Cybernetics"), Pierre de Latil explained how it worked. "You move a piece. The machine replies with a move as if made by a ghost. How?

"Each square on the board is built up of three metal plates electrically isolated from each other

144

by rubber strips. The black king of the player opposing the automaton has a metal base and makes contact with the plates of the square on which it is standing. This in turn causes two different currents to be sent to the automaton, informing it of the square on which the black king stands at the moment. The automaton's reply to the move made by man is made by electro-magnets which move under the chessboard and pull the white pieces, which have a metal ball hidden in their hollowed bases, into place. If the live player makes an illegal move, a sign 'First error' lights up and the automaton interrupts play until its opponent rectifies the error. If the man makes a second illegal move, a sign 'Second error' lights up. On a third illegal move, the automaton stops play. If the king is played on to a checked square, a loudspeaker cries out 'Jaque al Rey' ('Check to the king!'). When the machine wins, it cries 'Mate'."

The machine does not actually assess any situation. All possible play has been decided in advance. In effect, the black king mates himself. Wherever he goes, he automatically brings suicidal reactions into being. The entire play, in every conceivable situation, has been determined in advance and there is no possibility of the black king getting into a position from which he can escape mate.

At the Congress of Cybernetics in Paris in 1951, the inventor's son, Gonzales Torres y Quevedo, presented his father's "electro-magnetic chess player." A distinguished cybernetist, Professor Norbert Wiener, was duly defeated. It was jested at the time that this was the last triumph of classical mechanics over modern cybernetics, a victory of "determinism" over "organization."

We are now witnessing completely new attempts at harnessing machines to chess playing.

Scientists have designed complicated electronic computers which carry out in a split second complex mathematical operations whose solution in the ordinary way would require many exacting calculations made by a team of skilled mathematicians. Within the limits decided by their designers, these machines, or rather teams of electronic apparatuses filling large rooms, are able to select and carry out, as if by themselves, certain operations, eliminating irrelevant ones, and to reply to the mathematical question put to them, by scanning the possibilities of many combinations at tremendous speed. This automatic

"Prodigy Child" operated by transistors wins a simultaneous game against "valve" robots.
Cartoon by V. Kashchenko ("Tekhnika Molodiozhy").

"Whenever I stop to think for a moment, he immediately breaks the circuit."
Cartoon by V. Voyevodin ("Ogonyok").

search for mechanical selection of various combinations might seem to resemble actual thought, and it is tempting to call computers "artificial brains," but wrong.

The arrival of the computer has turned scientists anew to the idea of a chess playing machine. The "artificial brain" cannot think for itself. It can scan possibilities, and possible combinations of moves, at amazing speed. In a Polish popular-scientific monthly "Problemy," I. Kroszczyński has explained how computers work.

"Let us imagine how such a machine would play chess. At the same time, let us assume that chess cannot, any more than life itself, be calculated outright to the end. An ordinary chess automaton would be able to play one or more specimen

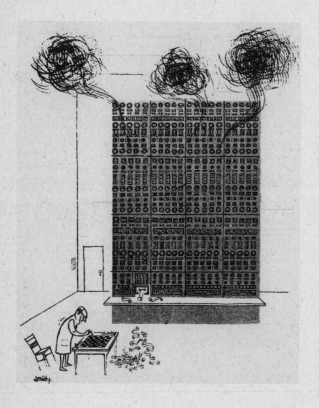

"Man has won!" Cartoon by D. Milty ("Szpilki").

games of the same standard as its designer could play them; neither better nor worse. But a homeostat, or an 'artificial man,' is quite a different thing. If properly programmed, it would move the pieces strictly according to the rules, and would endeavour to mate its opponent. This would demand only comparatively straightforward technique.

"The apparatus would make the first move quite accidentally, depending on the arbitrary choice of whoever prepared its programme. Its opponent would make a reply move; and then?

"It could move any piece. Each move could lead on to a number of different situations, some to the machine's advantage, some not.

"It could delve into great numbers of these possible situations. 'If I do this, he can do this. If I then do this, he can do this, or this or this.' Weighing up the attractiveness of the resulting end-situation from each train of moves, it could finally select and make the move which led to the best…

"A single analysis which might take a man several months, could be carried out by a computer in minutes, or even seconds, with less probability of error and with no possibility of fatigue.

"You might almost say that every move by the apparatus would be the calculated introduction to a deep combination. Nobody could win a game against it. On the other hand, a twenty-move deep apparatus would always lose to one which would 'think,' say, for fifty moves.

If we altered various controls, e.g. the anode tension of the valves, we could have various 'temperaments'; one apparatus, for instance, might tend to favour rapid violent operations, another more 'reflecting,' by collecting data and proceeding with caution."

So a chess playing automaton can be made. Its scope is more limited, but it does not need a man to be hidden inside it.

The role of the secret player is in this case performed by the designer who, instead of concealing a live man in the machine, has introduced

into it the result of his chess-and-mathematical speculations.

Here, however, we come immediately to the point of the problem. A computer is incapable by itself of devising a single independent move but is only able to select its moves according to a certain predetermined pattern of operation. This pattern is the programmed contribution by the designer who determines the tactics of the machine in the game and imposes a certain defined orientation. We know by now that chess theory has not as yet found any mathematical definition, also that nobody has so far been able, with the aid of algebraic equations, to analyse a complete chess game or to assess a definite chessboard situation. Thus even the best electronic computer cannot possibly be programmed with an objective unambiguous pattern of operation as would guide it towards success in scanning the astronomical number of various individual combinations. To simplify the problem, let us assume that the machine is to decide on

a move to its material advantage, provided that the opponent's strength is estimated by giving to various pieces a certain number of points and correcting the result, depending on, for instance, how many squares the piece may attack and on whether it will be isolated, in a combination, etc. The machine has finally finished selecting the variants and made its reply. The result — it has selected a move which will lead the opponent to win easily.

Chess play recognizes, for instance, the idea of "sacrificing" a piece when a material loss brings a strategic supremacy or victory to a well-organized, but substantially weaker player in the contest against the stronger, yet chaotically positioned set of his opponent. One could, of course, in the future improve such a "pattern," introduce a range of refined corrections in assessing the strength of each of the opponents, yet nothing whatever would make one achieve a fair substitute for the brain of a live player who skilfully will reject the disadvantageous

variants and who, through the analysis of the developments for several moves ahead, will select not only the one appropriate move, but also the train of further possible moves. A chess playing machine is incapable of strategy, and it also has to match millions of combinations, with all the irrational variants included.

There is also another essential factor which prevents machine from effective playing. This is the speed of calculation which, with the present state of technology of the electronic computers, is much too small for practical purposes of chess playing. The capacity of an "artificial brain" was until recently not above a hundred thousand operations a second. This speed, however, is not subject to limitations, and is being constantly increased by constructional improvements. Let us assume then that we have at our disposal a computer capable of a milliard counting operations per second — a very remote possibility as yet. Mathematicians have calculated that a five-move deep chess

automaton would have to analyse a single move seven days and nights. At seven-move deep playing, a single deliberation, or the selection of one individual variant from all possible situations, would take about ten thousand years to accomplish!

We are thus left with only one single solution in this situation — namely, to abandon all ambitions of constructing an ideal electronic chess player, and to allow the computing machines to play their best as they can. The machine would then plan for two or three moves in advance, availing itself of a simplified "memory" and performing certain standardized replies depending on the moves made by its live opponent. In an opening play, such an automaton could possibly defend itself against its opponent's attacks as long as the game followed one of the ordinary long-established variants. Confronting, for instance, a poor player who fashions his moves according to manual instructions, the "electronic brain" would oppose him by playing appropriate variants as outlined by some outstanding chess authority, and imprinted, as it were, in the automaton's "memory." However, to any odd, incorrect or simply irrational moves the machine would not react sensibly, since, as lacking the qualifying criteria, it is not capable of actual strategic assessment. For the same reasons it would equally be unable, even over a short distance of play, to conduct rationally a game which it has entered in the middle of playing.

Electronic computers were used to play chess for the first time in 1956. It has almost become a custom since to try out the chess playing ability of every new, improved model of computer. Machines, however, have not so far mastered this art satisfactorily.

Such machines produced more interesting results in simplified chess. Two American scientists, William and Stein, conducted experiments with an automaton playing chess on a chessboard of 6×6 squares, with a set of pieces diminished by the Bishops, and with the elimination of castling and the Pawn's privilege, on its initial move, of leaping over a piece. Here again, the machine lost against a good player and won in the contest against a bungler, but the course of the game was at least marked by some conspicuous logic which did not allow one to pass over the problem of mechanical chess players indifferently.

There is of course no vital necessity for constructing chess playing automata, and thus depriving people of the emotions they receive from this noble pastime. The possibilities of chess playing automatons are actually regarded as the proof of the perfection of their mechanisms — a perfection which does not really seem a desirable necessity.

In a science-fiction film directed by Kurt Maetzig, "Milcząca Gwiazda" (The Silent Star) (1960), a joint Polish-German production, which

A chess game with an electric robot; scene from the Polish puppet film "The Ghost in the Palace."

149

is partly based on the Polish writer Lem's novel "Astronauci" (The Astronauts), there are a few scenes of a game of chess being played in a space rocket between an American nuclear physicist and the "Omega," a universal robot constructed by a Polish cybernetist-designer, Sołtyk. The automaton dictates the moves and wins repeatedly, which depresses the scientist who does not want to yield to the intellet of a machine. Under such circumstances the game has lost all of its flavour. Fortunately, the designer, with a frolic of good humour, has, in secrecy from the persistent chess player, manipulated a few screws inside the "Omega" and endowed it with more human-like characteristics which will allow it to err in playing. The scientist now begins to triumph over the machine, winning one game after another.

Even earlier, a French writer, Pierre Boulle, ended his "absurd short story," as he himself called it, entitled "Le robot parfait" (The Perfect Robot) with a witty and more ingenious point of damaging the ideal chess playing robot.

The hero of the story, a certain Professor

Modern technique serves man: a paralyzed person can play chess with the aid of a hydraulic prosthesis enabling him to make any move with the paralyzed hand. The device was constructed at the rehabilitation centre for paralyzed persons in California.

150

Fontaine, is the outstanding designer of ever-improved computer models produced by an Electronic Computer Company. The firm has completely dominated the market, as the models designed by Professor Fontaine have achieved such perfection that the Company's advertising brochures now no longer speak of the calculations of its products, but simply of the "thinking processes" inside these mechanisms. Professor maintains that the electronic machine is a perfect imitator of the human mind, and as it admits of being equipped with an unlimited number of electric circuits, it is thus capable of surpassing the power of the human brain which operates with but a restricted number of physical cells. In order to confirm his hypothesis, he decides to construct a chess playing automaton.

" 'I maintain,' concluded the Professor, 'I maintain after the most careful consideration that an ideal chess player or a 'robot' which I intend to design will in every instance be able to bring the number of possible moves down to a single one. This the machine will achieve by automatic appraisal of all possible resulting combinations from a particular position in the game, outright to the end, and from the appropriate elimination of all incorrect moves."

This theory had propelled the scientist towards sensational achievements. He really succeeded in constructing a chess automaton capable of the most advantageous moves and unquestionably defeating every possible opponent. But his success alarmed competitors, arousing them to intensified efforts. One of them, following the same theoretical assumption, constructed an equally ideal 'robot' which, like its original counterpart, made no errors in playing. It was subsequently found out that all possible displays had thus been reduced to a single ideal game, constantly identical, which invariably ended in a draw. In this way the matter had lost much of its original attraction, and the universal enthusiasm shown for the chess playing automaton had quickly subsided."

A five-ton crane with electro-magnetic grab being demonstrated at an exhibition of automatic equipment in London in 1956. It made a number of moves with great accuracy, going through predetermined games with great precision.

Other automatons in this story are in no better position. They function faultlessly, but they exhibit none of the peculiar human characteristics. They therefore become objectionable on account of exaggerated technicality. Their designer is grieved, because his aim was a perfect machine, capable of matching all human achievements. Finally he strikes on a marvellously simple idea. It is only sufficient to damage these machines a little, and it will alter their abominable behaviour completely. This being done, they really begin to err in their operations, make blunders, and startle people with some unexpected replies. The famous mechanical chess players begin actually to lose. It is then unanimously agreed that Professor Fontaine has really succeded in constructing a perfectly human-like machine.

That was how the French writer facetiously presented his deeply sensible view on the problem of chess playing automaton. One could hardly find a better appraisal of the prospects of this problem. The writer's opinion is moreover in complete agreement with the opinions and views of present-day scientists and outstanding chess theoreticians. When Mikhail Botvinnik delivered his lecture on "Men and Machines behind the Chessboard" at the Humboldt University of Berlin in 1961, he thus concluded his considerations:

"The designers of computers have so far created highly accurate mechanisms, and have also attempted constructing a top accurate mechanical chess player. Unfortunately, it is very unlikely that such a mechanical super player could ever be constructed. However, should we rather not apply ourselves to an entirely different task — namely, to the construction of a mechanism which would be equally imperfect in thinking as the ordinary chess player, and which would err as easily as any of the mortal top masters? The task would then be much easier and it would probably reduce a million times the calculation of variants, bringing the realization of the project within the bounds of our present-day technology.

In other words, we shall continue to fail as longs as we attempt constructing a mechanical champion. The task may become practicable, I believe, if we try to construct a machine in our own image and after our likeness.

"Here, of course, great difficulties appear when it comes to the programming of such a machine. How can we expect ever to reach a machine to analyse 'in a human manner' if we are ourselves actually ignorant of the precise way in which a chess player's mind operates. What is the way in which we actually do that ourselves? And

yet we shall never know the answer until we begin working on such a machine. For we have had no need until now of learning about the way in which a chess player thinks. But once man starts designing 'electronic brains' analogous to human chess players, the inadequacies of 'chess thinking' will be revealed, and the checking of the various methods of programming will tell us how the live players really think.

"The machine will also emerge superior to a champion in that it will have a perfect memory at its command and an enviable strength, and that it will show complete indifference both to the noise in the playing hall and to the future journalistic reviews...

"It should be added that the task of programming such machines, as well as the research into the methods of a live chess player's speculation, can be carried out only with the joint co-operation of mathematicians, psychologists and other scientific workers."

Despite all the theoretical and technical difficulties involved in the programming of electronic chess players, a considerable progress has already been made, due in particular to the achievements of present-day cybernetics. In November 1966 the entire world became electrified with the news of a chess tournament which was arranged between the electronic computers of the Stanford University, U.S.A., and similar machines at the Institute of Theoretical and Applied Physics in Moscow. This match, which was played on four chessboards, had lasted for over a year and had ended with two games won by the Soviet-programmed machines and with the other two a draw.

This undoubtedly was the first important step that was made towards mathematical analysis and synthesis in chess playing.

(The English Editor does not necessarily accept the views put forward in this chapter).

VII. LOVE AND WAR AT THE CHESSBOARD

Death checkmating the king. An allegoric copperplate engraving of the 15th century, the work of an unknown artist from Alsace who signed with the letters BR and an anchor. The picture follows favourite mediaeval morality books depicting life as a game of chess.

The bloodless combat on a chessboard was originally conceived as an imitation of war. The ancient Indian name of chess (Chaturanga) meant an army, and the arrangement of pieces imitated the arms of the time (e.g. infantry, cavalry or elephant-drawn chariots). It seems that before becoming a pastime, chess in ancient India was a military game used to train officers and leaders; it was this which occasioned the military names of the pieces and the rules of the game. In the course of centuries some of the pieces assumed civilian guise (e.g. jester, bishop, and queen or dame) but they always remained human.

The chessboard — a battleground; the play — a struggle. This picture fired the imagination so strongly that chess idioms have affected everyday speech and literary language, and provide many a handy metaphor in day to day conversation.

"...A great game is waged incessantly by day and night on the chessboard of history by Polish organs of security which foil the plans of enemy intelligence services..." — "Cichy front" ("The Quiet Front") by L. Wolanowski.

"The moves of the four men on the chessboard of life were exhausted. The action of the novel... came to an end..." is a comment by E. Boyé, reviewing a novel "The Mist" by M. de Unamuno.

"...Carpentier ... to whom Churchill used to tell anecdotes, and who was backed by the President of the Republic... was just a pawn in the hands of powerful coteries financing sporting life in the West." — Z. Kałużyński in the Polish weekly Nowa Kultura.

In an article published in another Polish weekly, Przyjaźń (1954), entitled "Szachy i strachy pana Dullesa" ("The Chess and Stress of Mr Dulles"), the political situation was almost wholly analysed in chess metaphor:

"... the Washington strategists made a few moves on the diplomatic chessboard.

"... Next, Mr Dulles wished to move the other, more important pieces on his board..."

We find chess metaphors in crime fiction:

"... You see, the other side, the prosecution, has a lot of powerful pieces, and so far we have only a few pawns. You have to do wonders with pawns to beat castles, bishops, and rooks. All the same, we shall do it..." ("The Sloane Square Mystery," by H. Adams).

During the French presidential campaign in 1965, the following statement appeared in a French paper:

"... The election's chessboard has been prepared for the game. The king with due ceremony assumed his place. His adversaries are also all set. They are expecting — with more determination than ever — that they will at least make him go for another term.

Three pieces and a few pawns are to participate in the game — one of these is likely to give us a surprise.

The main piece is Charles de Gaulle..."

Quite an original turn of speech was used by a Polish poet, Andrzej Braun, in one of his poems:

We live at a time when choice is 'de rigeur'
and I was born as one of the pieces in chess...

In a long poem "The Waste Land" by T. S. Eliot, one part, which describes complicated personal relations between people, is entitled "A game of chess;" though chess is not presented at all, and is mentioned only once as a means of passing a worrying time in its hero's life (verses 138 and 139):

And we shall play a game of chess,
Pressing lidless eyes and waiting for a knock upon
the door.

The Austrian writer Franz Kafka, who is often obsessed with man's loneliness in a cruel world, uses an unusual image in his "Letters to Milena":

"... The thing I am afraid of, with my eyes wide open and in an unconscious plunge into fear..., this is only an inner conspiracy against me ... It consists in that I, who in the great game of chess am not even a pawn of a pawn, and even far from it, now wish to seize the place of the queen, against the rules... I, pawn of a pawn and thus a non-existent chessman which does not take part in the game at all. And next maybe I shall wish to seize the place of the king himself, or even a whole chessboard, and if I really wanted this it would have to happen in another way, more inhuman..."

Ilya Ehrenburg, writing in his memoirs, "People, Years and Life" referred to the Stalinist terror of 1937–38, when anybody could be arrested without warning or reason at any time: "I lived in a period in which a man's fate resembled not a game of chess but a lottery..."

Harold Wilson, ex-Prime Minister of Great Britain, once remarked: "Politics is like playing a game of chess: in difficult moments one does not make one's best moves."

And here is an example of events of the last war (referring to German-occupied Poland): "He found himself once again in the little town from which the Germans had evicted him a year before. He felt bad and realized that he was a small, miserable and laughable piece on a chessboard. Events had shifted him here and there, and here he was back in his old place, finding to his despair that every square of the chessboard had been fenced with German wire, and that nowhere in the small and bare area was there any nook to hide in. A hare in a burrow was safer than he. The chessboard on which he wriggled stubbornly, trying to escape his doom, was as glaringly lit as a boxing ring..." — "Granatowy" ("The Dark Blue Uniform") by M. Szczepańska.

Two French playwrights, Feuillet and Bocage, gave their play, produced in 1846, a chess title, "Echec et mat" ("Check and Mate"), although the game had no connection with the plot except in a metaphorical sense. The intrigues at the court of King Philip IV held their particular heroes in ... check. Other characters were "mated" and lost...

Chess provided quite an important theme in William Faulkner's story, "Gambit." The introduction of a chess term in the title symbolically emphasizes the risk of a gamble in a vital game by the heroes, and points to the analogy of situations and events to chessboard positions:

An allegoric water-colour by the Polish artist Jacek Żuławski. The earth, shown as a chessboard, with people of various races, classes and eras as chess men. Hovering in space, the face of Fate is seen behind a cloud.

Cartoon from the "cold war" period (1948), showing the organization of Western Europe's defence against the "threat from the East." The caption indicates the decisive chessmen on the European chessboard. Scandinavia is the bishop, Great Britain the queen, the Pyrenees the rook ("Leader Magazine").

A symbolical illustration from Melchior Wańkowicz's book "The Battle of Monte Cassino," at the beginning of a chapter entitled "The players set out their chessmen." The Polish detachments personified by Siren, the symbol of Warsaw, prepare to attack the German positions (Photo-montage by Z. and L. Haar).

"Then his uncle said:

'A knight comes suddenly out of nowhere — out of the west, if you like — and checks the queen and the castle all in that same one move. What do you do?'

At least he knew the answer to that by now. 'You save the queen and let the castle go.' And he answered the other one too: 'Out of western Argentina.' He said: 'It was that girl. The Harris girl. You bet him the girl. That he didn't want to cross that and open that stable door. And he lost.'

'Lost?' his uncle said. 'A princess and half a castle, against some of his bones and maybe his brains too? Lost?'

'He lost the queen,' he said.

'The queen?' his uncle said. 'What queen? Oh, you mean Mrs. Harris. Maybe he realized that queen had been moved the same instant he realized he would have to call the bet. Maybe he realized that queen and the castle both had been gone ever since the moment he disarmed the prince with that hearth-broom. If he ever wanted her.'

'Then what was he doing here?' he said.

'Why was he waiting?' his uncle said.

'Maybe it was a pleasant square,' he said. 'For the pleasure of being able to move not only two squares at once but in two directions at once.'

"They won't let us play chess..." A Polish political cartoon by J. Zaruba (1952), referring to the overthrowing of a pro-American government in Iran by the people ("Szpilki").

A Czech political cartoon by J. Pop (1958): "The White (House) opens the game but is losing"; an allusion to shady American oil deals in Arabian lands ("Dikobraz").

"Or indecision, since he can,' his uncle said. 'And almost fatal for this one, because he must. At least he'd certainly better. His threat and his charm are in his capacity for movement."

In Balzac's "La Comédie Humaine" the story "Vautrin's Final Incarnation" refers to a situation which develops between the opponents:

" 'My dear Sir, you have gained a complete victory,' said James. 'I have been defeated,' he added lightly, with the tone of a player who lost all his cash, 'but you have left a few men on a field... A costly victory...'

" 'Yes,' replied Corentin, taking up the joke, 'You have lost your queen and I am short of two rooks...'

" 'Oh! Contenson was only a pawn,' replied Collin derisively..."

Application of chess ideas and strategy helped the Polish literary critic, Henryk Vogler, to make an original comparison of the manner which contemporary heroes are presented in modern and 19th century literature. He writes about Lermontov's novel "A Hero of Our Time."

"... Such a typical hero is a young, rich and solitary man, bored with life and enjoyment, incapable of friendship, love or any other sentiments which would absorb his emotional life more intensively, treating people a little like pieces in a game of chess moved here and there so as to carry out certain combinations. Reading this book today, we see that Pechorin (Lermontov's hero) is no Botvinnik nor even a Sliwa,* that his chess combinations are only two or three moves deep and are mainly limited to little erotic intrigues. Thus it is rather a game of draughts than chess..."

And later, this reflection:

"The end of the 19th century, a century of scientific discoveries, development of industrial civilization, urbanization and mechanization, harnessed into the service of the new rich, gave new Pechorins new technical possibilities of satisfying their passions, and substantially widen-

_____
* A leading Polish master

ed for them the area of their chessboards without altering their relation to the wooden men…"

Finally, the modern period:

"… If the heroes' world, of whom Pechorin was one of the earliest, resembled a game of chess, then to the heroes of our time it rather resembles football. The hero of today probably suffers from everything but the lack of an enthusiastic and unrestrained attitude to life's phenomena. He likes quick thrills to which he surrenders with readiness and zeal. He likes jazz and sport and rapid clear decisions. He despises cool, analytical strategy, even that which only looks a couple of moves ahead. True modern football is often a considered and precise combinative game, but even the Hungarian arch-masters do not pretend to be chess players…"

Other examples of chess cant in literature:

"In Blok's plays (he was still a symbolist at the time), people — that is, main characters — are chessmen, their parts drawn in broad outlines, blurred, flickering, resembling living creatures." (Victor Shklovski, 1913).

"…A certain literary critic, an acquaintance of mine, told me a few years ago that Hamlet is not a neurotic, but a man who plays his part like a game of chess."

"… David Stacton's embittered splendid historical novels remind of a game of chess by some deceased masters of yore, reconstructed from faded notes. The author shifts both black and white pawns, anticipating the final result…" (Ameryka, No. 51).

Chess, with its infinite variety, offers itself for use in comparisons on a higher plane. It has lent itself to philosophical discussion; chess metaphors can be found even in sermons. In the Middle Ages it reflected social and state conditions, the rules governing the pieces on the chessboard mirroring morality, ethics and law.

In one morality, "Miracles de la Sainte Vierge" ("Miracles of the Virgin Mary"), by Gautier de Coincy, published in France from a 13th century manuscript, there is an allegory in a game of chess between Satan and God. Satan chases Man to the corner of the board, trying to mate him (for committing original sin). Then God creates the piece, the Fers (i.e. the Virgin Mary or the Queen) and defeats Satan. In the French original there is a play upon two words: *fierce,* from the Persian-Arabian name of the piece, and *vierge,* maid or virgin.

In an old German song, the King addresses Death:

Another Czech satirical cartoon by B. Cepleha referring to the American-Arabian political conflict of 1958: "Try to understand, Mr. Dulles, he who has lost his king loses his rook as well" ("Dikobraz").

"A Game with Death." Allegorical fresco from a church in Taeby, Sweden, the work of Albertus Pictor (15th century).

Will hands of Death to all kings show their goal?
Thus rule resembles chess and Royal Game.
My sceptre stretches from the South to North,
Now Death has smitten and has mated me.

The distinguished Polish preacher and writer of the 16th century, Piotr Skarga, praised the study of history:

"... You see how superb are the Kings, Lords and Soldiers on the chessboard; yet when the game ends they are only thrown into the box as if into a tomb. Read ancient history...!"

In Cervantes' work, "Don Quixote" the hero deliberates on acting and the theatre, remarking to Sancho:

"... 'when the comedy is ended and the actors take off their costumes, all the players become equal.'

" 'The same, then,' said Don Quixote, 'happens in the life of this world, where some play the parts of Caesars, others of Popes, and really all those parts which can appear in a comedy: but when we finally reach the end, that is when life ends, death will deprive everybody of those garments which made them differ, and they will become equal.'

" 'A prime comparison,' said Pancho, 'although not so new, since I've heard it more than once or twice. It is just as in chess: each pawn has its particular task for the duration of the game, and when it ends, everything is mixed up, made equal, loses value and is commonly put in a bag, almost like a corpse in a grave.' "

Similarly, chess was used to illustrate how social injustice only disappeared at death, by a German author, Gottlieb Konrad Pfeffel (18th century). Comparing chess with life, he concluded:

The Lord's game begins: to all the pieces
He gives out the parts, directing their course,
Dispersing next and mixing, great and small
In one dark sack. Likewise looks our world.

In a philosophical setting by Schopenhauer, the chess metaphor took this form:

"Life is like chess: we prepare some plan, but this plan is determined by whatever the opponent in a game, or fate in life wish to achieve."

In a water-colour by a Polish painter, Jacek Żuławski, a chessboard replaces the earth in the solar system Human figures in costumes of various periods, arranged as chess pieces, sym-

160

bolize the comparison between life and chess. An enormous face from behind a cloud on the far horizon looms up — of a Player? Fate? or Death? The artist does not answer the question.

Albertus Pictor used a chess game to represent death and fate in a 15th century fresco that he painted in a church in Taeby, Sweden. From this theme, the eminent Swedish director, Ingmar Bergman, produced the film "The Seventh Seal."

Chess has provided excellent analogies of the struggle between good and evil. Evidence of this is to be found in literature as far back as ancient Indian, Persian and Arabic times; in Old Spanish and Old French.

The Persian poet Omar Khayyám, in his "Rubáiyát," offered an especially suggestive picture of human fate as seen in a game of chess (English translation by Edward Fitzgerald, Stanza 49):

Tis all a Chequer-board of Nights and Days
Where Destiny with Men for Pieces plays:

Hither and thither moves, mates and slays
And one by one back in the Closet lays.

This inspired Walter E. Spradbery to paint a picture showing the struggle of Day and Night. The two sides were shown as Louis XIV, representing the peak of absolutism, and Napoleon Bonaparte, representing the French Revolution.

In a short film produced in the U.S.S.R. in 1959, "It Will Soon Rain," based on a popular Vietnamese fable, a Ruler of the World plays chess against the witch Drought. He loses rivers, lakes and streams but Drought had forgotten the clouds which finally bring the saving rain.

In the French-Swedish picture "Les Creatures" (1966) by Agnès Varda, a game of chess provides a rather original dramatic and philosophical motif. The main character, Edgar, who is a writer, carries out an observation of the inhabitants of a small island near the coast of Brittany in order to collect material to work out the fates of dramatis personae in his novel. He becomes engaged in an extraordinary game played with the

The knight playing chess with Death. A chess motif with an important dramatic function in the Swedish film "The Seventh Seal," directed by Ingmar Bergman; the motif taken from a mediaeval church fresco.

"The embarrassed Spaniard." France and Spain competing for influence in Europe. A 17th century French political cartoon.

An allegorical drawing — the chessmen personify the court of Louis XIV and the Revolution. The central column is shaped like a chess king. By W. E. Spradbery ("Chess Pie").

keeper of a lighthouse, inventor of a peculiar playing machine combining elements of chess, cards and dice, and provided with a radar-and-television screen projecting images from real life which resemble the situations on the chessboard.

Animated tiny figures of people appear in place of chessmen. Cards decide which is to be moved on the board, and dice — by how many squares. In the display appear appropriate episodes from the lives of the small creatures, depending on which of the players influences the course of events. A further complication is that the creatures endeavour to escape the influence of the players and make their own "moves." At this game of living chess, the man from the lighthouse represents an "evil fate." The game is played on his terms. To win the game, the writer has to save from destruction on the chessboard (and at the same time in actual life) at least a single couple — a man and a woman. The stake is the writer's wife. The finale: the writer, who has had enough of playing with human life... destroys the machine.

Attempts to philosophise from chess have often been based on phoney pseudo science but there have sometimes been quite interesting observations. For example, the following excerpt from Emanuel Lasker's article, "Philosophy of the Royal Game":

"... Struggles of all kind differ from each other only outwardly. The rules governing them are often identical. In this sense war is a competition, a pursuit of truth, beauty or happiness; all of these kinds of struggle resemble each other and chess. They are equally based on principles of simplicity, economy and harmony. The same principles are employed by a conscientious researcher in chemistry, physics, biology or art... The game of chess is a puppet-show but one in which the puppets perform with force and with vital truth. Chess teaches us how our life should shape, with equal chances and without accident. To that degree it is a mirror of life. Chess is the scene of a miniature drama of temptation, guilt, struggle, effort and the victory of justice..."

"When is this game going to end?" Louis Philippe against the Republic. A French cartoon by Desprez ("La Caricature").

"In check! Check-Mate!" The Republic checkmates King Louis Philippe. A French political cartoon from the time of the February revolution ("La Caricature").

Piłsudski and his government; a Polish political cartoon of 1931 by J. Zaruba ("Cyrulik Warszawski").

The reactionary government checkmated. S. Kobyliński's illustration to a pre-war revolutionary poem ("Świat").

The militarist goes on with the game although the king (the Kaiser) was checkmated in 1918. German satirical cartoon of 1924 ("Lachen Links").

Soviet cartoon of 1959 referring to the agricultural competition between the Soviet Union and the United States ("Krokodil").

An exhibition of amateur paintings by Polish miners, presented in Cracow in 1946, contained a picture called "A Game of Chess," by a noted self-taught, primitivist painter, Teofil Ociepka. His fantastic works combine reality with the products of a fine imagination. The game of chess represents man's struggle against Evil. A woman dressed in white symbolizes Goodness. A point made by one of the reviewers is probably right, namely that "...this picture can also be treated (as generically) without any symbolism."

Chess is particularly suitable material for use in satire, especially political.

Piotr Royziusz, a lecturer in law at Cracow in the middle of the 16th century, depicted in a Latin epigram a chess kingdom in which the king stood majestically motionless whilst the queen hopped about in all directions, prying into

165

"In check! Check-Mate! Hitler done for..." Scene from the Polish film "Others Will Follow You" (1949).

every corner of state affairs, an outspoken satire on the last years of the reign of Zygmunt I and the government of his queen Bona Sforza.

A Polish Jesuit, Franciszek Gościecki, visited Turkey with a legation in 1712–14. He described in humorous verse the continual intrigues and jockeying for government positions at the Court of Sultan Ahmet IV:

> *Now if you saw chess being played,*
> *Thus Turkish notables hold sway:*
> *Knight checks king, bishop strikes knight,*
> *Prison like rook has queen in sight,*
> *Pawn defeats bishop...*

One political cartoon from the early 17th century captioned "The Perplexed Spaniard," depicted France and Spain at the height of their struggle for political influence in Europe as opponents at chess.

A satirical drawing by Desprez, in a period when revolutionary feeling was growing during the reign of King Louis Philippe, was captioned "When Will This Game End?" The king, playing chess with a woman in a Phrygian cap (Republican France), has a very poor position and is unable to withstand the pressure directed from his opponent who is sitting safely on a barricade.

A later cartoon, captioned "Check and Mate!" showed Louis Philippe as a chess king mated by a white queen — the Republic. The white king symbolizes freedom; the white rooks, towers representing democratic associations; the bishops, jesters personifying the satirical journals, "Le Charivari" and "La Caricature"; the knights, centaurs with copies of the political papers, "La Tribune" and "Le National"; the pawns, the armed populace. The black pieces have suffered serious casualties; of those that remain, the rooks represent prisons, with judges in robes looking out; the knights — ministers on children's hobbyhorses; the bishop — a snooper with a jester's cap, the pawn — a guardsman.

In 1924, a German progressive satirical journal, "Lachen Links," published a cartoon showing death playing chess against a militarist. The chessboard contained armies and cannons; the fallen pieces were stacked in coffins on the floor. "Though the king was checkmated in 1914–18, he still plays on... What is going to happen?" asks the caption. The answer was not supplied until 1945.

A fine cartoon by Jerzy Zaruba, a Polish cartoonist, appeared in 1931 in the humorous weekly, "Cyrulik Warszawski," captioned "Szachy na Lachy" (Chess-fright). The chess pieces represented the Sanacja coup-government of the time, moved by the dictatorial hand of Piłsudski.

An anthology of Polish revolutionary satire of the inter-war period includes a quatrain directed against the ruling class:

A Game of Chess. Picture by the Polish painter Teofil Ociepka, a primitivist (1946).

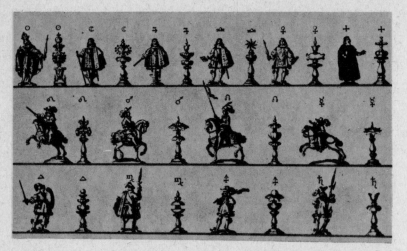

In Wickhmann's treatise on chess (1664), human figures were drawn alongside chessmen to illustrate their functions.

"Napoleonic" chessmen shown at the world exhibition in Paris in 1900.

Personified figures of the king, queen and bishops from a set of chessmen belonging to the Polish Hetman A. Sieniawski (18th century).

The chessmen of this Austrian set (1848) are carved in wood and personify historical characters. From the Hammond collection.

Not only those who know play chess,
Willy-nilly, you'll play it yet,
It's worst for those who never guess,
Quite often they will just hear: 'Mate!'

The films have also furnished examples.

In a Polish film, "Others Will Follow," 1949, directed by Antoni Bohdziewicz, there is an assault by partisans on a guard-house of the German military police, in which they surprise two Nazis playing chess. After successfully completing their operation, before they left the guard-house one of the partisans moved a piece and said, "Check, mate — Hitler kaputt..."

In the Soviet film, "October" (1927), directed by Sergei Eisenstein, the lonely Kerensky, bent over an empty chessboard, picks up the broken bits of a chess piece, puts them together and places a crown on top — a beautifully simple piece of political imagery.

Lenin jokingly compared Kerensky, the Prime Minister of the Russian Temporary Government of 1917, to a pawn moved about by the imperial-

Kings in Chinese sets made for export to Britain were often carved in the likeness of British kings. Here are four which portray George I, II, III and IV. From the Hammond collection.

ists. The Soviet satirical journal "Krokodil" in 1960 based a cartoon by its noted team of cartoonists, The "Kukriniksy," on this remark.

The Czechoslovak artist Kopriva in a Prague literary journal showed white doves (peace) checking and mating a black king (who looked like an atomic bomb) trapped in a corner of the chessboard. This climaxed a long picture-story and the final caption read:

Atomic diplomat stuck in a groove;
White checkmates him on the third move.

The idea of treating the chessboard as a battleground became, from the earliest times, an incentive for craftsmen, sculptors and engravers to fashion the pieces after human and animal models.

The world's museums contain thousands of chess pieces shaped as soldiers of various periods, nationalities and formations, and personified symbols, warring men and the animals taking part in the combat.

It is interesting to try to fathom why chess is so interminably linked with war. To quote only one example, an excerpt from an article by Ludo-mir Stępowski, published in 1913 in the Polish periodical "Szachista Polski."

"A game of chess resembles war in various respects: (1) the terrain; (2) the material forces; (3) the moral forces; (4) the time factor. In a game of chess, just as in war, not only the leader's talent and knowledge but also his character may influence the outcome. A player who is careful, persevering, who reflects coolly on the fluctuating chances of the game, and who calculates dispassionately the consequences of each move of the army, will always have a bigger prospect of success than a player who is impatient, nervous and temperamental... the cooler player will be able to concentrate the better." Few people go to the extent of drawing important conclusions from these analogies, diverting as they are.

Humour has its place in this field but a certain German writer of the inter-war period who specialized in military problems, was unfortunately lacking in it. He publicly protested against comparisons between war and chess, arguing that they disparaged the army! One French chess periodical published articles by a senior army officer, refuting meticulously any ideas of similarity between chess and war.

Chess, instead of being an image, has often been the cause of conflict, in consequence of the contestants' characters. A player, upset by failure at chess, would use the chessboard or a piece (and these were sometimes very large) to bash his opponent on the head. A breach of the rules which often led to a resumption of the battle elsewhere with other weapons.

This seemed particularly the fashion towards the end of the eleventh century.

Robert and Henry, sons of William the Conqueror, King of England and Duke of Normandy, during a ceremonial visit to Philip I, King of France, sat down to a game of chess with Louis, their host's son. A quarrel developed. Louis offended Henry who struck the French prince on his head with the chessboard and would have probably killed him had his brother not intervened. The quarrel led to war. A squabble over chess became the pretext for an armed invasion!

William and his sons invaded France, conquered Normandy and almost reached Paris.

Quite a similar event, although this time it can be safely supposed not a historic one, was described by a Polish writer, Wojciech Żukrowski, in a charming book for children and adults, "Porwanie w Tiutiurlistanie" ("An Abduction in Tuturlistan"). In a chapter entitled "Fatalna gra" (A Fatal Game) there is a story of a game of chess played by two kings, Cinnamon and Barrel. The dramatic game, in the course of which the almond Pawns were vanishing mysteriously from the chessboard, caused an outbreak of war between the peoples of Tuturlistan and Blabant. To be exact, one should point out that the notorious game rather resembled draughts but the fabulous kings played it with gusto, shifting the Pawns and using a fine call of "Chess, mess!" The text is supplemented with pleasant drawings by Adam Marczyński, very chess-like in its theme and details.

Still in the world of fiction... Uncle Benjamin, the hero of a novel of that name by Claude Tillier,

Battle on a chessboard depicted in grotesque style by an anonymous Italian artist.

was challenged to a duel by a notorious brawler, Monsieur de Pont-Cassé who asks:

" 'You have not forgotten, sir, why you came?'

" 'I have not forgotten and here is the proof,' replies Uncle Benjamin, pointing to a box on the table, 'I have made all arrangements to receive you.'

" 'And what do we need these toys for, since we are to fight with swords?'

" 'I do not intend to fight with swords,' Uncle replied.

" 'Sir!' said Monsieur de Pont-Cassé, 'I was insulted. I am the one to choose the weapons, and I choose swords.'

" 'Oh no! I was offended first and I'm not giving way; I have chosen chess!'

"He opened the box and, having set out the chessmen, gestured his opponent to take his place behind the table.

"Monsieur de Pont-Cassé became livid with anger.

" 'What's this? Are you sneering at me?'

A Czech set carved in wood depicts the battle fought in 1442 between the Hussites led by Jan Žižka (White) and the army of the Emperor Sigismund of Luxemburg (Black).

172

Personalities from old German peasant wars in chess guise. The piece on the extreme right personifies Thomas Münzer, the leader of a peasant revolt.

" 'Nothing of the sort,' replied Uncle, 'Every duel is a game in which two men fight for the stake of their lives: this can be achieved with pawns as well as with a sword. If you're not strong in chess, I am prepared to play you at écarté or faro'..."

The situation was solved in a very unusual way. The enraged Monsieur de Pont-Cassé tried to come to blows. Forced to defend himself, Uncle fetched his sword; unexpectedly proved a good swordsman and thrice knocked the sword out of the brawler's hand, taunting him that he could hardly have fared worse at chess.

From fiction to legend.

Going back a thousand years, we find a chess duel between Charlemagne and Sir Garin de Montglane, recorded in a lay of mediaeval minstrels.

Garin came to Charlemagne's court and was quickly promoted to an important position. Everything would have been well, had not Queen Galienne fallen violently in love with him. One day she asked him to her chamber under some pretext and... it is uncertain how matters would have progressed if the worthy knight had not fled, to her great annoyance of course. Her cries brought the king and when he asked for an explanation she, rather surprisingly, confessed that Garin had dared to spurn her love. The king agreed that this was a great insult and decided to punish the insolent man. Garin was summoned and, guessing what was happening, arrived with a sizeable body-guard. Asked why he had visited the queen's chambers, he replied that he had played chess with her. Charlemagne suggested playing a game with him also, stipulating tremendous stakes: If Garin won he would gain the crown and the queen! If he lost, he would lose his head. There was no arguing with the king, whose forces were superior anyway. Having sworn a solemn oath to abide by the conditions, the two sat down at the chessboard, a fine gift

A hussar   *Sultan Mohammed IV*   *A knight*

A standard bearer   *Camel*   *Peasant*

These Polish historical chessmen made by the sculptress Helena Skirmunt in the second half of the last century depict the victory of Jan III Sobieski over the Turks at Vienna in 1683. On the "Polish" side are King Jan III, Hetman Jablonowski, a bishop and standard bearer, a hussar and a knight, a lion and a bear (the rooks). The Turkish pieces represent Sultan Mohammed IV, the Vizier Kara-Mustapha, Janissaries, camels etc. The chessmen, cast in silver, were exhibited in Vienna on the occasion of the 200th anniversary of the relief of the city; these photos were taken at that time.

174

from Harun-al-Rashid. The tense atmosphere caused little misunderstandings to develop into brawls. Repeatedly the barons and courtiers had to intervene to persuade them to confine the fight to the chessboard. A new quarrel flared up into a general mêlée and bloodshed. Eventually the game was resumed. Garin gained an advantage and finally mated the king. However, he proved a sportsman. The victory won at chess satisfying him, he generously waived the stakes (in any case he probably realized it would be difficult to enforce them!) and became the king's life-long friend. Legend does not reveal whether there was any reconciliation with the queen.

Sadko, a legendary hero of the old Russian epic poems, the "byliny," engaged in a different wager over chess during a visit to the court of a maharajah in the course of a journey round the world. The maharajah coveted Sadko's bewitched horse, whereas Sadko wanted the phoenix bird in exchange. The maharajah suggested a game of chess to decide which should gain his wish. Vainly the maharajah tried to distract Sadko's attention with dancing girls and enchanting music. Sadko played calmly and on the advice of Trifon, a wise old companion, laid a trap by allowing his knight to be captured. The maharajah fell into the trap and lost the game, and Sadko gained the

A set of symbolical chessmen from Russia in the 1920's. Red (revolution) versus White (Bourgeoisie). The kings are a worker and a capitalist.

enchanted bird with a woman's head. This scene was screened in full by the U.S.S.R. director A. Ptushko in a film called "Sadko" which brought in a beautiful damsel as an additional stake.

A woman was not only the cause of conflict, even on a chessboard, in the climax of a short-story "Chess" by L.H. Lowe. It is poor literature and thoroughly unrealistic in its treatment of Arabian themes but certainly strikes an unusual note.

An orientalist, Mr. K., meets an Arab pasha on a voyage from Genoa to Alexandria. The men become rivals for the favours of a beautiful Englishwoman, Evelyn, travelling on the same ship. She first flirts with the pasha but eventually falls for Mr. K. After arriving in Alexandria, the young couple, not yet officially engaged, stayed at different hotels so as not to attract attention. Mr. K. is leaving his hotel to meet Evelyn for lunch when he unexpectedly encounters the pasha who seems pleased to see him and invites him to his house. Mr. K. accepts, having time to spare. Here the tale is taken up by the hero:

"In the room to which I was led, I was sur-prised to see the floor laid out as a chessboard. The squares were unusually large and the quaint, carved pieces were more or less of the height of a child. The pasha asked me to wait a little while he changed. ... I rose to look closely at the unusual chessboard. Then I noticed that all the pieces were there except the white queen. — When he returned I asked him about this and he said, 'The white queen will be here soon.'

"He clapped three times. A curtain in front of me was drawn aside and (my heart missed a beat in awe) a Negro led a chained naked woman into the room — it was Evelyn. With a cry, I started towards her but a row of Arabs with pointed daggers barred my steps.

" 'Didn't you want to see the white queen?' asked the Pasha. He spoke calmly as if he were talking about the weather. 'Here she is, and now we can start the game. If you win, Sir, she is yours, if I win, then...'

"... I realized that only I could save her. Swaying like a drunken man, I went to the chess-board by which stood low Arabian tabourets.

" 'Please, play White,' said the Pasha and sat

Carved ivory chessmen made by a Chinese artisan for export to Europe.

Bandits and hill-men. Chessmen carved by folk artists from Zakopane in the Tatra Mountains.

*Ancient German warriors at chess.
Porcelain statuettes by C. A. Luplau,
1772. There is artistic licence here,
as chess was not known among the
German tribes.*

opposite me. The game started and I soon realized that the Pasha was a better player than myself, and that he had prepared this subtle revenge in cold blood. I tried in vain to protect Evelyn. I moved her naked and shivering body here and there. — I don't know how long we played...

" 'Now you've lost!' cried the Pasha. Then he made some move. 'I've won,' he said quietly and politely and I saw that the queen was lost..."

And so Evelyn became the Pasha's prisoner. The unfortunate fiancé tried to rescue her but was struck unconscious... a few hours later he woke up in his hotel room. A search by the police produced nothing.

Moral: never neglect your chess, you never know when it may be useful!

More imaginative still is the similar situation which arose in a story by the Polish author, Anna Zahorska, "Check to the queen" (1932).

Ramski is sitting at a desk shaded by a green lampshade. The electric light streams down on typewritten sheets bearing the initials of clerks and managers as well as the stamp of the records department. His task is to abstract a pile of documents. — His work is going badly... At the foot of the page he has doodled a rook. A subconscious urge to play chess, like the lure of alcohol, is distracting him.

177

Contradictory versions of one report are set out like a chess game. The white and black squares are a scene of strife. The Board adjudicates: white should win. The provincial branches favour black. He is swept by a scorching wind of conflict.

The report is ready. He goes out into the street. It is a quiet summer evening. The stars are set out like pawns and bishops. Silver figures on a sapphire-black chessboard. A stifling desire blows like a desert wind, drying up the freshness of the night.

He reaches for a handkerchief in his pocket. His hand feels a packet. Medicine for Emma, bought on his way to the office. Emma is waiting. The maid has already left. ...

A few steps and he will be in a world of oblivion. A world of battling chessmen.

A café grins at him with two wide windows in which are chessboards of chocolate cake, with green icing or red jelly. Tall dough cakes tempt him with their resemblance to rooks.

Will he go on? Something draws him compellingly inside. It's hot. Damn it! "Everytime I reach for my handkerchief to wipe my brow there's always this medicine!"

Emma... She has no right to be ill. She has no right to intrude. In the queen's gambit the queen does not occupy the whole of the chessboard. Not she, she is lying on their couch, having laid an old rug on it; by a wall near the stairs. She is listening for steps. Maybe his? ...

In check! Checkmate! An amusing illustration by A. Marczyński to W. Żukrowski's book "Abduction in Tuturlistan."

Sadko, a hero of old Russian folk legends, beats the Maharajah at chess. Scene from the Soviet film "Sadko" (1953).

He sets up the pieces on the chessboard absent-mindedly. "We drew yesterday," his opponent remarks.

Ramski nibbles his moustache. "Why the deuce does he use so much scent? Lily of the valley... He has been with a woman. There are lilies of the valley in a small topaz flower pot on a wickerwork table by Emma's side... This man's sharp features repel me." He holds out the pawns in a clenched, hairy fist. "I've got White." If only he could think of a good opening to mate in two or three moves!

Then... KN-KB3. Billiard balls are clicking in the next room. "He will move P-QN3." Let it be, then. Queen's Indian Defence. The wind is howling outside... The waiter brings coffee...

Yesterday, he cleared everybody out so quickly that they had to agree a draw.

"Why is he pushing his queen at me?"... Well, he must remember the rule of the Indian Defence: "The struggle is not being waged for a mere initiative but for out–and–out defeat."

"Now I can attack. I have the advantage on the king's side. He is on the defensive."

Ramski promotes a pawn to a second queen. White gains control of the KR-QR8 diagonal. There is a black-haired queen with Emma's face.

"Check!"

"It's a long way to mate, though." His opponent smiles bleakly. Eliminate the queens! Then it will be easier. The idea is to destroy your opponent...

179

And it all began so innocently. Miniature from a French 15th century manuscript, describing the adventures of Renaud de Montauban.

to chase from the board this queen on whose round head keeps appearing Emma's face.

"Watch your queen!"

Black is doomed. But the black rook captures the queen. "No danger, my pawn on KB7 becomes another queen. I can attack yet."

He has captured and cast the helpless queen to one side. She must be silent. Now she can never interfere.

Black resigns. He departs with a perfunctory "good evening."

Ramski feels victorious. The fallen queen will never rise.

He reaches a gate, black, with bent metal flowers...

He unlocks the door carefully. Let her sleep. Her soft, sad voice need not call him.

His foot stumbles on something lying in the

180

Lancelot and the queen at chess. Illustration to Wacław Berent's novel "Żywe Kamienie"
("Living stones") by Maja Berezowska.

corridor... He turns the switch, his hand trembling and missing the familiar spot on the wall. Emma is here on the floor!... Her hands thrown wide. Fright in her eyes. She has had a heart-attack. He reaches for the little box with medicine. ... Yes, yes... This was to have helped...

He lifts the cold hand and lets it go. It thuds dully on the floor and lies stretched out on a darker square of the floor. As if on a chessboard. K-Q4. Ramski whispers to himself:

"Guard your queen!"

In a French film directed by Louis Daquin, "La patrie," after a play by Victor Sardou, there is a subtly-drawn picture of the eternal triangle which a game of chess resolves. The film is set in 16th century Flanders during the despotic rule of a governor on behalf of the King of Spain. Count Rysoor, a leader of the Resistance, played by Pierre Blanchard, neglects his young wife (Marie Mauban) who commits adultery with his friend and fellow-conspirator (Jean Desailly). The husband learns of this and by ambiguous remarks in the course of a game of chess makes it clear to his unfaithful wife and her lover that their affair has been discovered. Your nerves would indeed have to be strong to play well in such circumstances. When a player is in love, his standard of play (at chess of course) can woefully decline.

In a Czech picture entitled "Eroticon" (1929) directed by Gustav Machaty, is a scene with a husband and his wife's lover playing a game of chess. The wife who wants her lover to win the game, while unobserved by the husband, secretly advises the lover what moves to make nodding in consent or gesturing in disapproval.

The lover checks his opponent's king who never suspected the plot, but in a counter-attack — he was check-mated himself to the annoyance of the kibitzing woman.

In Pushkin's magnificent poem "Eugene Onegin" there is a fine scene in which the sweethearts, Lensky and Olga, linger in the park full of emotion:

Zbigniew Lengren: Professor Filutek plays chess.

At whiles, upon their elbows leaning,
In grave seclusion as is fit,
Above the chessboard they will sit,
And ponder each move's secret meaning,
Till Lensky, too absorbed to look,
With his own pawn takes his own rook.

Pushkin once wrote to his wife saying how glad he was that she was learning chess, saying no well-conducted family should be ignorant of this game.

Of Sharr Khan, son of the Grand Sultan Omar-Ibn-An-Numan, a story is recounted in the "Arabian Nights."

He is sent by his father on an expedition into a foreign country. One day he falls asleep on his horse. When he awakes he is alone on the bank of a woodland river, in which a beautiful girl is bathing, wrestling playfully with slave-girls. No-

ticing Sharr Khan, she challenges him to a match, and with extraordinary skill, defeats him three times, revealing meanwhile that she knew he was the leader of the invaders. However, despite this she is prepared to hide him in the palace. At supper, she makes him drunk and arouses his passion. The slave-girls bring musical instruments and begin to sing. The young lovers recite love poetry to each other. Two days pass in this way. On the third day the girl asks him, "Are you, oh, son of the Sultan Omar-Ibn-An-Numan, versed in the game of chess?" And Sharr Khan replies, "Yes, but you should not be like the one of whom the Poet has said:

My desire now rises and now ebbs,
Love's sweet foretaste quenching my thirst;
To my beloved I've brought a set of chess,

Was given a mirthless game by foes, now white,
*   now black.*
I felt that the king who just displaced the rook
*   Does meditate upon a battle against the Hetmans[1].*
If ever I surmise the message in her eyes

---

[1] Hetman (commander-in-chief) is in Polish the chess queen.

The power of her sight, my friends, will work my
*   ruin.*

They start playing but, whenever it is his turn to move, he keeps gazing at her and moving the wrong pieces. The girl laughs at him, "You must play better than this!" Sharr Khan replies, "This is only the first game and it does not count!" Eventually he loses and sets the men out again to resume the contest. He loses again and again.

Cornelis de Man (17th century):
Man and woman playing chess.
From the Budapest Art Gallery.

A. Johannet: A Game of Chess. French lithograph, early 19th century.

Finally she says to him, "You have been completely conquered!" "My lady," he replies, "whoever plays against you, how can he escape from being conquered?"...

In an old 13th century French poem by Huon de Bordeaux, the author depicts himself as the hero of a double game and describes love and chess in beautiful language.

The poet, dressed as a minstrel, goes to the court of Admiral Yvarius and recounts his many virtues, which include skill at chess. The Admiral, to test whether the young man is boasting, asks him to play his daughter. The stake: her hand, or his head. The game starts. Huon gazes more into the girl's eyes than at the board and plays very badly. She warns him that he will lose but he replies: "The game is not over yet, and one thing is certain, that you will be in my arms!"

These words visibly affect her and, her concentration ruined, he wins easily. The Admiral offers to give him money instead of the girl but she turns down the suggestion saying she has been well mated!

Another amorous game of chess which involves Lancelot, mentioned in various French and German tales of the days of chivalry, was described by the Polish author Berent in his novel "Living stones."

Lancelot arrived at the court of King Arthur and went into the queen's chambers... "Soon he was sitting beside her whilst a page hurried to the other end of the room, brought out a chess set and placed it on the carpet between Guinevere and her guest. Lancelot was bidden by the queen to kneel and set up the pieces so that the situation might look less suspicious to her ladies-in-waiting. She slowly unfastened her veil so as to free her lips for kissing. Then, as soon as her ladies looked elsewhere, she clasped his head, drew him over the chessboard and clung to his lips in a long, breathless kiss... he jerked himself forward to embrace her and scattered the chessmen. Soft-footed pages ran up to them and started to pick up the pieces like birds pecking at millet seed.

D. Chodowiecki: Education. An engraving from the 1790's.

In their corner of the room, the ladies-in-waiting tut-tutted severely..."

The Italian playwright Guiseppe Giacosa wrote a one-act play "Una partita a scacchi"— do we need to translate the title? — based on Huon's ballad. The play was immensely successful in Italy in the second half of the 19th century and was translated into many languages and staged in many lands. The story was set, for a change, in a 14th century ducal castle in the Aosta valley. The Duke had taught his daughter Paula to become an accomplished chess player. Her opponent, with the same stakes as in the old story, was the page Fernando. He too kept gazing at her and was similarly in danger of losing both the

185

game and his head. Luckily, the game slackened in pace and quickened in romance. The Duke tried to supervise the game so as to ensure that it was played strictly according to rule, but to no avail. Paula forgot all he had taught her, allowed her thoughts to stray and lost — which did not trouble her in the least. The page demanded that the stake be paid and the Duke, after some hesitation, acquiesced to the marriage.

Judging by the outcome, he must have been a better father than teacher, in fact equally a failure as a coach and an umpire.

Chess as a theme for a love game is far from uncommon in the literature of Poland. Lenartowicz in a long poem "Mate by the Queen" described a journey by young Jan Sobieski, the future king of Poland, about the middle of the 17th century, to the Court of France, to learn worldly ways and courtly manners. His chivalry made a great impression on his hosts. He himself was attracted by the carefree life at the court, the amusements, women and entertainment. It then happened that...

... in a queen's ladies' gilded room,
Where a chess table has been set,
And crystal fountains were humming,
A Polish knight sat by a maid.
A breeze, as if blowing on leaves,
Rustled through lace-work of her gown,
At which Jan gazed and listened,
While the young lady checked his king.
He gazed, so spell-bound, at the charms

Of little Mary delightful
Who, musing over the chessboard,
Propped with one hand her lovely face
And addressed her worthy partner:
'Here is my checkmate, Sir, with queen!
A knight should rather better watch;
Easier than knights, the kings are found.'
To this politely Jan replied:
'Against a queen it's a hard task,
She strikes from near and far alike,
And in her stroke she never fails;
Although the distance is so great,
She's sure to strike the target true.
A king, much as a knight, will fall,
Before this lady's skillful blow.'
'And every day, then,' she would ask,
'Will life allow us the same rights?'
And on the knight's hand placed her own.
He felt a clasping fair hand,
And was forever lost in gaze
Of his delightful conqueror.

This game led to marriage, and the girl who mated with a queen become a queen herself when Sobieski ascended the Polish throne as Jan III. A highly romantic contribution to our collection of links between Mars, Cupid and chess.

We may fittingly conclude with a quotation from a play by Aleksander Fredro, the great Polish comedy-playwright:

The art of love is like a game of chess;
All in it strive for secrets of success.

Jan Sobieski, the future king of Poland, as a guest to the royal court in Paris, becomes acquainted with Mademoiselle Maria Casimira d'Arquien, whom he married a year or two later. A Polish illustration (1871) to T. Lenartowicz's poem "Queen in Check."

VIII. LIVING CHESS

Scene from a living chess game in the Helsinki sport stadium in 1955. In the foreground is a white pawn; in the background a white knight.

Chess as a struggle between opposing individuals or armies inevitably invites personification.

The idea came very early of enlarging the board to the size of a court-yard and replacing wooden pieces by living actors — and we had "living chess." The scope for the spectacular is obvious. Staged games of chess, offered to an audience in a decorative setting, are as attractive today as centuries ago.

The oldest written account of living chess dates back five hundred years. An Italian Dominican Friar, Francesco Colonna, wrote a mystic sort of book in 1467 which purported to tell how a certain Poliphilus dreamt that he watched a game of chess played with living pieces on a monster board. This work, published in Latin in Venice in 1499 under the title of "Hypnerotomachia Poliphili," later appeared in French and in English as "The Strife of Love in a Dream" in 1592.

Poliphilus's dream provided a pattern for living chess displays which the ducal and royal courts of France and Italy followed for centuries. The game was staged as a masquerade or as a tournament; it was often made a great social occasion. Everything followed a set routine. The actors' hats and costumes, and their behaviour, followed a standard pattern.

These spectacles impressed the people of those days. Rabelais devoted two chapters to them in the fifth volume of his "Gargantua and Pantagruel." Or did he? It has been denied that the colourful description of live chess at Dame Quintessence's Court is his work at all. It was not to be found in his own manuscript and the first time the fifth volume describing the game appeared was in 1562, nine years after his death. Nobody knows what chess enthusiast inserted these two chapters. Anyway, here is the story:

At the palace of Dame Quintessence, who highly esteemed chess as an occupation demanding "a purely abstract effort of intellectual ability," the game was staged in the presence of Pantagruel.

"When supper was over, a ball in the form of a tournament — which was not only worth seeing but eternally memorable — was held in the lady's presence. Before this could begin, the floor of the hall was covered with a large piece of pile tapestry, designed in the form of a chessboard — that is to say in squares, alternately white and yellow, each one foot across and all perfectly regular. Then thirty-two yellow personages entered the room, sixteen of whom were dressed in cloth of gold. These were young nymphs such as the ancients painted in the company of Diana, one Queen, two Wardens of the Castles, two Knights, and two Archers. In similar order came sixteen more, dressed in cloth of silver.

"Each party had musicians, dressed in similar livery, one band in orange damask and the other in white. There were eight on each side with various fantastic instruments, all different yet perfectly tuned to one another and marvellously tuneful. These changed the tone, mood, and time of their music as the progress of the ball required; and this surprised me, when I considered the number and variety of the steps, back-steps, hops, leaps, returns, flights, ambuscades, retreats, and surprises. It was even more transcendently incredible, as it seemed to me, that the dancers should so quickly retreat. For no sooner had the music given the note than they alighted on the intended square, even though their moves were all different.

"When the two companies had thus assumed their places, the musicians began to sound in unison a martial strain, as alarming as the signal for a charge. We saw the two parties quiver and brace themselves to fight manfully when the hour for combat came and when they were summoned from their camp. Suddenly the musicians of the Silver band ceased and only the instruments of the Golden band played on. By this we understood that the Golden party was going to attack; which soon happened. For, as the music changed, the nymph placed in front of the Queen made a complete turn towards the King on her left,

Live chess at the French court; a copper engraving, 1640.

as if begging his leave to enter the battle and at the same time saluting the rest of the company. Then, in all modesty, she advanced two squares forward and made a half-curtsey to the opposite party, whom she was attacking.

"Then the Golden musicians ceased, and the Silver ones struck up. I must not fail to mention at this point that after the nymph had saluted her King and her party in order that they should not remain inactive, they returned her salute by making a complete turn to the left, except the Queen who turned to the right, towards her King. This salutation was performed by all movers, and was the convention observed throughout the whole conduct of the ball, by both sides alike.

"To the music of the Silver musicians the Silver nymph who stood in front of her Queen stepped forward and graciously saluted her King and all his company: a salute which they returned as the Golden party had done, except that they turned to the right and their Queen to the left. Then she alighted on the second square forward and, after curtseying to the enemy, stood in front of the Golden nymph with no distance between them, as if intending to fight, although these nymphs can only strike sideways. Their companions, both Golden and Silver, followed them in a broken line, and gave the appearance of skirmishing until the Golden nymph who had first entered the field struck the Silver nymph to the left with her hand, sent her off the field and occupied her place. But soon, on a new note from the musicians, she was struck in the same way by the Silver Knight. A Golden nymph made him move off; the Silver Knight

192

emerged from the camp, and the Golden Queen placed herself before her King. Then, fearing the Golden King's anger, the Silver King changed his position and retired behind his right-hand Warden, to a place which seemed well-protected and defensible.

"The two Knights on the left, the Golden one and the Silver, advanced and made large captures of the opposing nymphs, who could not retreat, especially the Golden Knight who devoted his whole attention to the capture of nymphs. But the Silver Knight had greater plans in his mind. He disguised his intentions and sometime, when he could have taken a Golden nymph, let her go and advanced further, to such effect that he came close to his enemies, into a position from which he bowed to the Golden King and said: 'God save you, sire.' Upon this warning to protect their King, the Golden party trembled; not that they could not quickly bring him aid, but because in saving their king, they could not avoid losing their right-hand Warden. Then the Golden King retired to the left, and the Silver Knight took the Golden Warden; which was a great loss to the Golden Party. They, however, resolved to work their revenge and surrounded him on all sides, so that he could not retreat or escape from their hands. He made countless attempts to get away, and his party tried innumerable tricks to rescue him, but finally he was taken by the Golden Queen.

"Deprived of one of their bastions, the Golden party tried desperately, by hook or by crook, to find a way of retaliating. Casting caution aside, they did great damage among the hosts of the enemy. The Silver party assumed indifference and awaited the hour of their revenge. They offered one of their nymphs to the Golden Queen, after laying her a secret ambush, which almost allowed the Golden Archer to surprise the Silver Queen. The Golden Knight then attempted to capture the Silver King and Queen, and greeted them with 'Good day!' The Silver Archer saved them, but was taken by a Golden nymph, who

was captured by a Silver nymph. The battle was sharp. The Wardens came out of their posts to rescue. Everything was in perilous confusion. The goddess of battles had not yet declared herself. Sometimes all the Silver forces penetrated to the Golden King's tent, but were quickly repulsed. Among others, the Golden Queen performed mighty deeds. In one sally she took that Archer and, darting to the side, captured the Silver Warden. At the sight of this, the Silver Queen advanced and struck with similar boldness, taking the remaining Golden Warden and some nymphs at the same time.

"The two Queens fought a long battle, sometimes trying to surprise one another, sometimes to escape and protect their own Kings. Finally the Golden Queen took the Silver one but was immediately afterwards taken by the Silver Archer. Her King had then only three nymphs,

The title page of Thomas Middleton's play "A Game at Chess," staged in 1624 at the Globe Theatre, London.

an Archer and a Warden, and the Silver King no more than three nymphs and his right-hand Knight; for which reasons they fought more cautiously and slowly for the rest of the game.

"The two Kings seemed grieved at the loss of their beloved royal ladies, and gave all their thoughts to the winning of new ones. They strenuously tried, therefore, to raise one of their three nymphs to the dignity of a bride, promising to love her joyfully, and swearing to receive her as the new Queen if she could advance as far as the enemy King's last line. The Golden nymphs succeeded first, and one of their number was made Queen. Whereupon a crown was placed on her head and she was given new robes. The Silver nymphs followed the same tactics. But only one file remained open for the advance towards a coronation, and this was guarded by the Golden Warden. The advancing nymphs therefore, stayed still.

"The new Golden Queen wanted to show herself brave, valiant, and warlike, upon her accession, and performed great feats of arms in the field. But during this by-play the Silver Knight took the Golden Warden, who was guarding the outskirts of the field; and so a new Silver Queen was made, who also wished to show her valour upon her accession.

"The battle has renewed more fiercely than before. Countless ruses, countless assaults, and advances were made by each party, to such effect that the Silver Queen secretly entered the Golden King's tent, and said 'God save you, sire.' There was no way of relieving him except by his new Queen, who, without more ado, stepped in the way and saved him. Then the Silver Knight, leaping in all directions, came up to his Queen, and together they so confused the Golden King that he had to sacrifice his Queen in order to extricate himself. Notwithstanding this, the Golden Archer and the two remaining nymphs defended the King with all their might. But in the end they were captured and sent off the field, and the Golden King was left alone. Then the whole Silver company made him a low bow and said 'Good day, sire,' which signified that the Silver King had conquered. At these words the two bands of musicians began to strike up, in unison, to proclaim victory, and the first ball was brought so joyfully to a close that we were

A game of living chess in the square of Marostica, the old township in Italy. The chessmen in 16th century costumes.

Two rivals for the hand of the beautiful Eleonora sit down at the chessboard, the course of the game being enacted by live pieces in the market place.

194

In a game of chess acted in Vienna in 1928, Wallenstein's army, fighting the Turks, was distinguished by characteristic hats and colourful costumes.

all beside ourselves with delight, like people in an ecstasy. Such mighty feasts, such dignity of behaviour, and such rare graces made us imagine — and not wrongly — that we had been transported to the sovereign bliss and supreme felicity of the Olympian heaven.

"When the first tournament was over both parties returned to their original places, and began to fight again in the same way as they had fought before, except that the music was half a beat faster than in the first battle. The moves also were totally different from before. This time I saw the Golden Queen, as though grieved by the previous rout of her army, called out by the music and taking the field among the first, together with an Archer and a Knight. Indeed, she almost surprised the Silver King in his tent, in the midst of his officers. Afterwards, when she saw that her plan was discovered, she skirmished among the Silver troop, and so discomfited the nymphs and other officers that it was a sad sight to see. You would have compared her to another Penthesilea the Amazon, raging through the Grecian camp. But the havoc was short-lived. For, exasperated at their losses, but disguising their grief, the Silver party secretly planted an ambuscade. They posted an Archer in a distant corner, and with him a Knight-errant, and by these two the Queen was taken and sent off the field. The rest were soon defeated. On the next occasion she will be better advised to stay near her King and not venture so far off. Or, if she must go, she will take a more powerful escort with her. So the Silver party were victors once again.

195

LEFT: *One of the live chessmen, a knight.*
RIGHT: *the triumphal carriage drawn by a pair of "dragons" in which a magician arrived to play the game. Sketches by J. M. Szancer for K. Libelt's story "A Game of Chess."*

"For the third and last dance the two parties stood up as before; and to me they seemed to have a gayer and more determined look than in the two previous ones. The time of the music was faster by more than a fifth, and was in the warlike Phrygian mode invented by Marsyas in ancient days. Then they began to wheel about and engage in a marvellous battle, with such agility that they made four moves to one beat of the music, all with the customary turnings and bows that have already been described. It was in fact just a series of hops, leaps and curvettings upon the tight-rope, one after another. When we saw them revolving on one leg after making their bow, they looked for all the world like small children's spinning-tops, which are whipped so hard that they seem to be motionless. For they spin at such a speed that their motion looks like repose and they appear to be quite still or, as the children say, to be sleeping. If we paint a point of some colour on them, it seems to be not a point but a continuous line...

"Then we heard hand-clapping and acclamations repeated at each move by both parties alike. Never was Cato so severe, Crassus the grandfather so unsmiling, Timon of Athens so misanthropic, or Heraclitus such as enemy to laughter — which is peculiar to man — that he would not have relaxed his frown at the sight of these young men with their queens and their nymphs, moving, advancing, leaping, vaulting, capering and wheeling in five hundred different ways to the swift changes of the music; and so nimbly did they move that one never got in the way of another. The smaller the number of those remaining on the field the greater was our pleasure in watching..."

There is no finer description of living chess extant. This was just a tale, of course. It would be interesting to know if there are any documents describing real live chess exhibitions, earlier than the 15th century. Source materials are almost entirely lacking. There are notes in various chronicles that Charles Martel (7th-8th centuries A.D.) took up chess from the Arabs and made it popular in Spain, crediting him with the introduction of living chess to Europe.

The fifteenth century produced some gruesome

196

A Brussels street becomes a giant chessboard for a few hours (1930).

variants. Sultan Mohammed I developed the engaging habit of sending captured men straight to the executioner. In Spain, a Dominican member of the Inquisition, Pedro Arbues, ordered unfortunate victims of persecutions to stand in as figures in a game of living chess played by two blind monks. Each time they captured a piece, they condemned someone to death. Tsar Ivan the Terrible, notorious for his cruelty, was also said to have played living chess for the lives of his subjects. "Dying Chess" might be a better name.

In China, living chess was practised earlier still and has survived unchanged up to the present day. When Alekhine visited China in 1933 he witnessed a spectacle of this kind in a city square.

Two bishops (jesters) on donkeys waiting for the order to move. In the background, the black king on horseback.

The ballet "Checkmate" was performed by the Sadler' Wells Company in 1947. LEFT: The Black Queen tempts the Red King. RIGHT: The Red Knight attacks the Black Queen.

The ballet tells of life, love and death, of the triumph of good over evil. RIGHT: The Red Knight finds he cannot strike the Black Queen; he succumbs to her words of love.

CHESS "MYSTERIES"

From Spain and France, chess "mysteries," living chess pageants, went to Italy where, frequently tinted with legend, they continue in some towns as annual events to this day.

The Italian town of Marostica witnessed in 1554 a chess duel between rivals for the hand of the local governor's daughter. An attempt to settle their problem by the sword had led to the arrest of both the admirers. The father of Eleonora — the lady concerned — suggested that the rivals, instead of duelling, should enter the lists of a chessboard. So that the townspeople could watch, the game was played in the open air with appropriately dressed and made-up living people. The winner, one Rinaldo de Angarano, gained the hand of Eleonora and a fine dowry. The two were very happy, and the father, satisfied with the outcome, ruled that the "duel" should be restaged in the main square of the town each hundred years afterwards.

Another living chess exhibition, in 16th-century Italy, was described by the Polish writer Karol Libelt (1807–75), in a fantastic short story "Gra w szachy" ("A Game of Chess"). Here is how he imagined the courtly game to be staged at Rome:

"The actors waited dancing in a magnificent room on a floor laid out as a chessboard. Then a herald announced that two famous wizards from Egypt and India had arrived and begged the permission of the Emperor as a connoisseur of the ancient game, to play the game in his presence, and later to judge which had won. The Emperor nodded approval, and a team entered the room among the sounds of trumpets. First the Bishops dressed as Harlequins, with caps of various colours, frolicking oddly. Then the Knights under the guise of Centaurs; their horses made of paper, two greys and two blacks. Next, the two royal couples: Ermina and Alexander, wearing the colours of Venice and their opponents the colours of Milan. Four Elephants (rooks) wound up the procession.

"They all paraded three times round the room past the Emperor, and halted at their appointed place. As soon as they took up their positions, the wizards entered, driven through two opposite double-doors on high triumphal chariots, one drawn by crocodiles and the other by dragons. Having hailed the Emperor with their magic wands, each one stood behind their 'men'."

A fanfare of trumpets announced the start of the game. Anastasio, the hero of the tale, soon found his opponent Bernardino a much better

In the American ballet spectacle "This Crazy Game," a mad game of chess is danced by a team of charming girls wearing chess emblems.

199

The Renaissance courtyard of the Royal Castle on Wawel Hill, Cracow, has more than once been the venue for spectacular contests of living chess. Here is a 1932 game acted by artists of the Cracow theatre.

player than he had made out during rehearsals. The fortunes of the game swayed to and fro. The pawns strode forward, the harlequins and centaurs weaved here and there, directed by the magic wands. Many departed, captured. The struggle became ever keener. The heavy artillery went into action. Suddenly Anastasio noticed that his own king had furtively moved to an inferior square. The "King" was a man named Alexander and happened to be Bernardino's nephew. So one of his own pieces was a traitor! Anastasio rose angrily from his seat and commanded Alexander to stay in his proper place. There was uproar for a while. Bernardino had been rattled by the discovery of his perfidy, however, and soon afterwards fell into a trap. He struggled against the inevitable but soon a second fanfare of trumpets announced his downfall. Anastasio knelt before the Emperor and was given a golden jewel set with a chessboard.

During the reign of Catherine II of Russia, King Gustav IV of Sweden visited St. Petersburg in 1796. Count Strogonov held a reception in his honour which was marked by the spectacle of a game of chess. In a park, on a lawn covered by yellow and green squares, the figures of a chess drama moved in mediaeval costumes.

In a play, "A Game of Chess," staged at the Globe Theatre in 1624, Thomas Middleton presented eminent political persons in the guise of chessmen. One of the politicians lampooned

Young people of Ströbeck walk onto the board for the traditional game of living chess.

Helsinki, 1955: chessmen that have been captured are carried away on stretchers.

Capablanca playing a game of living chess in a Berlin park in 1930, tells the herald his move.

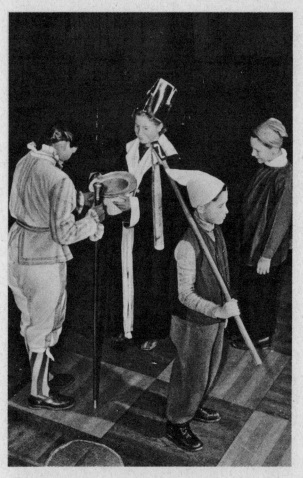

Ströbeck: The Black Rook checkmates the White King, who takes off his hat as a sign of surrender.

At Frankfurt-on-Main in 1936 street traffic was held up to permit the spectators to follow the game.

In Hans Richter's experimental film "8 × 8" (1957) the action took place in a world of live chessmen.

In the final scene of the Czechoslovak film comedy "The Proud Princess" (1952), the king running about the black and white chequered courtyard of the castle gave the impression of being a chess king trying to escape mate.

was the Spanish Ambassador, an unfortunate go-between in the matrimonial negotiations on behalf of Prince Charles, heir to the Spanish throne. The authorities prosecuted and fined the actors, and Middleton went to prison.

Living chess became a frequent subject for ballet on the stage either as a spectacle in itself or as a part of an opera or play.

1,700 witnessed the opening in Paris of a grand ballet-pantomime, "Jeu d'échecs," with music composed by Philidor L'Aîné. This chess masquerade was recorded in an eight-page pamphlet containing the score of the music. A chess ballet was the central scene in a five-act opera, "Magicienne," by Halévy, staged successfully in Paris in 1858.

Later Antonio Lozzi, the composer of an Italian musical comedy "The King, Rooks and Jesters" (Jester — the name for a chess Bishop in Italy), combined live chess with the development of the plot in subtler style. He used a story by a comic writer Luccio D'Ambra, describing the adventures of a young Prince Rolando, symbolised by a chess king. The courtly love affair was presented in a live chess ballet scene which ended with the King being checkmated.

In 1916, D'Ambra made a silent film. When Ernst Lubitch made in 1934 his famous film "The Merry Widow" with Maurice Chevalier, he not only borrowed D'Ambra's atmosphere, style, costumes, situations, but transposed the live chess sequence to a new ballet which, although not directly connected with chess, was based on black and white visual effects.

In the same year, 1916, a Russian director A. Uralskii made a film, "Chess of Life," a melodrama starring Vera Kholodnaya. The final scene was a masquerade with dancers on a large chessboard. The ballet was given an additional ambiguous meaning for the main characters, entangled in a matrimonial "triangle."

But the greatest artistic success in living chess was achieved by the Sadler's Wells ballet company who, at the Paris World Fair of 1937, pres-

ented "Checkmate," with music by Arthur Bliss and choreography by Ninette de Valois. The theme was the struggle of Love (Red) with Death (Black). The ballet was revived in London with new costumes in 1947.

Later on, in 1953, and also in London, at the Empress Hall, an effective ballet-pantomime, "Sindbad the Sailor on Ice," was presented, the first chess ballet on ice. Produced by Miss Eve Bradfield, advised on chess themes by Mr. R.C. Noel-Johnson, it featured in living chess the famous game played in 1858 in Paris between Paul Morphy and the Duke of Brunswick and Count Isouard.

In American choreography, living chess has been presented in the form of a "Ghost Revue." A press account reads: "One of the latest shows 'The Crazy Game' began with the lights suddenly going out. An infernal chill wind blew through the auditorium with a diabolical whizzing sound. Phosphorescent tentacles appeared on the ceiling,

and an electric current passed through the arms of the seats shaking the horrified audience in their seats. Soon afterwards, a large chessboard appeared on the stage with two ghastly chess players murdering each other. The chessmen, freed from their masters' control came out of the box and... a splendid ballet started: eighteen half-nude girls with chess emblems on their heads, danced to a furious Dixieland rhythm. Suddenly the girls lifted their legs which grew longer and longer, extending over the heads of the spectators sitting in the first rows, and suddenly flew up with a dreadful hiss, while the pretty ballerinas dropped below the stage, amid flames and pungent smoke..."

One of the most popular spectacles of live chess was for a long time the staging of historic battles, or mock skirmishes presented in the open air to mass audiences.

The Agricultural Exhibition in Vienna in 1898 featured a living chess presentation of the Battle of Zenta (1697) where the Turkish forces were defeated by Prince Eugene. Each chess piece was represented by a whole group of performers. Altogether, three hundred and forty men and sixteen horses took part, to music from a fifty-piece orchestra. The chessboard was laid out on a common marked with black and yellow squares.

The battle of the Polish knights commanded by King Jan Sobieski with the Turkish forces led by Kara Mustapha, at the time of the relief of Vienna in 1683, was the theme of a game of living chess presented on the courtyard of the Wawel Castle in Cracow in 1927 during celebrations in honour of a Polish poet Juliusz Słowacki whose body had been brought to Poland from Paris. This pageant was recorded by Janusz Stępowski. Here is an excerpt from his "Tournament of Live Chess":

The King wondered in Council whether to follow
The spearhead, or rather to open up the ranks.
Choosing the second course, amid the battle's run

He sent expendable pawn Francis to his doom
This sacrifice could be a heroic climax
If earlier 'twere not called a gambit in chess.'

Ströbeck in Germany keeps up a living chess tradition. For the last three centuries, the young people there have been acting living games. In feudal times the village was obliged by an edict to stage such a show at all royal coronations.

In the finale of a Czechoslovak fairy-comedy film, "The Proud Princess," directed by Borivoj Zeman, a grotesque King Miroslav is seen running in small steps around a floor laid with white and black squares, as if fleeing from a mate. But a scene in part two of "Ivan the Terrible," a fine film directed by Sergei Eisenstein, comes even closer to chess. Static figures of monks, knights, pages and ladies at the court of King Zygmunt III create a vivid chess image which is still further heightened by a sharply-defined chequered floor.

By making Zygmunt III rather unflatteringly like a lifeless chess king, the producer adds a satirical touch.

IX. WHO AND WHEN?

King Louis XI at chess in the Château de Plessis-les-Tours. French miniature of the end of the 15th century.

If you had asked "What is chess?" in a questionnaire circulated 1,000 years ago, you would have learnt that the game was a hobby of people in every walk of life, of every sort of occupation and social standing.

For some it was a passion, for others a pleasant pastime. It became an object of mathematical, sociological or moral investigation. Many artists and creative workers took chess as a motif in their works. Chess also had a few opponents who regarded it as completely valueless.

Library archives tell us a lot about chess players.

Chess has been reputed to have been in great favour with Charlemagne and his court. In the famous "Chanson de Rolland," Charlemagne is described as sitting in an orchard with Roland and Oliver at his side while the oldest and wisest of his knights are amusing themselves at chess or draughts (not then invented yet! — B.H. Wood).

A beautiful set of chessmen said to have belonged to Charlemagne has been preserved to this day. He is presented as an enthusiastic chess player in many literary anecdotes but a thorough historical investigation has left no grounds to suppose that he ever took any interest in the game at all.

In the Cluny museum in Paris there is a fine set of chessmen carved in gold, silver and crystal that once belonged to King Louis IX, the Saint. This did not, however prevent the same King from outlawing chess in an edict of 1254.

John Lackland, King of England (1199–1216), was a keen chess player.

The Spanish King Alfonso the Wise, was not only an excellent player, but the author of a treatise about chess, an historian, Maecenas and untiring popularizer of the game. He invited Arabian masters to his court. In the preface to a book dealing with chess, dice and other board games, he suggested a legendary origin. There were once three wise men, each with a different view on life and, consequently, on entertainments. The first declared that everything depended on Wisdom; he brought chess with him; the second said that Luck decided everything and brought dice; the third claimed that both Wisdom and Luck were important and brought board games. Today we might expect the third to like bridge.

Tamerlane, the Mongol ruler and conqueror of the 14th century, was a great chess enthusiast. He considered two pastimes worthy of a warrior: hunting and chess. Once he had just won a game with a fine rook move when two messengers arrived, each carrying news: one, that a son had been born to him and another that the town he had ordered to be built on the River Sichone was finished. To mark this happy coincidence of three events, he gave the name of Shahrukh to his newborn infant and that of Shahrukhie to the town (derived from the words "royal rook"). Tamerlane invited many chess teachers to his capital to instruct young people in the game. All were surpassed by Galaldin, who often gave his opponents the odds of a queen. Tamerlane used to tell him: "You are first on the chessboard, as I am first in the country. We are both invincible in our own domain."

The French kings Charles V and Charles VI prohibited chess, but Charles VII was so fond of it that he spent long hours over the board with his mistress Agnès Sorel in his castle in Touraine. Henry IV of France was also a keen chess player, of whom a rather low anecdote is told. He was playing with a nobleman called Bassompierre. Picking up the knight to make a move, Bassompierre made a loud rude noise. True, his opponent was the good King Henry, but he was a monarch all the same. Bassompierre blushed but hurriedly explained: "Sire, my knight will not move if he does not hear the trumpet call." The king smiled.

After being defeated by the Emperor Charles V, the Saxon Elector John Frederick found himself in a dramatic situation. We take the description from the novel "The Iron Crown" by a Polish writer, Hanna Malewska:

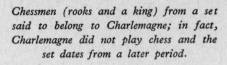

Chessmen (rooks and a king) from a set said to belong to Charlemagne; in fact, Charlemagne did not play chess and the set dates from a later period.

Chessmen of gold and crystal presented to the French king Louis IX, the Saint. From the Cluny Museum, Paris.

Miniature from the treatise on chess by Alfonso the Wise of Spain.

Margrave Otto IV of Brandenburg playing chess. Part of a 13th century German miniature from Maness's manuscript, "Grosse Heidelberger Liederhandschrift."

"The former Elector was taken prisoner by the Spaniards, together with Ernest of Brunswick. He had already completely regained the self-possession which had temporarily deserted him when he had learnt that his eldest son had been killed.

"He was playing chess with Duke Ernest when his captor's verdict was brought to him. The messenger looked at the unfinished game, then at the prisoner, and read:

'The former Elector is condemned to death by beheading with an axe for rebellion and lèse majesté.'

"Standing erect, the Elector, after listening to the sentence, said: 'I did not expect the emperor to treat me so severely.' He took the document from the hands of the messenger, put it on the table and turned back to the game. 'Cousin,' he said to the dismayed Ernest, 'pay attention to your game, because I'm about to checkmate you'."

Legend has it that Ivan the Terrible died playing chess. Among many accounts of the last hours of the Tsar's life, that of the English envoy who was in Moscow at that time is perhaps the most reliable. He describes how, feeling very ill, the Tsar ordered a table to be brought for a game of chess. He began to put the pieces on the chessboard himself. Just before he set the last king in its place, he died of a stroke.

Chess was a popular game at the court of Tsar Ivan IV, the Tsar himself inviting leading political personalities in Russia to play him. Among his opponents were Boris Godunov and Duke Bielski. Once, in a particularly good humour, he explained the game to a confidant, Maluta Skuratoff, of low origin. This was to a certain extent an infringement of court etiquette because

209

Kürfurst Johann Friedrich der Ältere of Saxony playing chess with a Spanish captain.

ite game; it advanced in popularity and was widely cultivated in Russia during her reign. In educating her son Paul she laid great emphasis on instructing him in both ordinary and four-handed chess. After her death, Tsar Paul issued an order that street doors, windows and lamp-posts should be painted in black-and-white squares as a sign of mourning.

Napoleon, contrary to general opinion, was a poor chess player. As a young lieutenant of the artillery he often visited the Café de la Régence in Paris to play. The table he played on has been preserved up to our times. He played boldly, seeking unusual situations and becoming very excited. When losing, he often lost his temper, pushing away the board and scattering the men. It made him angry to find that he could not master the game. This is probably why he said: "It is too difficult for a game and not serious enough to be a science or an art." At the height of his career he had to give chess up; it was taking too much of his time. He preferred draughts which did not last so long. He is said to have based tact-

ical moves on the battlefield on the moves of the chessmen. In his final exile at St. Helena he often played chess. He played, but never suspected what was hidden inside the chessmen, a secret that was revealed only years after his death. In 1933 an exhibition of Napoleonic relics organized in Austerlitz included a chess set in ivory and mother-of-pearl. They had been made by his friends, and inside some of the pieces were plans for his escape. The set was to have been handed to him by an officer who knew the secret, but who died during the voyage on the ship, the gift being finally delivered by somebody ignorant of all this. Napoleon accepted the set and kept it until his death. He bequeathed it to his son in his will, and it changed owners many more times before reaching the exhibition.

Chess players have been numbered not only among kings but among those who overthrew them. Marat and Robespierre, the tribunes of the French Revolution, liked chess. It was suggested at that time that the names of the pieces should be changed, and above all that the "king"

The Tsar at chess in a picturesque scene from the film "Ivan the Terrible" (Part I, 1944) directed by S. M. Eisenstein. Note his shadow.

on one side should be called "freedom." The story is told that a young woman came to the Café de la Régence dressed as a man and challenged Robespierre to a game. After being checkmated twice, he mentioned that they had not yet agreed the stakes. "Human life is at stake," answered his mysterious opponent. "You have lost, so please sign this," and she handed him an order to release the imprisoned aristocrat, Marquis de Meruy. "Who are you, young man?" asked the tribune, astonished at the demand which was a dangerous one for his opponent to make. "I am his fiancée," was the answer. Which just goes to show what true love can do!

Among military commanders and strategists, we find many keen players: Tadeusz Kościuszko (in the Warsaw National Museum there is a small chessboard with the chessmen he made himself); La Fayette (a box containing a chessboard and a few pieces carved in ivory are to be found in the Army Museum in the Hôtel des Invalides,

Paris); Suvorov. The Russian statesman and politician prince Potemkin, a favourite of Catherine II, was an intelligent player, liable to forget his duties when deep in a prolonged game. He suffered from insomnia, and requested opponents in the middle of the night. The victims were awakened by his guards and brought to him in spite of their protests. The famous French diplomat, Talleyrand, always beat Napoleon. Cardinal Richelieu was a great chess enthusiast and, going even farther back, so was the Italian politician and historian Machiavelli. In his novel "Goya" Lion Feuchtwanger wrote that Machiavelli, after being banished by the Medicis, lived in a small landed estate near San Caciano and used to go after dinner to the "inn to play chess with the innkeeper, the butcher and the miller and two brickmakers."

The two Poles who led the workers' battalions during the Paris Commune, General Jarosław Dąbrowski and General Walery Wróblewski,

The king of England John Lackland receives a delegation of French envoys while at chess. Drawing by Moreau le Jeune (1782).

215

were also ardent chess players. Stanislaw Strumph-Wojtkiewicz in his historical novels "The General of the Paris Commune" and "The Battle of Paris" describes, among other things, how after the failure of the Commune, General Wróblewski, who survived the defeat, sought to forget his losses in chess.

'He is surely courting death,' said Robert in despair, when the General, deaf to all persuasion and requests, used to go off to the Café de la Régence to play chess with anybody who happened to be there. The Poles who used to come to the café watched him in dismay; this man who had been one of the leaders of the Commune, and now seemed heedless of the raging terror.'

Martin Luther, the religious reformer, had a strange desire; all through his life he dreamed of being able to acquire a fine set of chessmen carved and moulded in gold and silver. His predecessor, the Bohemian reformer John Huss played chess in his youth, but later proscribed it. Speaking of the clergy, let us mention that a majority of popes and bishops have condemned chess classing it with gambling games. Pope Leo XIII was an exception, he loved the game. He had a regular opponent, a rather excitable monk. It is said that on one occasion when the monk was quite enraged about his position, the Pope halted play and delivered a short sermon about virtue, Christian resignation and self-control.

The Church authorities in Spain — and few people know this — proclaimed in 1944 the 16th century Saint Teresa patron of chess players. St. Teresa used to play chess with her father, relatives and brothers. In her religious writings she often uses chess to illustrate her meditations about ethics and faith.

The orthodox clergy, apart from a few exceptional cases, have taken a negative stand toward chess, but one Moscow patriarch of the 18th century ordered the old bells from a nearby church tower to be taken away and sold because they disturbed him when playing chess through the whole night.

Empress Catherine II with Kempelen's automatic chess player in the French film "The Chess Player" (1938).

"I make so bold as to point out to Your Highness that the King refuses to be captured." Drawing by Z. Lengren.

Napoleon Bonaparte at chess in his youth. Scene from the French film "Napoleon" (1926), directed by A. Gance.

The great scientist Isaac Newton liked a game of chess. The German philosopher Leibnitz valued chess, being intrigued by its immense mathematical possibilities of various combinations in the game. On one occasion when asked what was the use of chess, he replied: "It helps to improve one's ability to reason and one's inventiveness... People's ingenuity is best revealed in chess playing."

Benjamin Franklin, American scientist and politician, recommended chess as an excellent method of teaching young people self-possession, intellectual concentration, and a tactical approach to life. He emphasized that chess was not just an entertainment, but also a factor stimulating the development of many useful mental abilities invaluable in one's daily work and life in general. Franklin was the author of the first book on chess published in America, a valuable work containing many keen observations about its influence on society. Not a very good player himself, he did not hanker after the emotional thrill

of tournaments, but liked a quiet game at home.

Among historians, the Pole Joachim Lelewel (1786–1861) and the English writer H. T. Buckle, were both fine chess players. Buckle's short-lived chess career deserves particular mention. In 1847 as an amateur, he defeated a group of strong professional players in a local tournament; he won first place and thus qualified as a candidate for a match with Staunton but he refused the attractive proposal to play against the then World Champion, pleading lack of time. He was working on his "History of Civilization" which was to earn him immortal fame. Later his studies caused him to give up chess altogether.

The famous Russian physicist Lomonosov, the Polish historian Askenazy and the French mathematician Poincaré, all liked a game of chess. The Rumanian mathematician and astronomer W. Pauly became one of the world's most famous composers of chess problems. The house of the Russian chemist Mendeleyev, discoverer of the

"The King's Downfall." Napoleon at chess on St. Helena. Drawing by an anonymous French artist of the last century.

Jean-Jacques Rousseau at chess in the Café de la Régence in Paris. A contemporary aquatint by Gabriel de Saint-Aubin

periodicity of the elements, used to be a Mecca for chess enthusiasts. He was a fine player himself. He was fascinated by the theory of the game, studying text-books and making notes about his games. Though he used to play until far into the night, he was never tired; on the contrary, refreshed by his intellectual efforts at the chessboard, he returned with gusto to his scientific work.

Marx and Lenin played chess. The former in his memoirs refers to the frequent games with a close friend Helen Demuth. He played a lot of chess when he lived as an emigré in London.

Wilhelm Liebknecht, one of the leaders of the German working class movement, describes Marx's chess amusingly. "Marx took his chess much to heart and when he lost was eager for a return game. He once claimed to have invented a new sensational opening. He beat Liebknecht a few times but then lost. He insisted that they should resume the contest early next day, then spent the whole night analysing. Next morning he was ready for battle again. A victory exhilarated him greatly; but then he lost again. He took the next game very seriously, concentrated hard

and won again. All through the day the match went on with fluctuating fortunes. Midnight came again. When, at last Liebknecht won two successive games and rose considering the duel over, Marx tried to detain him by force and it was only thanks to his wife that he was finally persuaded to bring the marathon to a close."

About Lenin, the Soviet historian I. Linder wrote: "Vladimir Ilich Lenin liked to play chess in his hours of leisure. He learned to play as a child from his father, Ilya Nikolayevitch Ulyanov. As a young man, Lenin competed successfully with the best players of the town of Samara, playing in matches."

"He always took his game seriously, disliking what he called 'light games,' wrote Lenin's brother D. Ulyanov. What gave him the most satisfaction was the stubborn struggle to find the best move, the effort of finding a way out of a difficult, often desperate situation. The final result, whether he won or lost, was of secondary importance to him. He was pleased if his opponent played well, displeased if he blundered. If his opponent made it too easy for him, he would say with a smile: 'It is not I who have won the game, but you who have lost it.'"

A Soviet chess player of the older generation, P. Dolgov, casting his mind back to the years before the revolution, describes the following scene:

"As a child I often watched the chess matches that took place in our house in the evenings. Mostly there were six or eight players, and if Khardin was among them, simultaneous games were organized, or perhaps one or two consultative games. V. I. Lenin was often present at these chess evenings."

Nadezhda Krupskaya, in her "Reminiscences About Lenin" described how he played Lepeshinsky by correspondence. He was so preoccupied with the game that he sometimes cried out some remark like "If his knight moves here, then my rook should go there" in his sleep.

When an emigré in Paris, Lenin used to go to a café in the Avenue d'Orléans, at the corner of Place Montrouge. It was a very quiet café and Lenin liked playing chess there with his close acquaintances. Once he offered to one of his French friends that he should give him the odds of some piece and when the other refused he said, "So much the worse for you, I shall gobble up your knight," and when this prediction came true, he added, "Are you satisfied now?"

M. Gorki writes about Lenin's all-round interests and the passion with which he devoted himself to everything he did: "It was with equal enthusiasm that he played chess, read the 'History of Costumes' or discussed some problem with a friend for many hours at a time, or went fishing, or walking among the stony lanes of Capri."

After the revolution, the pressure of state duties caused Lenin to give up chess almost completely. Chess, he confessed, absorbed him too much, hindering his work. When the doctors ordered complete rest during his illness towards the end of his life, he occasionally returned to the game but was no longer the ardent player of the past. His chauffeur, S. Gil, writes in his memoirs: "Even during his long illness he continued his walks, boat trips, croquet playing and skittles.

Pope Leo XIII at chess.
A painting by Fritz Dietrich.
From a private collection.

If a good opponent were available he also enjoyed a game of chess. He, a good player as a young man, had been extremely fond of the game but later he preferred hunting. He considered that only physical exercise in the open air could bring relaxation after intellectual work."

Georgi Dimitrov, the great Bulgarian revolutionary, liked playing chess.

Among contemporary political leaders and statesmen, Josip Broz Tito, President of Yugoslavia (who even opened the Chess Olympiad in Dubrovnik in 1950 by playing a game hors concours), Gamal Abd el Nasser, late President of the United Arab Republic, and Fidel Castro of Cuba are all keen chess players.

Among writers and poets have been found many devotees of the game.

The 11th century Uzbek poet and sage, Alisher Navoi described chess in a poem entitled "The Language of Birds," comparing "the noble duel after which no trace of destruction can be found" to war. He also mentioned that "the rulers of the world should not be too proud for when the game is over and the pieces are thrown back into the

The Russian physicist M. Lomonosov liked chess. Scene from the Soviet film "Mikhail Lomonosov" (1955).

box, the king *(shah)* might be at the bottom and the pawns on top..."

The Polish poet, Jan Kochanowski, author of the poem "Chess," not only played well, but showed that he was deeply interested in chess. In his novel about Jan Kochanowski entitled "Poet and Courtier" Mieczysław Jastrun devoted a whole chapter to a chess match between the Polish poet and the Italian Vetello, his rival for the hand of Catherine. Here chess is a sort of symbolic duel offering scope for many allusions:

"The black-and-white boards divided into sixty-four squares, were alive with the movements of the ivory soldiers. The courtiers who were playing sat opposite each other, not yet completely alienated from their companions, as the game had only just begun and they had only made the first moves. Jan Kochanowski was sitting opposite Eneas Vetello and attentively watching his opponent's over-hasty moves...

"Now we see the poet in a role that should not surprise us. There is no doubt he was a fervent chess player and the whole plot of his poem 'Chess' published about that time was based on that game...

"He was so completely absorbed in the game that he was not thinking about the Italian as his rival at the moment and did not fully realize that, like the Ruthenian dukes Fiodor and Borzhuy in the poem, they were playing for something more... namely, Catherine.

"They were extremely polite to each other, not only because they were cultured men of wide experience; the world had given them polished manners and feeling for others; but also because each underestimated the other. The handsome Vetello underestimated Jan's poetical gifts, superior to him in matters of women and love-making; Kochanowski underestimated the Italian's good looks regarding him as a frivolous fop. Were it not for this mutual lack of understanding, who knows but that their words might have suddenly turned into knives. But no, there is no fear of that, it is not a princess who is at stake in the game of chess. Is is only one of many, many contests at the Jagiellonian court.

" 'I have heard,' says Vetello, repeating a thing he had once been told, but repeating it now only to conceal his satisfaction at the triumph he was soon to have: 'I have heard that in Moscow they play this game very seldom but very well indeed.'

"Kochanowski did not answer, but his anger against his opponent was rising. Then came a feeling of discouragement and fatigue. The Italian made one more move, quick as lightning, and he was checkmated.

" 'Don't worry,' said Vetello, 'he who is unlucky at games is lucky in love.'

"He could not have made a less tactful remark just then."

One of the characters in Łukasz Górnicki's "The Courtier," the Polish version of a work by the Italian Castigliano, proclaims singular views about chess.

"Mr. Kostka asked: 'And what do you think about chess, sir?'

"Mr. Myszkowski answered: 'Indeed, it is a fine entertainment for a quick mind. Chess is not for me, though, it needs too much skill. If you want to get anywhere with chess you must study diligently, wasting a lot of time on it, just as though you were mastering some noble science. And when at last you've learnt a lot about it, what do you know? You know how to play a game, and not even how to play it well. As I see it, it's better not to know too much about it than to be a great champion'."

The French writer and thinker Montaigne wrote: "I detest and avoid chess, because it is not a real game and is too serious as an entertainment. It seems a shame to give it attention that could be devoted to some better purpose."

What a contrast are Cervantes's words: "Life is a game of chess." Nor had the French rationalist writers, for instance, Voltaire, Diderot and Rousseau any prejudice against chess, although they were not very skillful at it. André Maurois de-

The eminent Russian chemist Dmitri Mendeleyev spent a lot of his leisure hours playing chess. A contemporary drawing.

scribes, in his book "Voltaire" how "Father Adam, who was very good at chess, played Voltaire every day. 'Father Adam is not a man of the world,' Voltaire used to say, 'but he plays an excellent game of chess.' When the priest won, Voltaire would sweep the chessboard off the table and cry, 'I've wasted two hours moving these bits of wood about. I could have written a scene of some play in that time'."

Voltaire often met Philidor at the Café de la Régence and played more than one friendly game with him. Rousseau, too, liked to visit the Café de la Régence, to try his hand at the chessboard but was no match for Philidor at all, even at the odds of a rook.

During one period of special interest in chess he worked out an elaborate strategic method of play which he considered sure to win. In practice, however, his sensational method did not pass the test. He was defeated by a third-rate player. This damped his enthusiasm. Later he had consol-

ation. Chamfort tells how after playing and beating Prince de Conti several times, he was told that he should allow a prince to win sometimes. "I don't see why," he replied, "I'm giving him a rook start!"

Diderot gave up chess because he came to the conclusion that he would never master the theory of it. In his "Neveu de Rameau" he wrote: "When it is cold or rainy, I take refuge in the Café de la Régence and amuse myself watching the chess. Paris is a centre of world thought and this Café is the centre of its chess. It is here that the profound thinker Légal, the subtle Philidor and the sober Mayot wage their battles of wits; you can see the most unexpected moves yet listen to the poorest conversation; because, although it is pos-

sible for a man to be a great intellectual and a great chess player like Légal, it is also possible to be a great chess player and as dull as Foubert and Mayot.

"One afternoon I was sitting there watching a lot, saying little and hearing as little as I could, when I was approached by one of the strangest persons I know, Rameau, the foster son of Rameau the famous.

"He came up to me. 'Ah, the philosopher, I believe? What are you doing here among these loafers? Are you too wasting time moving bits of wood?'

"I: 'No, but as I have nothing better to do, I am amusing myself looking at those who do it well.'

"He: 'Oh, then you are not often amused; apart from Légal and Philidor nobody else there has any idea of the game.'
"I: 'And Monsieur de Bissy?'
"He: 'Oh, he's as good a chess player as M'lle Clairon is an actress; both of them know all there is to know about their play.'
"I: 'I see you are hard to please; only the best will satisfy you.'
"He: 'Yes, in chess, draughts, poetry, rhetoric, music and other such trifles. Who can stand a poor performance in these things?'
"I: 'I agree with you almost entirely. But many must devote themselves to these arts so that one genius can emerge; and then only he is the one among many'."

The encyclopaedists gave evidence of their liking for chess by inserting an extensive article about the history, rules and practice of the game in their famous Encyclopaedia.

Goethe's words "Chess is the touchstone of the intellect" have become world-famous. When writing about the cultural achievements owed to India by the West, he said: "Zugleich hatte man aus derselben Quelle das Schachspiel erhalten, welches, in bezug mit jener Weltklugheit, allem Dichtersinn den Garaus zu machen völlig geeignet ist."

The great Polish writer Adam Mickiewicz (1798–1855), like every exuberant nature, eager to know the world and life, and trying to penetrate into all kinds of phenomena, was greatly absorbed by various games including chess. He even planned to write a treatise about the theory of the games.

One of the beautiful lyrics about his great love, Maryla, recalls the following picture of the moments they spent at chess:

In every place, come time, come tide,
Where I wept with you, where I played with you
Everywhere and always I'll be by your side
For a part of soul has remained there true.

Musing in your lonely chamber
Hand to harp unwittingly straying
At this hour, will you remember:
The same song to him I was playing.

And at chess when the first strands
Of the web round your king come closing
Do you think: as then so he now stands
Like that last game of ours when ending...

Maryla Wereszczakówna, the poet's stay in Tuhanowicze, the landed estate of her parents, love and chess, all this is reflected in Włodzimierz Słobodnik's poem about Mickiewicz, entitled "The Shadow of Love." Here is an excerpt from this poem:

Though fine was the night that is gone,
Know you a storm will rage on this ev'ning
And though the game of chess is still on
Know you the queen must take the king

The president of Yugoslavia, Josip Broz Tito is a great chess enthusiast. He personally patronized the Chess Olympiad at Dubrovnik.

223

For love blurs reason, upsets the array,
Of all your figures, my Kovno man
The mist of unreason, the flame you can't allay
Your defeat in chess must bring and can.

Your tricks one and all are of no avail
Each move forestalled, your king must fall
Like Solomon, he lies dead, this weapon cannot fail:
The ardent eyes that are a lover's call.

When Adam Mickiewicz was in St. Petersburg
in 1828 he became the frequent guest of a French
lady, Mme Roudoleur:

"After dinner we played whist or écarté, but
Mickiewicz did not take part in the game. He
only played chess, and if he did play cards, only
'druzbart'."

An episode from the same period, during a visit
by Mickiewicz to Moscow, has been recorded

224

Mickiewicz playing chess with Maryla.
Drawing by Tadeusz Popiel in the
Lvov edition of "Ballads and Romances"
by Adam Mickiewicz, 1891.

Adam Mickiewicz and Prince Golitsyn
playing chess in Rome in 1830. A con-
temporary water-colour by an unknown
artist in Celina Szymanowska's album.

by Władysław Mickiewicz, his son. The episode illustrates the mood of the Poles in those years of national slavery.

"Mickiewicz, together with his friend and companion in exile Daszkiewicz, attended a soirée in a Russian house. He started playing chess with a Muscovite. For some time the contest was evenly balanced...

"Gradually the other guests gathered round, the Muscovites round their countryman, the Poles round Adam who realized when he heard such remarks as 'Victory for Poland,' 'No, Russia will win' that he had become a representative of the Polish cause, and that a heavy responsibility rested on his shoulders. 'I was getting hot under the collar,' he said with a smile, recalling this scene, 'My opponent was going all out for victory and defeat would have been a calamity.' The stern looks directed at him by Daszkiewicz, standing close by, repeatedly emphasised that the honour of their nation was at stake, completing his confusion. But suddenly he discovered a weakness .in his adversary's game. He attacked it. The Mus-

covite was caught unawares and his defence collapsed. Mickiewicz, wondering himself why he had not seen his chance earlier, played more and more boldly and checkmated the Muscovite in about a dozen moves. His victory was loudly acclaimed by the Poles. Only Daszkiewicz kept silent. When they left and were walking home, Adam was very excited and pleased. But Daszkiewicz still kept silent. At last Adam asked, 'Why don't you congratulate me for defending our colours so bravely?' 'You have nothing to be proud about,' answered Daszkiewicz, 'Without my help you could hardly have won. When I saw this was no mere game but that our national honour was at stake, and realized that the Muscovite was a strong player, I stealthily took a knight of his off the board. That was what suddenly improved your position. All of you were so absorbed with the game that you did not notice anything.' And seeing his friend's astonishment and indignation, he added: 'For the love of one's motherland one can even steal a knight from the chessboard!' " (That a knight could be removed without

Mickiewicz (right) by the chessboard in A. Maliszewski's play "Ballads and Romances" staged in 1955 at the Polski Theatre, Poznań.

A set of chessmen used by Mickiewicz during his stay in Russia. From the collection of the Adam Mickiewicz Museum, Warsaw.

Leo Tolstoy at chess with his son-in-law M. Sukhotin. His family is watching the game. A photograph taken at Tolstoy's home in 1908.

a "strong" player or any spectator noticing seems a tall story — B. H. Wood).

In the Mickiewicz Museum in Paris is a reproduction of a water-colour painted from nature in the album of Celina Szymanowska showing the poet playing chess in Rome in 1830 with Alexander Golitsyn, then the Russian envoy to the Vatican.

Of the galaxy of nineteenth century Russian novelists, Pushkin, Lermontov, Chernyshevsky, Herzen, Turgenev and Tolstoy all played chess.

In a letter to his wife, Alexander Pushkin wrote: "Thank you, darling, for learning to play chess. It is an absolute necessity in any well organized family. I'll show you what I mean later."

In the collection of Pushkin souvenirs is a copy of Philidor's book once owned by the poet. Publishers and booksellers used to send new books on chess to him for review. His contemporaries relate in their memoirs how Pushkin played chess on the eve of his fatal duel: how, when he saw his enemy D'Anthès crossing the room, he said: "This officer is threatening me with a checkmate, I shall have to kill him." So saying, he took a knight off the chessboard as if implying that he was alluding to the game. Fate reversed matters.

D'Anthès, cunning and experienced, realizing at the very beginning that there would be no mercy in this duel, chose tactics that gave him the advantage and gained him time in the shooting. D'Anthès played the game with amazing caution and with a few excellent and faultless moves won the fatal game and the life that was at stake. This

The famous Polish writer Karol Irzykowski (d. 1944) was a life-long chess enthusiast.

The contemporary Polish writer Jerzy Putrament, a keen student of chess literature.

comparison with chess is in the description of the duel given by the Russian writer Leonid Grossman in his novel "D'Archiac Notes," which tells of Pushkin's tragic end.

Ivan Turgenev was a first-class chess player and participant in the championships. When in Paris, he was a regular habitué of the Café de la Régence. In 1862, he finished second to the excellent player Rivière in a tournament organized by the owner of the Café de la Régence for over sixty of the best chess players who were his regular guests. He was also a popular figure among chess players in Germany being elected vice-chairman of the chess tournament in Baden-Baden, 1870.

Turgenev wrote: "I was very keen on chess, even as a child." He used to get very excited when playing. The game aroused his fighting spirit. A witness of his exciting games recalls:

"Once he was in danger of losing the game. He became very excited. His eyes flashed, his moves were full of tension. But he concentrated all his attention on the game and, of course won in the end, though not without considerable effort. When the game was over, he breathed a sigh of relief."

On the contrary, Leo Tolstoy's passion in youth was card play and a very expensive passion it proved. It was only when he married that he gave up games of chance and went over to chess, which he played till the end of his days.

He liked the game to be keen, played with imagination; he went in for complex combinations and often defeated his partner with an ingenious mate. He yet had a very modest opinion of his abilities. He considered himself a weak player, was irritated by his own mistakes and really grieved when he lost. He greatly appreciated the beauty of the game and held chess masters in high esteem.

Here are a few of his opinions:

"I like chess because it is a good way of relaxing: true, it makes you use your brain, but in a specific and original way."

"One's main concern should not be to win at all costs but to go in for interesting combinations. Chess is a fine entertainment: when playing you feel fatigue falling away from you and you forget your troubles."

"When playing chess one should remember that the essence of the game is not in making sharp, unexpected and risky moves, but in calculating so as to make the whole set of chessman move forward harmoniously."

Among Polish classic novelists, Bolesław Prus and Henryk Sienkiewicz were both chess players. Prus also liked watching chess and would sit patiently watching others play for hours. He used to drop into a Warsaw café where chess enthusiasts gathered. The author of "The Puppet" was a close friend of chess champion Szymon Winawer and played with him at the Semadeni café near the Warsaw 'Teatr Wielki.' Sienkiewicz, author of "Quo Vadis," when in San Francisco, invited Captain Rudolf Korwin-Piotrowski to play him every evening. Piotrowski was well known among the Polish emigrants as a swashbuckling, original character. He became the prototype of Pan Zagloba, one of the main characters in Sienkiewicz's "Trilogy." Perhaps this was the reason why Sienkiewicz endowed his hero with a coat of arms originating from chess?

Karol Irzykowski, an outstanding Polish writer and critic, participated in tournaments at Cracow Chess Club and did well. Flamberg, the champion of Warsaw, was in one tournament in which Irzykowski did not intend to participate at first, only joining in the second round, yet winning the fourth place in the end. Here is an excerpt from a report on this tournament:

"This romantic of the chessboard who, above all, looked for the strange beauty enchained in the 64 squares that called up a splendid series of images in his dreaming head, was over-burdened with professional duties and did not feel equal to taking on this hard challenge, so he declined to take part in the tournament. After the first round, when Mr. Ameisen withdrew, Irzykowski,

A set of chessmen owned by the Polish painter Jan Matejko, in his former study in Cracow, now housing the Matejko Museum.

James Jones, a contemporary American writer, studies the theory of the game in his spare time.

The British film actress, Belinda Lee, played chess not only on the screen but also for pleasure, after work (A 1958 photograph).

230

drunk with the battle going on around him, took Mr. Ameisen's place and proved that modesty always goes hand in hand with skill. In the three games he played with particular finesse, he was not defeated once, not even by the powerful guest player Flamberg, with whom he drew, this was the only game the latter did not win. I look on Irzykowski as moral winner of the tournament."

Irzykowski's drama "The Victory" will be dealt with extensively in the next chapter. In her biography of that writer, H. M. Dobrowolska recalls the last years of his life in occupied Warsaw.

"... another passion of Irzykowski's was music, and next came chess. Recently he took part in a chess tournament organized in Warsaw (kept secret from the Germans — J. G.). He lamented the death of their best chess player, a Jew who was murdered by the Nazis in Warsaw, most probably in the Ghetto (this was the famous master Prze-piorka — J. G.). Towards the end of his life I sometimes found him sadly sitting over a chess-board without an opponent..."

Interested in chess matters from his early youth, he was on the Supreme Council of the Polish Chess Federation up till the war.

Franciszek Fiszer, the actors' friend, the most Bohemian of Warsaw Bohemians before and after the First World War, was a big chess player ("big" because of both his play and his extra-ordinary corpulence). He linked brilliant, almost Napoleonic attacks with a marked lack of patience and deliberation.

The English writer Lewis Carroll, author of the famous "Alice's Adventures in Wonderland" and its sequel with chess themes "Through the Looking-glass" solved chess problems and end-games as a relief from chronic insomnia.

Of contemporary Polish writers, let us mention Adam Ważyk, Melchior Wańkowicz, Stanisław Strumph–Wojtkiewicz, Marian Promiński and Jerzy Putrament; the latter was twice elected chairman of the Polish Chess Federation. He once remarked during an interview: "I like chess and find it a great pleasure to beat my colleagues at the game." "Those he could beat!" one or two

American film actors Cesar Romero and Walter Pidgeon having a game (1948).

Chessmen on a drum... Hollywood actor Fritz Feld (right) plays against the well known drummer Gene Krupa (1945).

of the more malicious of those colleagues were heard to remark.

Among French writers, André Stil, Tristan Tzara, Charles Dobzynsky, André Kédros and Eugene Guillevic are associated with chess. American chess-playing writers include James Jones who is as keen at analysis as at play.

Turning from literature to the fine arts, we find Rembrandt, Matejko and Repin among painters who relaxed in chess.

H. W. van Loon in his fictional biography tells of Rembrandt succumbing to chess quite unexpectedly. The book is written as reminiscences of a doctor friend of Rembrandt's.

"Rembrandt's meeting with my friends took place earlier than I expected.

"Saskia was confined to her bed. Rembrandt used to sit at her bedside and read the Bible. She knew she was going to die... she soon tired and fell asleep, lulled by her husband's voice... Rembrandt did not leave the room but occupied himself with various little jobs, for instance, correcting copper plates for engravings. He was shortsighted; working at his painting since early childhood had strained his eyes.

"So it was a relief to him to stop his work and we used to sit in Saskia's room playing dice. But even the noise of the dice rattling in the cup was irksome to her, so I mentioned to Rembrandt that I had been initiated into a most interesting game called 'chess' by Jean Louis and that this game, said to be the oldest of all, had been invented as an exercise for military commanders in Persia.

"Rembrandt was very interested in this game and asked me to arrange for Jean Louis to teach him it.

"I invited both of them to my home and they immediately became good friends...

"The rest of the evening was spent playing chess. Jean Louis brought a book he had obtained from Seville, written by a chess genius, Ruy

Soviet film artists: film director Alexander Stolper (left) and actor Alexey Dikiy at a friendly game (1949).

The German film director Kurt Hoffman enjoys a game of chess in the family circle (1960).

232

Franciszek Fischer and the poet Bolesław Leśmian in a Warsaw café. Cartoon by Jerzy Zaruba.

López. Following the indications contained in the book, he was checkmated by Bernard who had only started playing chess a month before. I was keen to see what Rembrandt's attitude towards chess would be. The previous evening, I had taught him the way the various pieces moved. He approached this completely new problem in the same way as he did his painting. A few days later I succeeded in getting his opinions.

" 'I like this new game, and I like your friend Jean Louis even more, doctor, and that is because when you play chess with a man you get to know his style... I don't know whether I have made myself clear. Every man has a 'style' of his own, a 'line.' Your Frenchman does everything he does in his own style. Even when he fries eggs. Even when he plays chess.'

"Rembrandt was soon to experience more pain and sorrow. Saskia's life was ebbing. I got two more doctors to come... We talked to her about painting and when she fell asleep we held a consultation. When the doctors went she was still asleep.

"Rembrandt and I sat down at the chessboard. His moves were planned and intelligent, but he was so absorbed with a combination in one corner of the board that he did not notice the danger threatening his pieces in another sector.

" 'Pay attention, or you'll lose your queen,' I warned him.

" 'Please, just a moment, I've got such a fine move here with the rook and the bishop, if you'd only be patient!'

" 'But you should play so as to win.'

" 'Of course, of course, but I can win this way too.'

" 'Are you sure?' And in one move, planned long before, I took the queen. The game was won.

" 'Let's have one more game, then you'll see.'

"He rose to look at the sleeping Saskia. She was dead."

There have been many chess players among musicians. The famous French chess champion

The Soviet film actor Nikolai Cherkasov playing with his son.

Two French film stars: Simone Signoret and Yves Montand.

American film actors: Anthony Quinn and Shirley Booth.

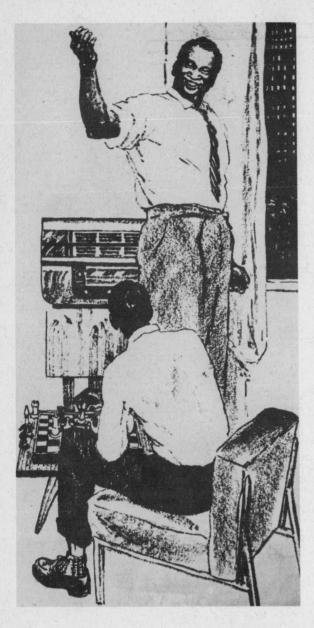

Paul Robeson and his son analysing a game of chess between Smyslov and Botvinnik. An illustration to the story "Joe Hill's Sunday" by the Soviet writer Boris Polevoy. Drawing by O. Vereysky ("Ogonyok").

Philidor was a composer. Beethoven and Chopin played chess. Ferenc Erkel, founder of the Hungarian national opera, liked it. The virtuoso Yehudi Menuhin plays chess almost as well as the violin. He could concentrate even in difficult conditions. It is said that at the age of twelve, after a recital at the Paris Opera House, he went to a café where he played chess and answered questions at the same time. The world famous Soviet composer and pianist Prokofiev was very keen on chess. When in Paris giving guest concerts in 1933, he could not refrain from the pleasure of joining Lasker's opponents in a session of simultaneous play that had been organized in the Café de la Régence. Prokofiev did not win, but this game was one of the most interesting played. In Warsaw before the war, he dropped in at the Chess Club as an observer after his concert in the Philharmonic Hall and met the famous Polish master Przepiorka, who gave him a book about chess with an inscription to mark their meeting. The Soviet violinist David Oistrakh is an excellent player. The well-known Warsaw composer and violinist Tadeusz Wroński invents chess problems, this being his all-absorbing hobby. Grigor Piatigorsky the cellist and his wife have financed a series of international chess tournaments of the highest calibre.

Film directors and actors supply us with a few anecdotes.

Recently the film town of Cinecittà, near Rome, was the scene of a fierce battle which lasted four hours; it took place on the chessboard and was between Vadim, who was shooting a new picture there, and the Soviet film director Bondarchuk, who was working on a new film with the Italian film director Rossellini. Vadim won; then Rossellini took up the cudgels for Bondarchuk and challenged Vadim to a return game. This was fought out in time stolen in between shots and lasted for a fortnight, ending with another victory for the Frenchman.

Fritz Feld, a comedy actor from Hollywood of German origin (from Berlin), has become

234

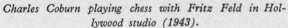

Charles Coburn playing chess with Fritz Feld in Hollywood studio (1943).

Chess in strange garb: actors waiting to go onto the set for a Polish film.

known for his persistent efforts to popularize chess among the artists in the American film capital. He keeps a chessboard in his dressing room, and entices some unsuspecting victims there, to suggest a quick game until the set is ready. Feld has played Charles Boyer, Lionel Barrymore, Humphrey Bogart, Douglas Fair-banks, junior, and many other stars. "Chess is not popular in Hollywood," he once said rather sadly (1948), "but there are always some stars eager to try their hand at it." And he philosophically added: "As long as there are film stars ready to spend an hour or two at chess, one can still hope for something good from this place!"

X. CHESS IN POETRY AND PROSE

A lithograph by Andrzej Jurkiewicz (1938).

From the earliest times, artists and writers have fallen under the spell of chess, so that it has become the subject, in fact the inspiration, of a great diversity of works of art and literature.

The famous Persian poet Firdausi when asked, a thousand years ago, why chess came into his poems, replied: "Its poetry inspires me."

Poems devoted partly or wholly to chess appear in English, Indian, Arabian, Persian, Chinese, Spanish, Italian, French, Scandinavian and other literature. Scholars have based valuable research on literary references to chess throughout the world; by examining the evolution of chess terms, they have often found it easier to establish the time when a given work was written, to establish foreign influences, manners and customs, ethnical indications, etc. The British orientalist H.J.R. Murray, in his fundamental work, "A History of Chess," makes extensive use of old literary works: reproductions of poems and excerpts from prose writings occupy quite a lot of its 900 pages.

Firdausi, who lived from 940 to 1020, finished his monumental work "Shah Nameh" ("The Book of Kings") nine hundred and sixty years ago. It tells the story of the Persian rulers up to the year 632. It describes the legendary birth of chess, according to which the game was invented by wise men who used it to convey to the mother of Prince Thalhand the news of how, unconquered in battle, he had fallen at the height of the fighting against the army of his twin brother Gen. The legend, which is entitled "Gen and Thalhand," contains a song known as "Preparing the Chessmen for Thalhand's Mother":

Those men of wisdom called for ebony
And two of them, ingenious counsellors
Constructed of that wood a board foursquare
To represent the trench and battlefield
And with both armies drawn up face to face
A hundred squares were traced upon the board
So that the kings and soldiers might manoeuvre.

Two hosts were carved of teak and ivory
And two proud kings with crowns and grace divine.
Both horse and foot were represented there
And drawn up in two ranks in war array,
The steeds, the elephants, the ministers
And warriors charging at the enemy
All combating as is done in war,
One in offence, another in defence.
The king was posted at the array's centre
With at one hand his loyal minister.
Next to these twain were placed two elephants
Supporting thrones, the hue of indigo;
Next to the elephants two camels stood
Whereon two men of holy counsel sat.
Next to the camels there were placed two steeds
With riders valiant on the battle day
And each wing ended in a warrior-rukh,
His liver's blood afoam upon his lips.
The footman's move was always to advance
That he might be of aidance in the fray
Till, having passed across the battlefield,
He sat — a minister — beside the king.
The minister might quit not too in battle
His king by more than by a single square,
But on three squares the noble elephant
Could move and for two miles survey the field.
The camel likewise moved three squares and raged
And snorted on the field of fight. The horse
Made too a three-square leap but in the move
Alighted on a square of diverse hue.
The warrior-rukh might traverse every way
And charge across the battle at his will.
They all contended in their proper lists
And each observed the limits of his move.
When one of them beheld the king in flight
Then would he shout and say 'Avaunt, oh king!'
Whereat the king would change his square till he
Was straitened where he stood. When rukh and horse
And minister and elephant and troops
Had blocked the way for him on every side
The king would look forth o'er that field foursquare
And see his men o'erthrown, their faces drawn,
Escape cut off by water and by trench

239

With foes to right and left and front and rear
And being moveless and foredone would die
For so the process of the heaven decreed.

Polish poetry has some matchless works on chess. Jan Kochanowski was a pioneer of poetry in his native language rather than in the previously universal Latin. One of his earliest poems, written four centuries ago, was entitled "Chess." The story soon unfolds. Tarses, King of Denmark, had a beautiful daughter, whom two suitors, Fiedor and Borzuj, both from Slav lands, were trying to win. They wanted to settle the matter by fighting a duel.

Tarses pointed to the chessboard and said:
Your tournament will take place in these lists.

The contest was set for two weeks ahead. Each competitor was given a copy of the rules of the game. The placing of the pieces on the board, their moves and all the other rules of the game are discussed down to the minutest detail.

The rivals came to the contest with hope in their hearts, but fear as well. The king gave a magnificent banquet and, after it was over, ordered a chessboard to be brought in. He appealed to the two contestants to play fairly and forbade the courtiers who had crowded round to interfere with the game in any way or make audible comment. Borzuj began to set out the white pieces, Fiedor the black ones. Lots were drawn, and Borzuj won the right to move first. That White should invariably move first is a comparatively modern convention.

The game that was to decide the fair maid's fate began. The rivals were not always able to control their nerves and soon came the first dispute: had a certain piece been touched or not?

Next Fiedor got into trouble for making an illegal move with his bishop. Players, onlookers, the poet himself all succumb to the tension. The fortunes of battle fluctuate to and fro. Attack, defence, counter-attack, strategy, losses and gains — all are described in detail.

The fight reaches a climax.

In the commotion, a knight of Borzuj's that had previously been captured somehow reappears in play. Borzuj is in disgrace but the struggle goes on and both try hard to avoid any further infringements of the rules.

Borzuj gets a new queen which naturally improves his prospects. Fiedor is in a bad way. Checkmate threatens. Night falls and the game is adjourned. The chessboard, with the pieces as they stand, is locked up in the chamber with guards on duty outside. Fiedor is depressed, thinking he has not the slightest chance of winning; his friends try to console him in vain. The princess, however, who had watched the game attentively throughout, had no intention of submitting meekly to her fate. The rival suitors were by no means equal in her eyes. With the help of her maid, she managed to steal in and examine the position. She saw a chance of victory for Fiedor. She reflected a moment, turned round a rook as to point its tusks in a particular direction as a sign, and stole from the chamber.

The rivals sat down at the chessboard again. The guards explained why the rook had been turned round. Very sure of himself, Borzuj awaited his turn to move. Fiedor thought long and profoundly. Suddenly his face lit up. Of course! The beautiful Anna had been right, and he mated his opponent in three moves.

Borzuj left the castle. He could not bear to wait to see the wedding.

This brief résumé of a poem which numbers 602 lines in all gives only a general idea of the scope of this original work; for original it was, in the fullest sense of the word. For long it was regarded as a translation of a poem in Latin by the Italian Marco Girolamo Vida. Even stranger, such Polish writers as Krasicki and Mickiewicz, not to mention a number of literary historians, when they did not call it a translation, called it "an imitation." It is enough to take Vida's work and compare it with Kochanowski's "Chess" to see that they were two separate works. Vida,

Frithiof playing chess. An illustration by M. Jurgielewicz to a chapter of "Frithiof's Saga" by Esaias Tegner.

Bishop of Alba in the Duchy of Montferrat, had written his "Scacchia ludus" about 1525. After it came out in print in 1527 (it has not been possible to ascertain whether there were earlier editions), it was translated repeatedly into Italian, French and English. Here is a summary of the plot:

Jupiter and all the Gods of Olympus were invited to the wedding feast of Ocean and Earth. After the feast, the God of the Sea ordered a chessboard to be brought in with beautiful chessmen made of boxwood and gave a pithy and delightful explanation of the game to the interested guests.

Not surprisingly, the gods took a liking to the game, and at Jupiter's orders, Apollo with the black pieces and Mercury with white sat down to a game surrounded by the Immortals, who had been committed to neutrality.

The game is a lively one. Mercury, seemingly inattentive, moves a pawn, and Apollo makes a sudden movement as though to take it, but Venus gives him a sign with her eyes. He withdraws from the intended move. This brings forth a heated protest from Mercury who then, by a wrong move with his bishop, worsens his situation, to the joy of all. Mars secretly replaces a bishop that had already been taken off the chessboard. Vulcan tells Apollo, Mars goes pale, and Jupiter orders the unfortunate onlooker — and the bishop — to be removed.

Both players lose their queens. Mercury promotes a pawn to another, which plays havoc among the black army; but through his eagerness to take one more pawn, he loses her through a double check by the knight. Apollo takes a rook, queens a pawn and starts the battle all over again, but loses the new queen too, by a double check. Then Mercury finally checkmates the black king...

This summary was given by M. Dzieduszycki in a treatise on the history of chess in Poland in 1856. He warmly maintained that Kochanowski's work was original. He conceded that Kochanowski had probably read Vida's poem when in Florence about 1550 and that he also

met the Bishop of Alba personally. The Polish poet probably borrowed his romantic theme from a work of Olaf Magnus, Archbishop of Uppsala, that was very well known at that time and which refers to the testing of rival suitors for a young lady's hand through a game of chess as an old Swedish custom.

Massmann (1839), the German chess historian, in a list of literary works on the game, quotes Kochanowski's poem as an original work; and Alliéy, a collector and lover of chess, Mayor of the department of Ardèche in France, published, in a small volume in 1851 his translations of four poems about chess by Vida, Kochanowski, Jones and Fischer respectively, which he obviously regarded as separate works.

Kochanowski's poem was finally accepted as an original work. Chlebowski, a historian of Polish literature of the last century, expressed

Russian ivory chessmen from the time of Ivan the Terrible (16th century). From Platt's collections.

the general opinion of today, that the young poet's artistic feeling infused the whole with such vitality, wit, courtliness and grace, as to turn a dry lecture on the rules of chess into a tale full of charm.

In an edition brought out in 1918, Henryk Galle derides an often repeated theory that the poem had a hidden political allusion, that Tarses, King of Denmark, was really King Zygmunt August, the Princess Anna his sister Anna Jagiellonka; and Fiedor and Borzuj (the suitors for Anna's hand in marriage) the Danish Prince Magnus and the Tsar Ivan the Terrible.

A historian of Polish literature, Julian Krzyżanowski, pointed out among the poet's merits, the independent spirit, originality and good literary taste, revealed in the way he removes the scene from the heights of Olympus to the court of the Danish King, replacing mythical personalities by human beings in the persons of two young rivals for a beautiful princess and, moreover, making his rhymed story radiant with flashes of real humour, which the reader of the original Polish still finds irresistible today.

Though many attempts have been made to reconstruct the game the poem describes, the problem has proved intractable. Something can be made of the last few moves only. In 1912, the Polish chess magazine "Szachista Polski" announced a competition for the best effort on these lines. Only one entry was received; it came from an Aleksander Wagner and went to 77 moves. Professor S. Gorawski devoted long hours of arduous work to the problem, his solution, delayed by the First World War, appearing in the same magazine twenty years later.

For another poem on chess we have to go back some centuries. Rabbi Abraham Aben-Ezra, doctor, astrologist and poet, who lived in Spain in the 12th century, wrote a poem about chess in Hebrew which was translated into Latin by Thomas Hyde in 1689. Another well known poem, "Caissa," was written in 1763 by a British poet William Jones, a student of Sanskrit engaged in research on ancient Indian literature (he was the first to publish the Indian source material on *chaturanga*). The story is taken from mythology: Mars, the God of war, succeeds in winning the favours of the dryad Caissa only when he invents the game of chess. "Caissa" as the name of the mythical goddess of chess has become more famous since than the poem itself.

Now swell th'embattl'd troops with hostile rage,
And clang their shields, impatient to engage;
When Daphnis thus: a vary'd plain behold.
Where Fairy Kings their mimic tents unfold,
As Oberon and Mab, his wayward Queen,
Lead forth their armies on the daisy'd green:
No mortal hand the wond'rous sport contriv'd, —
By gods invented, and from gods deriv'd.
From them the British nymphs receiv'd the game,
And play each morn beneath the crystal Thame.
Hear then the tale which they to Colin sung,
As idling o'er the lucid wave he hung: —
A lovely Dryad rang'd the Thracian wild,
Her air enchanting and her aspect mild:
To chace the bounding hart was all her joy, —
Averse from Hymen and the Cyprian boy;
O'er hills and vallies was her beauty fam'd,
And fair Caissa was the damsel nam'd.
Mars saw the maid; with deep surprise he gaz'd,
Admir'd her shape, and ev'ry gesture prais'd:
His golden bow the child of Venus bent,
And through his breast a piercing arrow sent.
The reed was Hope, the feathers keen Desire,
The point her eyes, the barbs ethereal fire.
Soon to the nymph he pour'd his tender strain:
The haughty Dryad scorn'd his am'rous pain.
He told his woes where'er the maid he found,
And still he press'd, yet still Caissa frown'd:
But e'en her frowns (ah! what might smiles have
                                                    done!)
Fir'd all his soul, and all his senses won!(...)
A Naiad heard him from her mossy bed,
And through the crystal rais'd her placid head,
Then mildly spake: "O thou whom love inspires,
"Thy tears will nourish, not allay the fires!

"The smiling blossoms drink the pearly dew,
"And rip'ning fruit the feather'd race pursue;
"The scaly shoals devour the silken weeds,
"Love on our sighs and on our sorrow feeds." (…)
"Canst thou no play, no soothing game devise,
"To make thee lovely in the damsel's eyes?" (…)
"Kind Nymph," said Mars, "thy counsel I approve;
"Art, only art, her ruthless breast can move; —
"But when? or how? thy dark discourse explain:
"So may thy stream ne'er swell with guishing rain!
"So may thy waves in one pure current flow,
"And flow'rs eternal on thy border blow!"
   To whom the maid reply'd, with smiling mien:
"Above the palace of the Paphian queen
"Lov's brother dwells, — a boy of graceful sort,
"By gods nam'd Euphron, and by mortals, Sport;
"Seek him; to faithful ears unfold thy grief,
"And hope, ere morn return, a sweet relief:
"His temple hangs below the azure skies —
"Seest thou yon argent cloud? Tis there it lies."
This said, she sunk beneath the liquid plain,
And sought the mansion of her blue-hair'd train.
Meantime the god, elate with heartfelt joy,
Had reach'd the temple of the sportful boy:
He told Caissa's charms, his kindled fire,
The naiads counsel, and his warm desire. —
"Be swift," he added, "give my passion aid;
"A god requests." — He spake, and Sport obey'd:

He fram'd a tablet, of celestial mold,
Inlaid with squares of silver and of gold;
Then of two metals form'd the warlike band,
That here compact in show of battle stand:
He taught the rules that guide the pensive game,
And call'd it Caissa, from the dryad's name
(Whence Albion's sons, who most its praise confess,
Approv'd the play, and nam'd it thoughtful Chess).
   The god, delighted, thank'd indulgent Sport;
Then grasp'd the board, and left his airy court.
With radiant feet he pierc'd the clouds; nor staid,
Till in the woods he saw the beauteous maid:
Tir'd with chace, the damsel sat reclin'd,
Her girdle loose, her bosom unconfin'd.
He took the figure of a wanton fawn,

And stood before her on the flow'ry lawn;
Then shew'd his tablet: pleas'd, the nymph survey'd
The lifeless troops, in glitt'ring ranks display'd;
She ask'd the wily sylvan to explain
The various motions of the splendid train;
With eager heart she caught the winning lore,
And thought e'en Mars less hateful than before: —
"What spell," said she, "deceiv'd my careless mind?
"The god was fair, and I was most unkind."
She spoke and saw the changing fawn assume
A milder aspect, and a fairer bloom;
His wreathing horns, that from his temples grew,
Flow'd down in curls of bright celestial hue;
The dappled hairs that veil'd his loveless face,
Blaz'd into beams, and shew'd a heavenly grace;
The shaggy hide that mantled o'er his breast,
Was soften'd to a smooth transparent vest,
That through its folds his vig'rous bosom shew'd,
And nervous limbs, where youthful ardour glow'd
(Had Venus view'd him in those blooming charms,
Not Vulcan's net had forc'd her from his arms);
With goat-like feet no more he mark'd the ground,
But braided flow'rs his silken sandals bound. —
The dryad blush'd; and, as he press'd her, smil'd,
Whilst all his cares one tender glance beguil'd.

   He ends: "To arms!" the maids and striplings cry;
"To arms!" the groves and sounding vales reply.
Sirena led to war the swarthy crew,
And Delia those that bore the lily's hue. —
Who first, O Muse! began the bold attack;
The white refulgent, or the mournful black?
Fair Delia first, as fav'ring lots ordain,
Moves her pale legions tow'rd the sable train:
From thought to thought her lively fancy flies,
Whilst o'er the board she darts her sparkling eyes.

   At length the warrior moves, with haughty strides,
Who from the plain the snowy King divides:
With equal haste his swarthy rival bounds;
His quiver rattles, and his buckler sounds. —
Ah, hapless youth! with fatal warmth you burn;
Laws, ever fix'd, forbid you to return!
Then from the wing a short-liv'd Spearman flies

"Chess composition." A photograph by the American photographer Ben Rose for the Magazine "Town and Country" (1954).

245

Unsafely bold — and, see! — He dies — he dies!
The dark-brow'd hero, with one vengeful blow,
Of life and place deprives his iv'ry foe.
Now rush both armies o'er the burnish'd field,
Hurl the swift dart, and rend the bursting shield.
Here furious Knights on fiery coursers prance;
Here Archers spring, and lofty tow'rs advance. —
But, see! the white-rob'd Amazon beholds
Where the dark host its op'ning van unfolds:
Soon as her eyes discerns the hostile maid,
By ebon shield and ebon helm betray'd,
Seven squares she passes, with majestic mien,
And stands, triumphant, o'er the fallen Queen.
Perplex'd and sorrowing at his Consort's fate,
The Monarch burn'd with rage, despair, and hate:
Swift from his zone th'avenging blade he drew;
And, mad with ire, the proud virago slew:
— Meanwhile, sweet smiling Delia's wary King
Retir'd from fight, behind the circling wing.

Long time the war in equal balance hung,
Till, unforeseen, an iv'ry courser sprung;
And, wildly prancing, in an evil hour
Attack'd at once the Monarch and the tow'r.
Sirena blush'd; for, as the rules requir'd,
Her injur'd Sov'reign to his tent retir'd;
Whilst her lost Castle leaves his threat'ning height,
And adds new glory to th'exulting Knight.
   At this, pale fear oppress'd the drooping maid,
And on her cheek the rose began to fade;
A crystal tear, that stood prepar'd to fall,
She wip'd in silence, and conceal'd from all;
— From all but Daphnis: he remark'd her pain,
And saw the weakness of her ebon train;
Then gently spoke: "Let me your loss supply,
"And either nobly win, or nobly die;
"Me oft has fortune crown'd with fair success,
"And led to triumph in the fields of Chess."
He said: the willing nymph her place resign'd;

246

And sat at distance, on the bank reclin'd:
Thus when Minerva call'd her chief to arms,
And Troy's high turrets shook with dire alarms,
The Cyprian goddess, wounded, left the plain,
And Mars engag'd mightier force in vain.

Straight Daphnis leads his squadron to the field
(To Delia's arms' tis e'en a joy to yield);
Each guileful snare and subtle art he tries,
But finds his art less powerful than her eyes:
Wisdom and strength superior charms obey;
And beauty, beauty wins the long fought day.
By this a hoary Chief, on slaughter bent,
Approach'd the gloomy King's unguarded tent
Where late his Consort spread dismay around,
Now her dark corpse lies bleeding on the ground.
Hail, happy youth! thy glories not unsung,
Shall live eternal on the poet's tongue;
For thou shalt soon receive a splendid change,
And o'er the plain with nobler fury range.
The swarthy leaders saw the storm impend,
And strove, in vain, their Sov'reign to defend:
Th' invader wav'd his silver lance in air,
And flew, like lightning, to the fatal square;
His limbs dilated, in a moment grew
To stately height, and widen'd to the view;
More fierce his look, more lion-like his mien,
Sublime he mov'd, and seem'd a warrior Queen.

As when the sage, on some unfolding plant,
Has caught a wand'ring fly, or frugal ant,
His hand the microscopic frame applies,
And, lo! a bright-hair'd monster meets his eyes;
He sees new plumes in slender cases roll'd,
Here stain'd with azure, there bedropp'd with gold:
Thus on the alter'd Chief both armies gaze,
And both the Kings are fix'd with deep amaze.
The sword which arm'd the snow-white Maid before,
He now assumes, and hurls the spear no more;
Then springs, indignant, on the dark-rob'd band,
And Knights and Archers feel his deadly hand.
Now flies the Monarch of the sable shield,
His legions vanquish'd, o'er the lonely field:
So when the morn, by rosy courses drawn,

With pearls and rubies sows the verdant lawn:
Whilst each pale star from Heav'n's blue vault retires,
Still Venus gleams, and last of all expires:
He hears, where'er he moves, the dreadful sound —
Check! the deep vales, and Check! the woods rebound.
No place remains: he sees the certain fate,
And yields his throne to ruin and Checkmate.

A brighter blush o'erspreads the damsel's cheeks,
And milder, thus the conquer'd stripling speaks: —
"A double triumph, Delia, hast thou won,
"By Mars protected, and by Venus' son;
"The first with conquest crowns by matchless art,
"The second points those eyes at Daphnis' heart."
She smil'd; the nymphs and am'rous youths arise,
And own that beauty gain'd the nobler prize.
Low in their chest the mimic troops were laid,
And peaceful slept the sable Hero's shade.

"Frithiof's Saga," a beautiful poem by the Swedish writer Esaias Tegner, who began to publish his works in the first half of the 19th century, has also become world famous.

Tegner gave literary form to sagas that had been passed down for generations by word of mouth, the oldest dating back to the 7th century though most are from the 12th or 13th — the golden age of the sagas. The sixth song "Frithiof Plays Chess" describes a game between Frithiof and his friend Björn. Old Hilding comes in. There is a conversation about the situation in the country, about political matters and personal affairs. Frithiof is in love with the royal princess Ingeborg. The whole conversation echoes with allusions to chess, for instance, "The king is in danger, only the peasants (pawns) can save him."

There are deliberate anachronisms. In Frithiof's days, the 7th and 8th centuries, chess was not known in Scandinavia. Nor was the name "queen" introduced until many centuries later, this piece being for a long time — when chess did come — the vizier or its equivalent, and not by any means the strongest piece.

Here is, substantially, the entire "song":

Frithiof plays chess

By the chessboard, fair to view,
Frithiof sat with Björn the true;
Squares of silver decked the frame,
Interchanged with squares of gold.

Hilding entering, thus he greeted —
"On the upper bench be seated,
Drain the horn until my game
I finish, foster-father bold."

Hilding quoth: "Here come I speeding,
For King Bele's sons entreating;
Danger daily sounds more near,
And the people's hope art thou."

"Björn," quoth Frithiof, "Now beware
Ill thy king dath seem to fare.
A pawn may free him from this fear
So scruple not to let it go."

"Court not, Frithiof, king's displeasure
Though with Ring they ill may measure.
Eagle's young have wings of power
And their strength thy strength outvies."

"If, Björn, thou wilt my tower beset,
Thus easily thy wiles I meet.
No longer canst thou gain my tower
Which back to place of safety hies."

"Ingeborg, in Baldur's keeping,
Passeth all her days in weeping.
Thine aid in strife may she not claim,
Tearful maiden, azure-eyed?"

"What wouldst thou, Björn? Assail my queen
Which dear from childhood's days hath been —
The noblest piece in all the game?
Her I'll defend, whate'er betide."

"What! Frithiof, wilt thou not reply?
And shall thy foster-father hie
Unheeded from thy hearth away
Because thy game is long to end?"

Then stood Frithiof up, and laid
His hand in Hilding's hand and said
"Already hast thou heard me say
What answers to their prayers I send.

"Go, let the sons of Bele learn
That, since my suit they dared to spurn
No bond between us shall be tied;
Their serf I never shall become."

"Well! follow on thy proper path;
Ill fits it me to chide thy wrath!
All to some good may Odin guide"
Said Hilding, and he hied him home.

Two of Jan Staudinger's epigrams touched on chess.

Execute kings! It is their lot.
Only one is immortal: the king in chess.

They say that chess, as cards, has kings and
queens.
What of the aces? They play too!

It is impossible to do justice in translation to the word-music and neatness of phrase of these poems. Boris Pasternak, Nobel-prize winner, in his poem "Marburg," achieved a delicacy of imagery which sets even harder problems. No translation could do justice to this lovely poem. Marburg was the German university town at which he studied. The last two verses describe, in the form of a chess metaphor, the poet's sleepless nights in the town of Grimm and Luther.

The nights are playing chess with me
On the parquet moonlit floor.
There is the scent of acacia blossom through
windows open wide

And emotion, like a witness, grows grey in the corner.
The poplar is the king. I play with sleeplessness.
The queen is a nightingale. I reach out to it
But night wins the game, the pieces step aside
And I recognize the face of the white morning.

Note by B. H. Wood:

That aristocratic litterateur Lord Dunsany, a magnificent patron of chess in Ireland in his day, more than once touched on chess in his stories; he was no mean player. Here are two of his poems contributed to my magazine in 1942–3:

"Bartolomeo fell madly in love with her." Illustration by M. Berezowska for L. Niemojowski's story "Check and Checkmate."

A cloistral room I've seen
Where hangs a hush sublime;
And men sit calm and keen
And almost free from Time

Though forty clocks are there
And twenty of them tick,
Till all the smoky air
Forgets their rhetoric

And round that room the cares
Of troubled days and o'er
The long street, set their snares;
But none come through the door.

The reference in verse two to chess-clocks is indeed neat.

The second was an epitaph on Capablanca, with a reference back to war days:

Now rests a mind as keen,
A vision bright and clear.
As any that has been.
'And who is it lies here?'

One that, erstwhile, no less
Than Hindenburg could plan
But played his game of chess
And did no harm to man.

Among the many German poems devoted to chess (Alfred Kiefer compiled a noteworthy anthology) "The Chess Knight" by Ferdinand Freiligrath, a revolutionary poet of the last century, is important.

In 1913 a poetic description of a duel at chess by a Polish author, Aleksander Zdanowicz, entitled "A Game of Chess with Mr. Rembach" had a chess diagram incorporated into the text, to illustrate the final position. The author added a problem of his own composition. The story is uncomplicated. The author visits a Mr. Rembach at Wieliczka and is persuaded to play chess with him. He gets badly beaten but eagerly starts a return game which he also loses. In a third, Mr. Rembach again gets a distinct advantage. The game is described in detail. The struggle is a stubborn one. Finally...

"There was silence. Two kings, two black pawns and one white knight only were left...

"Mr. Rembach was sure of victory... but he allowed his concentration to desert him. Instead of advancing his king, he threw forward the pawn. I saw I could trap his king. On came his pawn in threatening style... but with my knight I check-mated him."

A poem "Death" by the outstanding Polish poet Julian Tuwim, which builds up an atmosphere of hopeless boredom in a small town, is composed against a background of games of chess between two old adversaries, the doctor and the priest.

"Two friends are playing chess, muttering to themselves things like 'If I take your pawn, I can defend myself with the knight' and so on. Whilst they play, Death appears at the window. The players hear him but are too engrossed to open the door for him. The doctor takes a pawn... 'There is somebody at the door now.' 'Let him knock,' says the priest: 'I am going to take your rook.' The doctor: 'I've lost again. This is tedious. More wine, Mary!' "

Bezyminsky's poem "Chess" (Moscow 1927) passes from an exposition of the rules of the game through analogies with life, to deliberations on the fate of the world and the prospects of the Russian revolution.

Anatol Stern's "Piłsudski" strays further into politics than chess. It has one particularly weird feature, the use of the word "Capablanca" as a metaphor for "hunger."

Ho Chi Minh, leader of the Viet Cong in the Vietnam war, was a gifted poet and whilst in prison for his political activities in 1942–3, composed a poem about chess:

We play chess just to pass the time
But knights and infantry perish in thousands.

250

Storming attacks, controlled retreat;
Skill, impetuosity — these assure victory.

Understand the whole, weigh up the chances;
Once you've decided, strike without pause.
Hold back your rooks — you might miscalculate.
At time a pawn leads all to victory.

At the start the two sides' powers are equal
But in the end only one can win.
Attack, defend with stubbornness
And the leader's banner will be honoured by the
people.

In 1957, the Polish poet Dworak paid a rare compliment to Botvinnik in the form of a sonnet addressed to the World Champion:

Two pairs of eyes are riveted on the board
On which there will be military engagements.
Here all the centuries from Homer, from Diogenes

Are deciding what we shall play...
A hand is stretched out. The armies clash.
Botvinnik has well assessed the mental flights
That Alekhine — Alexander the Great — has
created.
A hand stretches out. Their eyes stray to the clock.
Oh mighty thoughts! About this game
Mickiewicz* wrote 'The throne of kings is cast
down —
In a world of inspiration and harmony.'

The grand master has woven a net of moves;
A piece of wood is moved five centimetres
Yet in that moment, the womb of continents is
convulsed.

Mentions of chess in prose are overwhelmingly numerous. Chess stories and excerpts from novels

---

* Adam Mickiewicz (1798-1855), an outstanding Romantic poet and political writer.

could fill a library. We must confine ourselves to work of real literary merit.

To the interesting short stories of Karol Libelt and Ludwik Niemojowski, Polish writers of the last century, we have already referred.

Libelt's story, entitled "The Game of Chess," is modelled on the Italian novels of the 16th century. The hero of the story is a young man Anastasio. As a child he was saved after shipwreck by a mysterious doctor-alchemist, who taught him mathematics, and on dying bequeathed him one hundred sequins. The young man set out on a journey to Syracuse, Naples and Rome. But his fortune was short-lived; the money flowed like water, for Anastasio indulged all his fancies, and one day he found he had not enough money left to pay his hotel bill. He had come to his senses too late. So he decided to sell something of the personal possessions inherited from his mysterious guardian, pay his debts and go to Palermo to earn his living by teaching mathematics.

"...The first question was, what could he spare? His mathematical instruments? No, they would be needed for teaching. Clothes? He had given away his old ones and he could not sell the new ones. Suddenly he cried: 'The chessmen! I can manage without them. I'll find somebody who is interested enough to give me a little money, for them...'

Illustration by D. Mróz to Stefan Zweig's story "The Royal Game."

"Before parting with them, he decided to have one more look at the chessmen and took them out of their case. Then he noticed, wrapped round the edges of the chessboard, a paper on which closer scrutiny revealed drawings of over a dozen chessboards marked with different combinations. There was an almost illegible sentence in the doctor's handwriting which he finally deciphered to read: 'An infallible way of winning every game of chess.'

"Then Anastasio remembered that he had often played chess with the doctor and had lost every time. He became so absorbed that he spent several hours in study, completely lost to the passage of time. Suddenly he remembered he must go and pay his debts. With a sigh, he took his purse, put the case of chessmen under his arm and went downstairs. Some old friends were there. Embarrassed to confess his plight before them, he cried out with feigned surprise: 'The deuce! I've forgotten to bring one more sequin; I'll bring it later. But now, look at this lovely set of chessmen. Would anybody like to play me a game?'

" 'Chess?' said Pescatini, the hotel keeper: 'Indeed I will: we'll play for the sequin so you may not have to trouble yourself going up for it again.'

" 'He'll have to go up for two sequins,' said somebody. 'You are an excellent chess player, Signor Pescatini.'

"Anastasio thought: 'In my situation, what is there between one sequin and two?' He accepted the challenge. He lost several pawns, all according to the doctor's precepts, but then checkmated and won.

" 'Per Baccho!' cried the hotel proprietor, slapping his bald head, while those present laughed heartily. 'Fancy me letting myself get caught so easily, but we'll play again, I double the stake.'

"Anastasio planned his moves carefully, the game took a little longer, both players brisk and alert, one taking a piece then the other, until finally...

" 'You're checkmated again, Signor Pescatini!' cried the spectators.

" 'Am I getting stupid? Am I drunk?' cried the hotel proprietor angrily, to the general amusement. 'I'll raise the stake and play for six times as much, young man!'

" 'All right,' said Anastasio, who was beginning to have more and more confidence in the doctor's method.

"So the battle began again. There were pauses tense with strained attention; the game was balanced for long on a knife edge. Signor Pescatini was no mean opponent; but at length Anastasio, by a brilliant triple sacrifice, was able to deal a deadly blow. 'Your king and queen are both under attack!' he cried. A few more moves and Signor Pescatini was again checkmated.

" 'This is unbelievable!' cried the hotel proprietor banging his fist on the table in a rage. 'Do you mind if I raise the stake again? We'll play for the rest of these twenty four sequins. Do you agree signor?'

" 'Why not, indeed?' replied Anastasio. The hotel proprietor put the gold in the centre of the table and they began to play again. The game took longer than any of its predecessors. Pescatini had obviously learnt to deal with the combinations already employed, yet only a few minutes passed before Anastasio again delivered checkmate. The onlookers laughed heartily, and Pescatini walked up and down the room in silence. Then another man, one of those present, sat down to play with Anastasio, who won every time. Upstairs in his room, Anastasio counted his winnings; his purse now contained 90 sequins..."

The next day, the hotel proprietor came to him with a proposition. He was to pass himself off as a foreigner, a champion of the royal game, and could earn a nice tempting income. "A fine chess player is lauded more today than a virtuoso or an artist. The whole world wants to know him, to see him," said Pescatini persuasively, offering his services as manager and partner. "You will play with everybody for a stake not less than ten sequins, and we shall charge half a sequin each to spectators."

There followed a series of triumphs for Anastasio. He won fame, popularity and a fortune, but was also the object of hate and intrigue. He tried to win the hand of his beloved Erminia, but her uncle, the powerful Doge of Venice, had him imprisoned on the charge of being a cheat. The price of his release was disclosure of his secret of winning. But Erminia organized his escape. They eloped together and, far from the noise of the great world, were very happy.

Anastasio started teaching mathematics and never played chess again. Pointing to Erminia, he used to declare his last move to have been the most fortunate in his life.

Niemojowski's story "Check and Checkmate" is in a different style, weirdly grotesque. The adventures of a chess genius Bartolomeo arise from his pathological passion for the game. The defeat of the chess "automaton," which climaxes the story, we have already quoted. Earlier he writes:

"... The story of his (Bartolomeo's) life was simple and short. His only passion, chess, brought about his downfall."

"The son of a rich merchant, who brought him up in keeping with his rank, he was sent to work by his father in the counting house of one of the most eminent bankers... but the banker demanded great accuracy from his young assistants, and the would-be financier, who had already acquired a passion for chess at school, often forgot his duties. However often he promised to reform, at the sight of a chessboard he would succumb again.

"One day, he was given a very important financial operation to handle, whose success or failure depended on quick completion of the work. The young man, remembering his promises, got down to work at once. Unfortunately, however, he had hardly sat down at his desk, when he saw a chessboard in the corner, left behind and forgotten by a visiting clerk.

"The sight of the chessboard aroused the passion latent in his soul.

" 'Just one game,' he said softly to the colleague working with him.

"His colleague allowed himself to be persuaded. Bartolomeo played like a champion — after a dozen or so moves, he gained the advantage. 'Check!' he cried in triumph.

" 'And checkmate!' said the banker, entering at that moment, seeing the important papers scattered about on the desk.

"The incorrigible chess player was not only dismissed himself, but caused his colleague to lose his job too.

"The story of this incident got around. From that time on, no business wanted to employ a young man so forgetful of his duties. Bartolomeo's father would not take him into his own counting house either but got the idea that a wife might reform him.

" 'That's the only way,' he thought to himself, 'to rid him of this ruinous passion. The beautiful form of the queen of his heart' — he said jokingly to his friends, 'will make him forget about the bony form of the chess queen.'

"He chose a wife for his son himself. She was the daughter of a rich factory owner with whom the old merchant had traded for many years. What is more, the young man not only did not object to the planned marriage, as is usually the case when parents take the matter into their own hands, but on seeing the bride his father had chosen for him, fell madly in love with her.

"Everything seemed to favour the plans. Unfortunately, the bride's father was a keen chess player, who spent all his spare time at the game. Unlike his future son-in-law, who was a champion, he played very badly. Moreover, being very conceited, he would not admit his mistakes and blamed his opponent for them, never forgiving anybody who beat him.

"As he was rich and influential, his friends, knowing his weakness, deliberately lost to him. A good dinner, a bottle of excellent Lacrima Christi, or even some financial service, were sufficient reward for their docility.

254

"But Bartolomeo could not bring himself to play like this. His passion for chess blinded him to the promptings of reason. Despite the warnings of his father, who, overjoyed at the coming marriage which had already been settled, trembled to think what would happen if the factory owner were to be offended, the young man beat him every time.

"On the day set for the announcement of the young people's engagement, before the ceremony of exchanging rings began, the host, father of the bride-to-be, said to the guests that had gathered for the occasion:

" 'First of all, I must convince every man present that my future son-in-law is just a beginner at chess, compared to me.'

"The injustice of this remark cut the young man to the quick.

"They sat down at the table, and each set out his chessmen. Bartolomeo, flaming with indignation at his opponent's conceit, was blind to his father's imploring glances and warning gestures.

"After eight or nine moves, the superiority of his position was evident. 'There is still time!' his father whispered to him, 'Lose the game, for God's sake lose the game!'

"But Bartolomeo heard nothing. His pawns penetrated into the very centre of the enemy's ranks like black devils...

" 'Steady now!' Bartolomeo laughed mockingly, as he took the knight.

"The factory owner's eyes became bloodshot, a shudder ran down his spine, and a suppressed groan escaped him.

" 'And now we shall see who knows how to play and who is a beginner,' Bartolomeo cried in triumph, moving a pawn.

" 'Checkmate!' The game ended.

" 'Checkmate!' shouted the bride's father in a rage, jumping up from the table and throwing the chessmen to the floor. 'Checkmate, but you, you scoundrel, for beating such an excellent chess player as I am by a trick, you will never marry my daughter.'

"All the efforts the distressed merchant made to save the situation were of no avail. After this affront, the intended father-in-law refused even to look at the man who had beaten him. After a year had passed he gave the hand of his daughter in marriage to a painter. The artist was poor, he had no talent at all, but he had one invaluable quality: he lost every game of chess to his father-in-law..."

Illustration by D. Mróz to Stefan Zweig's story "The Royal Game."

256

Composition on the theme of chess. Drawing by Jerzy Skarżyński.

This story, numbering more than fifty pages of print, not only brings some striking, fantastic action based on the chess theme, but also a profound dramatic effect through the rhythmic repetition of the cry "Checkmate," at the decisive moments in the life of the unfortunate hero. The final scene falls into the pattern almost uncannily:

"... Yes, it was he — Bartolomeo; but the change that several months of illness had wrought was even more terrible than that which had made such an unpleasant impression on me previously.

"When we entered the little room, he was sitting on the bed and moving pawns on the chessboard in front of him. Looking at his emaciated body, nobody would believe that not so long before he had been a picture of health and physical strength... He did not see us coming in, did not hear me when I spoke to him, did not realize what was happening around him.

"He just went on moving the chessmen from square to square: his moves were violent, quick and feverish; mechanical, involuntary moves, terrible to see.

"He was playing his last game of chess with himself!

"A moment or two later, his eyes became fixed, he put out his hand and made one more move; his head fell back heavily on the pillow and from his open mouth came a cry of triumph: 'In check, checkmate!'

"Those were his last words. When we reached his side, the poor fellow was dead..."

A description of a mania for chess that took hold of a man because of unusual circumstances is described in masterly fashion, taking the reader to the borderline of psychological weirdness, by the Austrian writer Stefan Zweig in his story "The Royal Game."

This story was found among Zweig's papers after his death in 1940. It was first published in Stockholm in 1943, then translated into many languages. In Poland, it was printed in the weekly "Przekrój," with fine illustrations by Daniel Mróz which we reproduce. In spite of this great literary success, a film based on the story (1960) failed.

The great chess champion Mirko Centovic is on board a liner, going to Argentine for a chess tournament. The author is told of his fantastic career by a fellow passenger. Centovic was born in a small village on the Danube. Left an orphan, he was taken into the home of the local priest who brought him up. Mirko was not a bright boy; on the contrary, he was intellectually dull. In the evenings, he liked to watch the men playing chess. One day, he happened to beat the village bailiff and his guardian, causing quite a sensation in the village. He was taken to town and placed under the care of Count Simczic, a chess enthusiast. Mirko went from success to success, studied the theory of chess and made it his career. He won many prizes and titles, finally becoming an international champion... He was an original character. Not very intelligent, what intellect he had was underdeveloped; he had no idea of mathematics and very little imagination, but at the chessboard he became another person, one who thought logically and shrewdly.

The author became interested and tried to get in touch with Centovic who, however, avoided people, keeping to himself. All he did was study chess. This only increased the author's curiosity. One of the passengers, a Mr. McIver, challenged Centovic to a game. Centovic said that he would play only for a stake. Conditions were agreed; the stake was to be pretty high. Mr. McIver sat down, lost and asked for a return match in which five other chess players were to consult with him. He lost this game too. McIver's blood was up. He asked for another game, and suggested doubling the stake. The champion agreed. And this time too, it looked like defeat for McIver when a certain Doctor B. who had kept silent so far, came up and suggested an unexpected move to the consultants, obviously seeing several moves ahead. This time, the champion had met his match, and had a hard job to draw.

257

The champion was shaken. He had risked his prestige on the eve of a tournament. Now it was he who demanded a game, with the Doctor, but the latter who seemed unknown to the rest of the passengers, did not want to play, explaining that he had not sat down at a chessboard for twenty--five years. Nobody believed him. To the author, he then disclosed the story of his life.

He was an Austrian, who had been a barrister in Vienna, one of his duties being that of legal adviser to the management of several large estates. After Hitler's annexation of Austria, the fascists arrested him, thinking that he would have confidential knowledge of certain political and financial affairs. He was imprisoned and subjected to a peculiar torture: he was kept in solitary confinement, completely isolated in a room with no furniture, equipment or in fact any object whatever. The complete loneliness and emptiness of his cell became almost unbearable. Without books, pen or paper, solitary, deprived of the least possibility of occupying his mind, on top of all this, he was from time to time taken suddenly out of his cell for interrogation, where he was cross-questioned from all sides without respite in efforts to catch him out if he was lying, and wring a statement out of him.

"There was a door, a table, a bed, a chair, a wash-basin, a barred window. The door, however, remained closed night and day; the table remained bare of book, newspaper, pencil, paper; the window gave on a brick wall; my ego and my physical self were contained in a structure of nothingness. They had taken every object from me: my watch, that I might not know the time; my pencil, that I might not make a note; my pocket-knife, that I might not sever a vein; even the slight narcotic of a cigarette was forbidden me. Except for the warder, who was not permitted to address me or to answer a question, I saw no human face, I heard no human voice. From dawn to night there was no sustenance for eye or ear or any sense; I was alone with myself, with my body and four or five inanimate things, rescueless-

ly alone with table, bed, window and basin. I lived like a diver in his bell in the black ocean of this silence — like a diver, too, who is dimly aware that the cable to safety has already snapped and that may never be raised from the soundless depths. There was nothing to do, nothing to hear, nothing to see; about me everywhere and without interruption, there was nothingness, emptiness without space or time. I walked to and fro, and with me went my thoughts, to and fro, to and fro, ever again. But even thoughts, insubstantial as they seem, require an anchorage if they are not to revolve and circle around themselves; they too weigh down under nothingness. One waited for something from morn to eve and nothing happened. Nothing happened. One waited, waited, waited; one thought, one thought, one thought until one's temples smarted. Nothing happened. One remained alone. Alone. Alone..."

Dr B. was soon at the end of his tether. The Gestapo had nearly gained its end. At last he broke down and decided to tell what he knew. But... whilst waiting in the hall for interrogation, he succeeded at great risk in stealing a book from the pocket of a police official's coat that was hanging there. A book! What joy! To be able to concentrate one's mind on words, sentences, to see printed letters — what an occupation for his mind! But he was in for a bitter disappointment: this little book, the object of his dreams, secured at the risk of his life, turned out to be a chess textbook with a collection of a hundred and fifty examples of games played by champions. His first impulse was to throw the book out of the window. He was not a chess player. But as he had nothing to do he began to study the games, learnt how to keep the score and recalled now that he had tried the game when a schoolboy.

The blanket in his room had a check pattern. He made chessmen from bread, used them to play through the games described in the book and after a week or two was able to go through the games without using the chess "board"

and men, picturing all the play in his mind. He became proficient in playing the whole game from memory. He began to take a delight in beautiful combinations, to understand the subtle differences among champions in style and method. This was food for his mind at last. His mental equilibrium returned. He could think once more. When interrogated, he began to give logical answers instead of parrying his persecutors' catch-questions as of old.

"...This happy time, in which I played through the one hundred and fifty games in that book systematically, day by day, continued for about two and a half months. Then I arrived unexpectedly at a dead end. Suddenly I found myself once more facing nothingness. For by the time I had played through each one of these games innumerable times, the charm of novelty and surprise was lost, the exciting and stimulating power was exhausted. What purpose did it serve to repeat again games whose every move I had memorized long before? No sooner did I make an opening move than the whole thing unravelled of itself; there was no surprise, no tension, no problem. At this point I would have needed another book with more games to keep me busy, to engage the mental effort that had become indispensable to divert me. This being impossible, my madness could take but one course: instead of the old games I had to devise new ones myself. I had to try to play the game with myself or, rather, against myself.

"I have no idea to what extent you have given thought to the intellectual status of this game of games. But one doesn't have to reflect deeply to see that if pure chance can determine a game of calculation, it is an absurdity in logic to play against oneself. The fundamental attraction of chess

259

lies, after all, in the fact that its strategy develops in different wise in two different brains, that in this mental battle Black, ignorant of White's immediate manoeuvres, seeks constantly to guess and thwart them, while White, for his part, strives to penetrate Black's secret purposes and to discern and parry them. If one person tried to be both Black and White you have the preposterous situation that one and the same brain at once knows something and yet does not know it; that, functioning as White's partner, it can instantly obey a command to forget what, a moment earlier as Black's partner, it desired and plotted. Such cerebral duality really implies a complete cleavage of the conscious, a lighting up or dimming of the brain function at pleasure as with a switch; in short, to want to play against oneself at chess is about as paradoxical as to want to jump over one's own shadow.

"Well, briefly, in my desperation I tried this impossibility, this absurdity, for months. There was no choice but this nonsense if I was not to become quite insane or slowly to disintegrate mentally. The fearful state that I was in compelled me at least to attempt this split between Black ego and White ego so as not to be crushed by the horrible nothingness that bore in on me.

"Before a real chessboard with real chessmen you can stop to think things over, and you can place yourself physically first on this side of the

The dramatic game of chess played by Werner von Basil (Curd Jürgens), chief character of the film version of Stefan Zweig's story, and the Champion Mirko Centovic (Mario Adorf).

table, then on the other, to fix in your eyes how the scene looks to Black and how it looks to White. Obliged as I was to conduct these contests against myself — or with myself, as you please — on an imaginary field, so I was obliged to keep fixed in mind the current set-up on the sixty-four squares, and besides, to made advance calculations as to the possible further moves open to each player, which meant — I know how mad this must sound to you — imagining doubly, triply, no, imagining sextuply, duodecimally for each one of my egos, always four or five moves in advance.

"...From the moment at which I tried to play against myself I began, unconsciously, to challenge myself. Each of my egos, my Black ego and my White ego, had to contest against the other and become the centre, each on its own, of an ambition, an impatience to win, to conquer. After each move that I made as Ego Black, I was in a fever of curiosity as to what Ego White would do. Each of my egos felt triumphant when the other made a bad move and likewise suffered chagrin at similar clumsiness of its own.

"All that sounds senseless, and in fact such a self-produced schizophrenia, such a split consciousness with its fund of dangerous excitement would be unthinkable in a person under normal conditions. Don't forget, though, that I had been violently torn from all normality, innocently charged and behind bars, for months martyred by the refined employment of solitude — a man seeking an object against which to discharge his long accumulated rage. And as I had nothing else than this insane match with myself, that rage, that lust for revenge, canalized itself fanatically into the game. Something in me wanted to justify itself, but there was only this other self with which I could wrestle; so while the game was on, an almost maniacal excitement waxed in me. In the beginning my deliberations were still quiet and composed; I would pause between one game and the next so as to recover from the effort, but little by little my frayed nerves forbade all respite. No sooner had Ego White made a move than Ego Black feverishly plunged a piece forward; scarcely had a game ended but I challenged myself to another, for each time, of course, one of my chess-egos was beaten by the other and demanded satisfaction.

"I shall never be able to tell, even approximately, how many games I played against myself during those months in my cell as a result of this crazy insatiability; a thousand perhaps, perhaps more. It was an obsession against which I could not arm myself; from dawn to night I thought of nothing but knights and pawns, rooks and kings, and a and b and c, and 'Mate!' and 'Castle'; my entire being and every sense embraced the chequered board. The joy of play became a lust for play; the lust for play became a compulsion to play, a frenetic rage, a mania which saturated not only my waking hours but eventually my sleep, too. I could think only in terms of chess, only in chess moves, chess problems; sometimes I would wake with a damp brow and become aware that a game had unconsciously continued in my sleep, and if I dreamt of persons it was exclusively in the moves of the bishop, the rook, in the advance and retreat of the knight's move.

"Even when I was brought before the examining Board I was no longer able to keep my thoughts within the bounds of my responsibilities; I'm inclined to think that I must have expressed myself confusedly at the last sessions, for my judges would glance at one another strangely. Actually I was merely waiting, while they questioned and deliberated, in my cursed eagerness to be led back to my cell so that I could resume my mad round, to start a fresh game, and another and another. Every interruption disturbed me; even the quarter-hour in which the warder cleaned up the room, the two minutes in which he served my meals, tortured my feverish impatience; sometimes the midday meal stood untouched on the tray at evening because the game made me forgetful of food. The only physical sensation that I experienced was a terrible thirst. The fever of this constant thinking and playing must already have manifested itself then. I emptied the bottle in two gulps and begged the warder for more, and nevertheless felt my tongue dry in my mouth in the next minute.

"Finally my excitement during the games rose — by that time I did nothing else from morning till night — to such a height that I was no longer able to sit still for a minute; uninterruptedly, while cogitating on a move, I would walk to and fro, quicker and quicker; to and fro, to and fro, and the nearer the approach to the decisive moment of the game the hastier my steps; the lust to win, to victory, to victory over myself increased to a sort of rage; I trembled with impatience, for the one chess-ego in me was always too slow for the other. One would whip the other forward and, absurd as this may seem to you, I would call angrily, 'Quicker, quicker!' or 'Go on, go on!' when the one self in me failed to riposte to the other's thrust quickly enough.

"The time came when this monomania, this obsession, attacked my body as well as my brain. I lost weight, my sleep was restless and disturbed, upon waking I had to make great efforts to compel my leaded lids to open; sometimes I was so weak that when I grasped a glass I could scarcely raise it to my lips, my hands trembled so; but no sooner did the game begin than a mad power seized me: I rushed up and down, up and down with fists clenched, and I would sometimes hear my own voice as through a reddish fog, shouting hoarsely and angrily at myself 'Check!' or 'Mate!' "

Suddenly Dr. B. found himself in hospital — after an attack of chess madness. When he was convalescent, the Gestapo released him, having lost all hope of getting any secret information from him. He had to leave Austria within a fortnight. It was a very strange experience for him, when free, to see people playing chess. He had been used to seeing the symbols and play in his imagination. This concrete, materialized game

seemed quite alien to him. He regarded the two living players as the two embodied selves of his schizophrenia...

And this brought us to the end of Dr. B's reminiscences. Against his will, he was persuaded to play Centovic. He treated the game as a test to see whether he could play a normal game with a real opponent instead of an abstract one. The duel began, with a big audience standing round. It was a stubborn fight from the start. After a dramatic game, the arch-champion was beaten by the dilettante. Routine lost to fantasy. Centovic asked for a return game. Dr. B. agreed. It was obvious that the game was exciting him, as he began to betray signs of nervousness and impatience. Quite unnoticed by him, the symptoms of schizophrenia began to appear. He walked about as though in his cell, not seeing his opponent, and what was worse, blind to the position on the board. He was playing against himself, paying no attention to Centovic, having in his mind quite a different situation on the chessboard. When he began to rave and get mixed up in his moves, we had to stop the game for fear that he would have some sort of seizure. Dr. B. composed himself, apologized and declared himself beaten. Not knowing his opponent's history, Centovic was triumphant. In his opinion, in a decisive game, the amateur would always turn out to be — just a dilettante.

Another story, in lighter vein, was "Chess," by the Hungarian novelist of the last century M. Jokai, based on Arabian motifs. Here the man who plays chess against himself certainly does not suffer.

"From time to time, Don Hurtado travelled round Spain, visiting the most important towns, and he always returned with an abundant harvest. One day, jogging along slowly on his mule, by the River Guadalquivir, he saw an Arab sitting in the middle of the road, playing a game of chess by himself. Surprised, Don Hurtado could not refrain from asking:

"He saw an Arab sitting in the middle of the road playing chess with himself." Illustration to M. Jókai's story *"Chess."* Drawing by A. Marczyński.

"He took a black pawn off the board..."
Illustration to a feature story by Boleslaw
Prus, "Players and Bunglers." Drawing by
A. Uniechowski.

" 'What are you doing here?'

" 'I'm playing chess, as you can see.'

" 'All by yourself?'

" 'I am not alone.'

" 'Who is with you?'

" 'He who is everywhere, the only lord, the great Allah.'

" 'Quite a powerful opponent?'

" 'Well, he is a just one.'

" 'And who is winning?'

" 'It looks as though I shall lose. Do you see any hope for me? One more move, and I'm mated. I can't play any more today.'

" 'Why not?'

" 'I've lost all my money.'

" 'So you play with Allah for money?'

" 'Yes, always. I've just lost fifty pieces of gold in that game.'

" 'And how will you pay Allah?'

" 'Oh, the usual way. When I lose, Allah sends me some worthy, pious man who takes the sum

I have lost from me and distributes it among the poor. That is just the same as giving it to Him. Today I believe that you are the man sent by Allah; so please take these fifty pieces of gold and distribute them among the poor.'

" 'How happy an idea!' Don Hurtado thought to himself: 'it must be a great experience to play chess like that.'

"So when, after travelling around Spain for some time, he returned by the same road to Cordova, he kept a look-out for the pious Arab to ask him how his subsequent games had gone.

"Yes, there he was, sitting in the middle of the road as before, absorbed in a game. I stopped and waited until he had finished.

" 'Did you lose today too, Abu Rizlan?'

" 'No, not today, fortune has smiled upon me today. One more move, and I shall mate Allah.'

" 'Oh, that's good. So you won today?'

" 'Yes. I've won five hundred pieces of gold from Allah'.

" 'And how will he pay you?'

" 'Oh, as usual. When Allah loses, he sends me a worthy pious man who pays me the sum I have won. Today he has sent you to pay me.'

"Saying which, the worthy Arab pointed a pistol at the terrified Don Hurtado who handed over his bag of money with a very sour look..."

One of the Polish author Bolesław Prus's chess columns in "The Illustrated Weekly" in 1911 was titled "Players and Bunglers" and was full of allegories based on chess; it was a time when there were growing conflicts between the imperialist states (a detail connected with the subject). One of the author's friends, a Jew, was supposed to have pointed out two men playing chess in a coffee-house and used their contrasting temperaments and styles to illustrate the "Polish question" of the day.

" 'That one is Gadulski,' ('Chatterbox'), he whispers. 'He was once a village landowner but now he's looking for a job, if only as a bank clerk.

Meanwhile he plays chess. And the other man, the one that says nothing, he is called Szulc. They quarrel a lot, but are good friends.'

"Szulc moves a pawn.

" 'Got him!' shouts Chatterbox. 'Your knight goes west!'

"He takes the black knight off the board. His opponent does not seem worried, however.

" 'Now watch and see what's going to happen in a minute,' whispers the Jew.

" 'The Bungler!' roars Chatterbox. 'He's after my queen, but doesn't see that I'm going to take his rook as well as the knight. Got him again!' And off goes the rook.

"But his opponent remained unconcerned.

"Some of those looking on began to smile. Szulc moved the bishop. My friend nudged me.

" 'That is the Polish game!' he said under his breath.

" 'Right you are, it's the Polish game all right!' shouted Chatterbox. 'We rush in, like a hurricane, smashing everything upside down. Got him again! That pawn's mine.'

"Now he takes a pawn.

" 'What a bungler!' — whispers an onlooker.

" 'I called him a bungler first,' thunders Chatterbox.

" 'But I am calling you a bungler,' replied the onlooker.

" 'Me?' Chatterbox is offended.

" 'I mate you in two moves,' says Szulc quietly.

" 'What?... what?...' shouts Chatterbox. 'Do you mind if I take back my last move?'

" 'No, I'm not taking moves back, I'm mating you.'

" 'What sort of bungling is this?' protests Chatterbox, not so loudly this time. 'I'll give you back your knight and rook and move my king and everything will be all right.'

" 'Next game! Next game!' replies Szulc starting to set up the pieces for the next game.

" 'Well! If that's the way we're going to play,' says Chatterbox indignantly. My Jewish friend takes my arm and leads me from the room.

"We sat down by the window, far from the noise. My friend ordered black coffee and said:

" 'You saw that game of chess between Chatterbox and Szulc? That is no game of chess, but the whole Polish question. Although Szulc is a Pole too, a cruel Pole, his father was a German and... he inherited something from him; not only a factory, but some brains.'

"He sipped his coffee and went on: 'I've watched them playing here in this coffee-house for a year or more. At the start, Chatterbox was playing just as he plays today. Szulc hardly knew which piece was which or how to move them. Chatterbox is a quick thinker, full of good ideas. Szulc is slow and phlegmatic but he is willing to work, whereas Chatterbox wants everything to drop into his lap for nothing. Szulc took my advice and bought a book on chess. He learnt a lot about combinations, how to play the openings. He learnt even a dozen or so outstanding games by heart, in fact he is still swotting up new games. We came here every day. Every day they played and every day Szulc did a little better. Chatterbox never improves...'

" 'And now you tell me. If there are two players of whom one always knows what he wants to do and the other never knows; one knows a little but the other knows nothing; one concentrates all the time, the other never; one always calculates, the other goes on impulse; one takes care not to be mated, the other bothers only when he is mated... just tell me who is going to win and who to lose?'

"Here, my friend took my hand, shook it feelingly and asked: 'Now do you see now what the Polish question really is?...'

"This chat about chess," concluded Prus, "came to my mind when I thought about the situation of Poland today. I found myself reflecting that life is very like chess, only our forces are, instead of rooks and knights, work, endurance, attention, firmness and skill.

"In a game of chess, each player wants to win. In life, peoples and nations want to win. What do they want to win? They want to win physical and spiritual perfection, that is, they want to increase their ability to work, their knowledge, to improve their health, their skill, to win the friendship of other people or nations, to win riches, honesty, dignity and these are the main necessities if we want to win the game of life..."

Prus reverted to chess in his novel "The Emancipated Women." Among a gallery of small-town characters, he paints a humorous picture of an old major and the parish priest who played innumerable games against each other. It was a daily ritual and usually ended in a quarrel.

"Shouts were heard coming from the summerhouse: the major had been mated and was telling the priest he had no idea how to play. The game had actually ended a move before the end, for the major absolutely refused to be mated. It would never have happened, he protested, had not his queen been quite accidentally on that file, his knight on this square, his rook on that!

" 'Yes,' replied the priest, 'And if your king had gone off into the garden he might not have been mated on this board.' "

In another episode, the two were called away from the chessboard to a man who was dying after having shot himself. The priest granted absolution. As they were leaving his home, 'You might have behaved a little better at a time like this, Major,' says the priest.

" 'I was saying prayers, wasn't I?' grunted the major.

" 'Yes, but muttering about chess as well and puffing away at your pipe till the smoke nearly choked us.'

" 'And you granted poor Cynadrowski absolution with a knight in your hand.'

" 'By the Passion of Christ!' cried the priest. 'I really have a knight in my hand. I'll never play chess again after this!' "

Another Polish novel is really interwoven with chess. It is Wacław Sieroszewski's historical novel "Beniowski." A Polish officer Maurycy Beniowski, arrested by the Tsarist authorities in 1769

"... Beniowski, oblivious of the onlookers gathered round him, cautiously laid his plans..." Illustration to Waclaw Sieroszewski's novel "Beniowski." Drawing by A. Uniechowski.

and sentenced to exile in Kamchatka, was an excellent chess player; the famous "smothered mate" by a knight is called a "Beniowski mate" in Poland. While in exile, Beniowski watched a game between two Russian generals and remarked after the game that the loser could at one stage have won in a few moves by sacrificing a piece. The officer, too proud to admit it, bet a large sum that it was not so. Beniowski showed he was right and won the bet. The novel varies this authentic chess episode a little. Beniowski starts to play the commandant of the local police and wins three games and so a stake as well but exasperating the commandant into fury at being beaten by a political outcast.

As Beniowski and his comrades were planning an organized escape, he did not want the least

The champion sacrificed pawns, and other pieces too... Illustration to the novel "Twelve Chairs" by Ilf and Petrov. Drawing by H. Chmielewski.

trouble with the local authorities. He offered back the money he had won. But here he was in for a surprise. The commandant suggested that they should go into partnership to play for high stakes against rich merchants coming to the island to trade in furs. The commandant was to supply the capital, Beniowski the skill.

Beniowski agreed, thinking this might help his cause. Every game brought victory for him and the partners filled their pockets with money won from merchants keen on chess. A third person, another local authority joined them; the chess "company" began to expand. Beniowski's fame quickly grew — but also the number of his enemies, he having worsted a great number of people. Meanwhile, under the cover of this diversion he was able to carry on with his secret plans. The defeated merchants sent for an excellent chess player Koleskov from the mainland to play against Beniowski. So an exciting duel was thus arranged during a festive ball. Most of those present were backing Koleskov. Big bets were placed. The music and dancing began, but most of the dancers found themselves drawn away to watch the match...

"People were standing on benches and looking over the heads of others to where, in the centre of the room, the elders were sitting on stools in a semi-circle and, in the centre of all, Beniowski and Koleskov. Next to them were piles of gold and silver roubles and other coins, as well as goblets of vodka, which nobody was drinking, by the way. Koleskov was red in the face, ran his fingers nervously through his hair and, whilst waiting for his opponent to move, tapped on the table with a pawn he had taken; Beniowski was pale, but apart from this, betrayed no emotion.

" 'It's check — checkmate!... A certainty!' cries Koleskov joyfully.

There is a stir in the crowd, many people jumped to their feet. Excited voices argue.

" 'He's won!... He's won!'

" 'Just a fluke!... Pure luck!'

" 'We win!'

"The second game starts. Oblivious to the spectators around him, Beniowski cautiously develops his pieces: Koleskov attacks amid mingled joy, apprehension and excitement from the two opposing camps of spectators.

"Beniowski seems to see nothing but the pieces. He weighs every move with care and plays delicately, coming down to pick up the piece lightly. Koleskov mutters to himself.

"Beniowski loses a second game. There is a great burst of noise. The merchants shout and stamp with joy.

" 'That Beniowski of yours is no good at all. All that fuss about him!...'

" 'What do you think you're doing, you damned outcast? I'll have you bastinadoed, you swine... what are you up to? Haven't you got eyes? Are you so stuck up that you don't bother to think out the moves?... Anybody could see that your knight couldn't move when he put his queen there,' shouted Chernykh, frothing at the mouth, jerking Beniowski's arm.

" 'Let me go! We haven't finished yet!' said Beniowski.

"His lips were trembling, his moustache was bristling, but he mastered his anger and looked boldly round at the wall of inflamed faces, flashing eyes, teeth bared in wolf-like grins, bristling beards and tousled hair that surrounded him. Chernykh put his hands to his head and blundered into the crowd.

" 'Ten thousand roubles... ten thousand! And all the furs,' he muttered over and over again, pushing towards the exit...

" 'We've lost everything. Skin the rascal alive! Who knows, perhaps he's in league with Kazarin? He'll lose and share the money with him afterwards! I'll demand an investigation! To the torture chamber with him! When they brand him, stick burning splinters under his nails, he'll confess it all. I'll see he doesn't get away with it!'

"When Beniowski was setting out the chessmen for the third time, he looked around the now quieter crowd for the first time. Suddenly among the rows of hostile faces he saw the loyal and tender eyes of a girl, dimmed with fear. It seemed to him as though a ray of sunshine had broken through the clouds. She stood behind her father's chair, alone, pure, virginal and appealing, among all those brutal men. He smiled at her...

" 'Come on, play!' he heard Koleskov saying impatiently.

"But Koleskov had not won his last game. Beniowski beat him. Then he beat him a second time, then a third and the fourth. The spectators began to get bored and move away. The music had stopped, the ballroom was emptying. The girl had gone home and the first light of the dawn was stealing in through the windows when the players at last rose from the table. With trembling hands, Czernykh counted their winnings.

" 'Twenty five thousand roubles... and all the furs...' "

This time, however, the infuriated merchants and Koleskov held up Beniowski in the forest and said he must "throw" the next match to them. He refused. They assaulted him. In defending himself he struck Koleskov who died from the blow next day. The subsequent events were to eclipse in seriousness any game of chess.

"Twelve Chairs," a satirical novel by the Soviet writers Ilya Ilf and Eugene Petrov, describes the adventures of the great rogue and trickster Bender who roamed the Soviet Union in the twenties. Bender used to lecture about "A guaranteed win in the opening at chess," then arrange a simultaneous chess exhibition.

"... From early morning a tall thin man, advanced in years, wearing gold pince-nez and very soiled shoes splashed with paint, could be seen walking about the streets of the town of Vashuki. He was sticking hand-written posters on the walls.

"The great champion himself soon went into action. Having hired the club rooms for three roubles, he went straight to the chess club, which for some unknown reason was in the corridor of the administrative office of the racehorse stables.

"He found a one-eyed man sitting there reading a novel by Spielhagen, edited by Pantelayev.

" 'I am the arch-champion Ostap Bender' — he introduced himself sitting down on the table. 'I am organizing a session of simultaneous games of chess in your club.'

" 'Chess!' continued Ostap enthusiastically, 'A game that spells progress in culture. Do you know that your 'Four Knights' chess club could completely transform the town of Vashuki if things were properly arranged?'

"He had eaten nothing all day. This always made him exceptionally eloquent.

" 'Yes!' he thundered, 'Chess increases the prosperity of the country! If you approve my idea, you will be walking down marble steps from the town to the quay! Vashuki will become the capital of ten countries... I tell you, it is absolutely essential to arrange an international chess tournament in Vashuki.'

" 'How?' cried those present; the noise had attracted a crowd.

" 'It is easy! With my personal contacts and your energy you have all you need to organize an international tournament here. Just think, how wonderful that will sound: International Tournament at Vashuki in 1928. Participants: José Raul Capablanca, Emanuel Lasker, Alexander Alekhine, Aron Nimzowitsch, Richard Réti, Anton Rubinstein, Siegbert Tarrasch, Milan Vidmar and Mikhail Botvinnik. I am also prepared to participate myself.'

" 'But what about the money!' — groaned the worthy men of Vashuki. 'All this must be paid for. It will cost an enormous sum. Where is it all to come from?'

" 'All has been thought of. We shall get money by selling tickets.'

" 'But who in our town could pay the prices we shall have to charge? The people of Vashuki...'

" 'No, not the people of Vashuki. They will not be paying out money, they will be raking it in. It's all so simple, people will want to come from all over the world to see a tournament with such world-famous experts. There will be hundreds of thousands of visitors, rich and well-to-do people coming to Vashuki. Now, first and foremost, with such a crowd wanting to come, our present transport will be totally inadequate. The People's Railway Commissariat must build a new railway line, Moscow to Vashuki. That is point one. Point two — hotels and skyscrapers for the guests to live in. Point three — improvement of farming methods for thousands of kilometres around the town. Our guests must be fed! We must boost vegetables, fruit, caviar, chocolate production five hundred per cent. Then, the palace in which the tournament will be held. That is point four. And now point five — garages for our guests' cars. To be able to tell the whole world how this sensational tournament is going, we shall have to build a gigantic radio station. That is point six. Now, regarding the construction of the Moscow-Vashuki railway line. There is no doubt that it will not be enough to bring all the people who want to come to Vashuki. So

"...He took a handful of chessmen and threw them at the head of his one-eyed adversary." Illustration to the novel "Twelve Chairs" by Ilf and Petrov. Drawing by H. Chmielewski.

the logical conclusion is to build an airport "Greater Vashuki" with direct air links with all parts of the world, not excluding Los Angeles and Melbourne.'

"Dazzling visions of the future appeared before the eyes of the Vashukian chess lovers. The very room they were in seemed to have grown into a vast hall. The mouldy walls of the racing stables receded and disappeared and were replaced by a thirty-storey chess castle in the air, throughout which, in every marbled recess, even in the high speed-lifts as they flashed up and down, people were playing on chessboards inlaid with malachite.

"Marble steps lead down to the blue waters of the Volga. Ocean-going vessels are anchored in the river. A long line of cars moves between rows of marble hotels. In a sudden hush, the champion José Raul Capablanca is seen going for a stroll. He is surrounded by exotic foreign ladies. A policeman salutes: he is dressed in a special chess-chequered uniform embroidered with golden knights. The one-eyed chairman of Vashuki's 'Four Knights' chess club goes up to the champion with dignified step. Their conversation is interrupted by the arrival of Dr. M. Botvinnik and the world champion Dr. A. Alekhine. Shouts of welcome are heard all over the town. A wave of the hand by our one-eyed chairman, and marble steps are pushed up to the plane. Doctor Botvinnik descends them, waving his new hat in all directions and discussing the errors that Capablanca might make in the coming match against Alekhine...

Illustration to W. J. Kasiński's story "The Knight." Drawing by G. Rechowicz ("Kierunki").

"Ostap Bender continues to depict the mirage of the magnificent and flourishing development awaiting Vashuki as a metropolis of chess. Soon this little town will grow so important that — to the envy of the other Soviet towns — it will become the capital of the country. And then would come the time to establish contacts with chess players from other planets, for even an inter-planetary congress of chess players suddenly seems quite a possibility. But to inaugurate these plans, capital would be needed; money and more money. Where was it to come from? To begin with, it was necessary to collect a small working fund. The small sum collected by Bender was to be augmented by profits from further simultaneous chess exhibitions...

"The night of the display came at last. Those who wanted to try their hand at playing with the 'champion' and their impatient fans gathered in the club.

"The great champion entered the room. He felt very sure of himself and knew very well that the first move P-K4 would not present any difficulties. He was rather vague about the rest of the moves, but the Great Trickster was not a man to worry about such things. He had thought up an unexpected way of getting out of even the most hopeless of situations.

"He was greeted with applause...

"He bowed, and with a gesture that was meant to convey that he did not consider himself worthy of such acclaim, walked on to the platform.

" 'Comrades,' he began in his resounding, impressive voice, 'Comrades and fellow chess players, the subject of my lecture, as I said a week ago, and I must admit not without reason, in Nizhni-Novgorod, the subject of my lecture — is the victorious idea of debut. Comrades, what is a debut and what is an idea? A debut, Comrades, is 'quasi una fantasia.' And what, Comrades, attention please, is an idea? An idea, Comrades, is human thought taking the logical shape of chess. One can be master of the whole chessboard with practically no effort at all. It all depends on the person we are playing against. Let us take, for instance, that fair man in the third row. Let us assume that he plays well...'

"The fair man in the third row blushed.

" 'And another man, let us say, that dark fellow over there, is not such a good player.'

"Everybody turned round to stare at the dark man.

" 'So, Comrades, we have a fair man who plays well and a dark man who plays badly. And no lectures can change this relation of forces if each individual does not systematically practise the art of wielding the sword... I beg your pardon, I meant, the chessmen... And now comrades, I will give you a few instructive accounts taken from the practical experience of our honoured hyper-modernists — Capablanca, Lasker and Dr. Grigoriev.'

"Ostap entertained his audience with a few antediluvian anecdotes that he had read as a boy in the 'Children's Friend.' That concluded his introductory lecture.

"The curious form of the lecture rather surprised those present. The chairman did not take his one eye off the great champion's boots for a moment.

"But the start of the simultaneous chess session diverted all suspicions for the moment. He helped the others to arrange the tables in the form of a horseshoe. Thirty chess enthusiasts had come to play the champion. Some of them seemed worried and kept looking into chess textbooks to refresh their memories about little stratagems that might help them to keep going for, at any rate, twenty moves or so before they could resign with honour.

"Ostap first took a look at the ranks of the 'blacks,' which surrounded him on all sides, then looked at the closed doors, and ... got down to the game. He went up to the one-eyed man who was sitting at the first chessboard and moved his pawn from K2 to K4.

"The one-eyed man at once clasped his head with his hands and began to think very profoundly. A whisper ran round the tables:

" 'The champion has moved his pawn from K2 to K4.'

"Ostap did not spoil his opponents by varying his moves. He made exactly the same move on the other twenty nine chessboards — P-K4. One after another, the chess enthusiasts clasped their heads in their hands and did some really hard thinking. Those who were not participating in the games gazed at the champion...

"At the third move, the word went round that the champion was playing a Ruy López on eighteen boards. On the remaining boards his opponents had resorted to the rather obsolete but well tried and tested Philidor Defence. Ostap would have been very surprised if he had known what difficult games he was playing and what tried and tested defences he was up against. The fact was that he was playing chess for the second time in his life.

"In the beginning his opponents, especially the one-eyed chairman, were almost paralysed with terror. The champion's great personality was only too evident. With the most unconcerned air in the world he sacrificed pawns and other less and more important men. He even sacrificed a queen to the dark man he had been so hard on during the lecture.

"The dark man was so worried about this that he was on the point of giving in and declaring himself beaten. It took a tremendous effort on his part to go on with the game.

"Five minutes later, like a thunderbolt from a blue sky, came a hoarse cry 'Checkmate!' It was the dark man, trembling with excitement.

"Ostap analysed the situation and condescendingly congratulated the dark man on his victory. There was a stir among the chess enthusiasts.

Illustration by G. Rechowicz to W. J. Kasiński's story "The Knight."

" 'Time to be off,' thought Ostap, walking calmly round the tables and negligently moving.

" 'You can't move the knight like that,' gasped out the one-eyed man. 'You've made an illegal move!'

" 'Oh, I beg your pardon, forgive me,' said the champion, 'I'm a little tired after that lecture.'

"In the next ten minutes the great champion lost ten more games.

"Shouts of amazement could be heard coming from the Cardboard Workers' Club. Ostap lost fifteen more games, one after the other, and then three more. At last the only player left was the one-eyed man. At the beginning he had made so many mistakes from fright that he was now having difficulty in ending the game to his advantage. Ostap took a black rook off the chessboard when nobody was looking and put it in his pocket.

"A crowd was gathering round.

" 'Where's my rook? It was here a minute ago,' shouted the one-eyed man, 'and now it's gone.'

" 'It isn't there now, so it couldn't have been there before,' replied Ostap.

" 'What do you mean, it wasn't there? I remember perfectly well that it was!'

" 'Of course it wasn't there.'

" 'Then where is it? Did you take it?'

" 'Yes.'

" 'When? On what move?'

" 'Why are you making such a fuss about that rook, why don't you say outright you want to throw up the sponge!'

" 'But, Comrade, I've got all the moves written down.'

" 'They write things down in offices!' was Ostap's riposte.

" 'This is scandalous,' howled the secretary. 'Give me back my rook!'

" 'Admit you're beaten and stop this fuss!'

" 'Give me back my rook!'

"At these words, the champion realized that delay would be disastrous. He took up a handful of chessmen and threw them at the one-eyed man's head.

" 'Comrades!' screamed the one-eyed man,

Illustrations by John Tenniel to the English edition of Lewis Carroll's book "Through the Looking-glass." LEFT: it was in this chess garden that the strange story of Alice began. RIGHT: Alice was changed from a pawn into a queen and sat down next to the real chess queens.

274

'I'll call you as witnesses. You saw him attack me!'

"Vashuki's chess players looked blank and nonplussed.

"Ostap lost no time. Throwing a chessboard at the lamp and tumbling over people in the dark, he ran out into the street. The chess enthusiasts of Vashuki, pushing and shoving each other in their hurry, rushed after him..."

A dramatic chase after Bender followed but the "chess" was at an end, in this story anyway.

Let us turn to something less boisterous.

In the novel "Schach of Wuthenow" by the 19th century German writer Theodor Fontane, the main character, Schach, has to suffer a lot of unkind puns on his name.

Owing to an irresponsible love affair with Madam von Carayon whilst he was officially a suitor for her daughter Victoire's hand, he finds himself the victim of malicious gossip. Numerous caricatures and jokes circulate around the town concerning this relationship of his, one of them being a drawing with a French caption "Le choix du Schach" ("Schach's Choice"), showing a Persian shah who could not make up his mind which of two slaves (whose faces had a distinct likeness to certain persons) to choose.

"But Schach found the third drawing the hardest to bear. The scene was Madam von Carayon's salon. On a table was a chessboard on which all the pieces had been scattered as though swept aside by the loser. Sitting next to the table was Victoire — a very good likeness — and at her feet, Schach kneeling, again with a Persian cap on his head as in the first drawing. But this time the cap was torn and crumpled. The drawing was captioned 'Checkmate.' The aim of the repeated attacks had been attained..."

Arnold Zweig, in his novel against war and imperialism "When the Guns Went Silent," depicting the situation in 1917 on the Russian-German front, began and ended his story with a chess scene.

Two keen chess players at the front are Greulich, an N.C.O. of progressive views, and Sergeant Pont. From the first chapter, entitled "The Game", we quote...

"On the encrusted black and white chequered chessboard, the pieces indicate an unfinished game... Amid clouds of pipe-smoke the two soldiers had pondered over the chessmen — beautifully carved out of ivory, once the property of the former owner of the house... Yes, it looks like being a long game. The players are educated sons of the German bourgeois class, one a teacher, the other an architect. Both are patient men, shrewd and fond of the noble game, a game that has united chess players in coffee-houses all over the globe into a mysterious clan with its own language and way of thinking. What unfortunate man, who has not been initiated into the secrets of this clan, could hope to guess what a 'gambit' is or a 'knight's move' or the real meaning of 'check?' Yesterday evening Greulich, the teacher, had had a passing idea whilst thinking about how to repel Pont's new attack...

" 'If the war were to end now, Pont,' Greulich had packed the tobacco down in his pipe with the hardened fingertip of the confirmed smoker, 'let us assume that every fallen soldier is given a square metre of ground. About two million Russians have been buried, about one-and-a-half million of our men, a similar number of Frenchmen and Austrians, and about half-a-million each Italians, Serbians, Englishmen and Turks. Now how many will that be altogether...?'

" 'Let's have those figures again, Greulich,' Pont had quickly totted them up on a piece of paper, 'Eight-and-a-half million killed.'

" 'Hm! eight-and-a-half million square metres,' said Greulich, staring at his king, almost completely surrounded, the queen ready to spring and the one remaining rook supporting the knight, 'How big a chessboard would be needed to get an idea of that great cemetery of fallen heroes?'

"Laurenz Pont gave a start, 'You pedagogues get the funniest ideas,' he muttered, 'But let's get

More of John Tenniel's drawings for Lewis Carroll's book "Through the Looking-glass." LEFT: The chessmen's world. RIGHT: The King in Alice's hand.

back to our game. If this bloody business doesn't end we'll have to wait days and days for the next move.'

" 'Oh, we shan't have to wait as long as that,' answered Greulich and with a cunning expression on his thin wrinkled face, puffing out smoke from under his yellowed moustache, he moved a small red pawn forward, one of the few men still on its original square.

" 'Oh, ho! So you want to get your rook back?' said Pont, 'But we see everything my friend. We clerks keep an eye on everything that goes on.' He moved.

"Greulich, threatened, feigned surprise and pushed forward a bishop to the rescue: 'Check!'

" 'Oh dear, oh dear,' said Pont to himself. He must have overlooked something. That's what happens when you watch a little pawn too closely for fear it will be promoted; somewhere else, a pawn almost grows into a rook.

" 'Which of our men,' asked Greulich, 'Could, do you think, turn from an ordinary foot-soldier back into a duke overnight, if the war were to end?'

" 'Hm,' replied Pont, 'I must think that one over.' He moved his king away. 'Our landsturmer Bertin has been passing himself off as a clerk of Judge Poznanski for a long time. He had just got his chance of promotion when they mobilized him in 1915 and at Verdun he married that pretty girl whose photograph stands in the place of honour on his desk in the military court office.'

" 'And he's learnt a lot meanwhile,' said Greulich, agreeing with his friend's words: 'He's gone through a lot and tucked away a lot of knowledge in that brain of his. So Bertin is one of the pawns to me... I suggest we finish playing for today. This is beginning to get interesting. 'He knows all there is to know about life, he will tell us what we want to know,' as old Faust said. But it's a quarter to nine and, if I am not mistaken, they will be ringing up from Kovno any minute now and I'd rather be downstairs.'

" 'To be continued,' smiled Pont and went to move the table into the corner of the room.

" 'Not by yourself!' cried Greulich, worried: 'With one pair of hands you can't carry that properly, any insurance company would tell you

276

that.' So he took the table from one side and Pont from the other, keeping watchful eyes on the pieces, which quivered despite their care. It would not take much to overturn them and spoil an interesting game.

" 'If you look on us all as pawns,' said Pont, 'For Bertin is only an example as far as you're concerned, then who are the officers in the end-game of the war?'

"Greulich, as a liaison soldier, a discriminating reader of the newspapers, glanced musingly at the board.

" 'They are not people at all. They are the big firms, some of them mysterious abbreviations that would not have meant a thing to our fathers. Maybe Krupp would have meant something to them but Albin Schiller as the queen, AEG and IG-Farben as the rooks would certainly not mean anything, nor would Kloeckner, Voegler, Hugenberg...'

" 'Our grandchildren will find them in any lexicon,' said Pont, 'And what about the other side?'

" 'Vickers-Armstrong, Rothschild, Schneider-Creuzot, I.C.I. — those are the great rival British abbreviations — and colonial ministries that haven't yet got a name.'

" 'And the junker Lenin, how do you assess him?'

" 'He' cried Greulich turning round at the door, 'isn't in the game at all yet, and that's just what gives him his chance.' "

The novel ends with a chapter symbolically called "A Draw?" After many adventures we find the same two players sitting over another game.

" 'It's snowing, it's snowing — a white carpet growing,' muttered Greulich under his moustache, cautiously bearing the table with the still unfinished game into the light under the green shade of the office lamp.

" 'So the Somme didn't cure you of your childish rhymes?' remarks Pont."

The two men are in no hurry to finish the game, although curious in their hearts how it would end. It really was snowing there in Merevinsk, the north-west wind blowing thick swirling flakes across the window. Meanwhile, the two soldiers lit up their cigars and puffed away, the office becoming pleasantly homelike with the fragrant smoke, and became absorbed in the position on the board... In spite of all the events of the last week, these chessmen always kept a little place in their minds. The only sound that broke the profound silence was the ticking of their watches.

Alice and the White Queen. Another illustration by John Tenniel to Lewis Carroll's book "Through the Looking-glass."

Illustration to C. D. Simac's story "Once on Mercury." Drawing by A. Orlov ("Znanie-sila").

"Pont, bent over his white pawns, summed up the situation fairly quickly. He knew what he was going to do. It was his move; his king had already evaded the danger Greulich had threatened by moving up his red pawns from the opening position to activate his bishops and queen. 'Red pawns,' thought Pont, 'There are no such things. All over the world, they are either white or black, clerical or free-thinkers — never red. That would be the end of the world as we know it.'

"He moved his queen cunningly just two little squares forward, forking his opponent's king and rook.

" 'Check!' he said softly, as though rather surprised himself and not too convinced.

" 'Pont,' he remarked, 'You have created a new situation, just like General Allenby, when he broke through our front in Sinai three weeks ago and took Jerusalem. Looking at things today, I see that Bertin was right in suggesting that

278

a German Palestine corps of Jewish volunteers should be sent there.'

"Pont, concentrating his attention on his opponent's thrust, asked: 'Why are you worrying your head about Jerusalem, you child-tamer? Hic Rhodos, Hic salta!' and he pointed to the square he was threatening.

" 'The mountain fortress of Jerusalem is just such a key position for the whole of the Middle East,' said Greulich.

" 'And how do you know that?' mocked Pont, blowing cigar smoke at Greulich.

" 'From studying geography,' was the reply, 'You catholics don't know your Bible. We protestants get, in every copy of the Bible, coloured maps of the Holy Land in the times of Moses, Solomon and Jesus. In each of them the main communication routes of the whole area intersect at the fortress of Jerusalem, the north-south route from Damascus to Heliopolis or On in Egypt, and the east-west route from Ur in Chaldea to Jaffa or Joppa on the Mediterranean. Today, the northern route goes further up, to Turkey — and if the Balkan front were to weaken, Turkish and Bulgarian divisions have been stationed there since 1912... The Jewish legion so enthusiastically urged on us by Bertin would have been very useful to us then.'

"Pont was put out. 'Do you want to sap our will to win? You'd do better to beat me here and leave it at that!'

"Obviously Greulich had got under his skin that day. He abruptly interposed a pawn hoping that his opponent would fall into the trap, grab the rook and leave himself open to attack.

"But Pont just nodded his massive head, deep in thought. His glance rested for a moment on the two iron crosses on his friend's breast then returned to the board.

" 'Have you told Bertin that he is to go to the Press Department?'

" 'Don't bother me, you — schoolmaster!' said Pont, parrying what he considered an attempt to distract his attention. 'He'll know in due course, when our field hospital is transferred.' He decided to leave the rook where it was. He brought up his knight near the red king.

"Greulich stroked his moustache and moved a pawn to attack the knight.

" 'Are we playing chess?' asked Pont, 'Or war?'

" 'Chess and war,' replied Greulich, giving Pont a keen look, for he had moved his queen so that the pawn could not take the knight without leaving his own king unprotected. He sat looking at his friend in surprise when suddenly the telephone rang..."

There was fresh news from the front. There were new positions to be marked on the staff maps; forecasts came through of the future course of events. The war game had entered a critical stage. Greulich looked at the table with the maps, but felt himself irresistibly drawn back to the chessboard.

" 'Downstairs,' he thought, 'Our red and white pieces are waiting in the light of the one electric bulb for the end of the game. I'll have him mated in three moves. If something new keeps coming up then we shall have to abandon the game as a draw. But I know that the game is already decided. White has lost!' "

In Kazimierz Brandys's novel "The Wooden Horse" published in Poland just after the war, the main character is a keen player. During the years of the Nazi occupation, when living a life of enforced loneliness, he often played chess with a neighbour, the Doctor:

"... The Doctor was no champion. He was impetuous, played unevenly, changed his plans half-way; his ideas ran away from him. Sometimes I let him win; he never suspected. Once he made a wrong move; I smiled, for this gave me the game.

" 'Chess is strategy, Doctor. I'm afraid you wouldn't be a very good commander.'

" 'Don't you think so?' he replied, with his keen eyes upon me. His mouth was a thin line of anger. 'So you don't think I would be a good commander?' he repeated quietly.

"I was rather alarmed at the tone of his voice.

" 'Surely you are not taking me seriously,' I faltered, ready to concede him the talents of Caesar if he preferred it.'

" 'Just my little joke, Doctor, nothing but a joke...'

" 'Oh, well,' he muttered grudgingly, shrugging his shoulders in the way he did when offended.

"It occurred to me that either loneliness had made me brutal or I was playing with a madman. I let him win the game. And he disarmed me in the end, when I put up my hands in a gesture of helplessness after the last move; he burst into a peal of loud childish laughter and held out his hand to me over the table.

" 'Ha! ha!' he laughed, 'Now tell me who is a good commander.' "

The hidden meaning of this scene becomes evident as the plot unfolds and it is found that the Doctor was a commander, the chief of the Regional Revenge Command, a Polish fascist underground organization. Chess themes permeate the whole final chapter. The hero of the book, now a convalescent, is playing a certain pharmacist, who has just been freed from a prison camp. They plan an escape, interrupting the conversation from time to time to make a move:

" 'So I shall go this way,' I said, with my mind only half on what I was saying as I listened to the last echo of the clock striking the hour. 'We'll go together until we are beyond that forest. But let's leave things as they were... We won't discuss it now.'

" 'Of course,' agreed the pharmacist, 'Your move now.'

"I moved a knight.

" 'A rather thoughtless move!' smiled the pharmacist. 'You've got ideas but you lack practice. That move will cost you dear. It's not so easy as you think to control a wooden horse.'

" 'It's not easy to control a wooden horse,' I muttered to myself."

With these words the story ends. That the title "The Wooden Horse" was meant to symbolize a knight in chess seems obvious. At the beginning we had been told about a wooden horse — a toy on which the hero of our story went galloping as a little boy. This symbolized his personality: the pampered son of a bourgeois family, he had sat motionless on his wooden horse for hours, as he was not allowed to play with other children. So the wooden horse symbolized social isolation as well, something which was to burden the hero all through life. But life is strategy too — and here the horse of the novel takes on chess shape. Another little detail, but eloquent: there is a picture of a toy wooden horse on the cover of the book, but the back of the book is decorated with chess knights.

In a story by another Polish author, Jerzy Władysław Kasiński, entitled "The Knight," this piece was the subject of macabre treatment.

The story was written in 1942 when the recent outbreak of war was vivid in the author's mind, but was not published until 1957. The scene is a mental hospital on the eve of Hitler's invasion of Poland. One of the patients is suffering from a specific type of persecution mania.

"The light and dark chequered pattern of the parquet floor served as a chessboard. A man with a large bald head was moving about it in careful jumps, with an expression of deep concentration on his face. The unreal-looking creature imagined

Scene from the sketch "Check and Checkmate" from a variety programme "We're off to the Olympic Games" at Cracow's Satirical Theatre (1956).

An illustration by Jerzy Skarżyński to Karol Irzykowski's play "The Victory."

himself as a knight of the chessboard. So it is not surprising that he was known as "The Knight."

" 'Ha, ha! Our knight's off again,' said the tall thin man known as 'Assistant Pieta,' bending over the thickset figure of Doctor Punicki, while the man-knight, having managed to get into the 'chequered' recreation room, began his complicated expedition. Hardly had he crossed the threshold when he bent his bald head over the alternate coloured squares of the parquet and then went forward in precise knight moves; a sudden jerk forward and sideways, always eventually from white square to black, or from black to white muttering the while 'Queen's knight's square — queen's bishop three — queen five — king six...'

"Here and there he darted, skirting round people met on the way, always keeping strictly to the rules of the game.

"Doctor Punicki, a keen chess player, had a special liking for this unfortunate man. As he stood in the doorway, watching the patients under his care, people misunderstood by the world and unable to understand it, his glance always rested a little longer on the bent back of 'The Knight,' checking on the correctness of his move and guessing the next.

"The Doctor imagined sometimes that he was at a real chessboard, that the patients and attendants were chessmen on a board delimited by the knight, who tried not to go beyond his chosen sixty four squares.

"The others were only pawns, the only piece on the imaginary chessboard being the knight, always on the move, throwing himself about now here, now there. He decided how the game was to be played, settling its course with lightning decisions, eluding the player's hand, a living thing moving automatically. He doubled and trebled in the eyes of the onlooker, approached, receded, played havoc among the sluggish pawns...

"And sometimes it seemed to the doctor that instead of a bald human head, with long pointed outstanding ears, he saw the stylized carved head of a wooden knight."

To see if it would help the knight to rid himself of his obsession, the doctor ordered the floor to be covered with unpatterned linoleum. When the patient next came in, he was greatly upset to find his squares gone:

"... Despair and helplessness were written on his face... He looked long and hard at the empty floor, at this smooth expanse that only yesterday had squares of alternating colours to guide his eyes. He knelt on the floor, his fingers feeling the smooth linoleum, as if he were looking for something in the dark. Finally he stood up, straightened his back and, staring wild-eyed at the floor, began to move forward. Uncertainly, falteringly, he followed the well-beaten path of the Knight, forward and sideways. It was as though he wanted to pierce through the pitiless desert of linoleum with his eyes, to see the squares hidden beneath.

"And on and on he went, in the same old way, but sad and silent. He even stopped murmuring the names of the squares.

"Doctor Punicki felt his experiment had failed, and ordered the linoleum to be changed back again.

"Back in his own world once more, the knight went mad with joy... he danced a zig-zagged dance of delight on the chequered floor that had been charmed back into existence. This was no longer just chess, it was the dance of a knight come to life. From that day on, he was happy again..."

The writer goes on to deal with other characters and conflicts, but returns to the knight in the end. War broke out. German planes scattered death and devastation. The mental hospital did not escape. The knight survived the bombing, emerging from the building into the courtyard, which was pitted with bomb craters.

"... Where had he come from? From the chessboard of the empty recreation room. He had got out by an adroit jump from the last eight-man-group when it was going towards the death field and played his great game on the two-coloured squares. Nobody got in his way, there was nothing to hamper him in making the moves he had worked out, so he zig-zagged happily and freely across the floor.

"Waves of melodious sound came from the radio on the table. Suddenly, the music stopped, a voice said: " 'Attention! Attention! He is on the way, P 27.' "The knight stopped, listened, and pondered. Here was something alien, something invading the old order of things: QB5, Q7, KB6 he knew. This was something new. He looked for a square P 27 but could not find it. His chess mind was working hard, going over the 64 squares. An idea occurred to him. It was just a mistake. A chessboard with a square marked 27 would have to have several hundreds of squares. The knight smiled. He returned to his customary progress.

" 'They have got through!' cried the radio.

"And again came the whining waves of sound. The knight moved rhythmically forward to the beat of the music, he had resigned himself to searching for square P 27, going beyond the boundaries of the chessboard. Crosswise there were now squares from A to Z and beyond, even beyond the mere alphabet; and the row of figures defining the squares lengthwise — they, starting at one, went on to infinity.

"In the pursuit of that last number which would mark the boundaries of the chessboard, he plunged on into infinity... the way led through the door, down into the courtyard.

"He stopped on the last step. Before him he saw a shell crater. He had to go round that.

"He had already covered the courtyard in his imagination with a network of squares that now extended into the distance without end. As he moved on again, making the knight's moves without a mistake, he suddenly drew back, terrified. There were some pieces lying about in his way.

"Here was somebody lying in front of him. With a sudden shock, he saw a new sort of piece — it was a human body lifeless and inert. From it ran blood in a dark red stain into a pool from the battered head.

"He seemed rooted to the spot. He looked at the pool of blood, at the battered human head, and then at the crater torn in the earth. He looked round him and he saw more dead men.

"He moved towards the centre of the courtyard. He was walking straight. It seemed to him that he had always walked that way. He didn't know where he was... it seemed an unknown world. A terrible dead land..."

From the world of cruel reality and pathological delusions let us turn to the land of fairy tales and then the realm of science fiction.

In "Alice in Wonderland," which is known the world over, many of the characters were taken from a pack of cards. In the sequel, "Through the Looking-glass" the same author makes his characters chessmen. For instance, among the white ranks we have Tweedledum and Tweedledee as rooks, the Knight and the Unicorn as knights, the Sheep and the Old Man as the bishops. The black men include Humpty Dumpty and the Lion as rooks, the Carpenter and the Knight as knights and the Crow and the Walrus as bishops. Among the pawns we meet flowers, the Daisy, Rose and Tiger-lily, and animals, the Frog, Oyster and Fawn. At the beginning, Alice does not belong to any side but, tempted by the possibility of winning a queen's crown, she agrees to be the white queen's pawn, starting from the second square with the promise that she will become a queen when she reaches the eighth. Her journey up to the eighth square, the adventures she has with the strange pieces she meets on her way in the land of chess, make up the story.

In a fantastic story "Once on Mercury" by the British writer Clifford D. Simac, we read about the adventures of some astronauts on that distant planet and here too enters an original chess theme. The conquerors of the Cosmos set up an observatory on Mercury. On the planet live strange creatures, the mysterious Bubbles who are able to change themselves into any shape that human beings think of. So the astronauts are in terrible danger as it is soon difficult to tell who is really a member of the research expedition and who a double created by the Bubbles. At the end, when the chief of the expedition is writing his report to the Solar Energy Council, he looks through the window and sees Bubbles changing into chessmen and jumping about around the observatory. There are more and more chess pieces every minute. The members of the team had been playing chess and, of course, thinking about the pieces.

In a story by the Frenchman Gerard Klein, "Le Gambit des Etoiles," published in 1958, the action takes place in the distant future, after man has conquered the Cosmos. Space ships manned by human beings are travelling at the speed of light among the stars near the Milky Way. The hero Jerg Algan undertakes a pioneer expedition outside our galaxy to find whether there are living creatures in areas hitherto unknown to man. The key to these unknown areas is a strange chessboard, picked up in an antique shop on one planet, with symbolical drawings on its squares. As the complicated story unfolds, higher beings living outside the Milky Way play a game in which planets, stars, human beings and history are elements of a cosmic version of chess. The hero is treated as a gambit pawn in a game between rival societies living in various parts of the Milky Way. Algan's expedition reveals that chess was invented by beings with a culture superior to that of the human race, dating back a million years before man first inhabited the earth.

Now we come to drama. Here we begin with some excerpts from Wolfgang Goethe's play "Goetz von Berlichingen." The second act opens

284

in a room where the Bishop and Adelheid are playing chess. Liebetraut plays idly on the zither. (we quote Act. I, Scene 6 in John Arden's adaptation).

"Bishop: Engaged to be married... I can hardly believe it.

"Adelheid: You are not paying attention to the game. Check!

"Bishop: Oh, yes, I am. I am feeling my way into the moves, that is all.

"Adelheid: Unless you are more careful, there will be no way left for you to feel. Check!

"Liebetraut: If I were your Eminence, instead of merely the blower of your Eminence's majestic nose, I should not only decline to play this game myself, but I should forbid it altogether throughout my dominions.

"Adelheid: Why?

"Liebetraut: It doesn't suit me, that's why.

"Adelheid: You are quite right: it does need a keen brain.

"Liebetraut: That is not my reason. How can a great Prince, who is given power and command over his fellow men, endure to sit at a little table and listen without rage to this continual nagging cry 'Check, check, check!' For who is being checked? His majesty himself. And who is it who checks him? Knights, squires, fortified castles, inferior clergy — it is the most subversive game under Heaven!

"Adelheid: I have checkmated you!"

The author introduces two contrasting views here, but Adelheid's belief that chess is a test of mental abilities has been taken as Goethe's personal opinion.

Plays have fairly often touched on a chess theme. In some it has been prominent. In 1876, the Palais Royal put on a one-act play "A Game of Chess" by Paul Ferrier. The play begins and ends with a game of chess with which the events have a direct metaphorical association. The comedy came out as a book the same year. The principle was similar in a one-act vaudeville show "The Game that was Won" by George

E. Vail, which was a great success (over 100 performances) when staged at the Paris Gymnase Dramatique in 1892. The pseudonym "Vail" was adopted by an American writer George Frost who published another version of the play under his real name. This version, entitled "Double Check," was published in 1909 as a supplement to the French chess magazine "La Stratégie."

A most original item was introduced into a comic opera "Beat Philidor!" with music by Amédée Dutacq to the libretto by Abraham Dreyfus. The first night was at the Opéra Comique in 1882. The story is not complicated, the interesting idea is to create situations in which

Illustration to Karol Irzykowski's play "The Victory."
Drawing by J. Skarżyński.

the great Philidor tries his hardest to lose. But do not let us spoil things by saying too much.

It is the year 1777. The scene is the famous Café de la Régence in Paris. Philidor has just won a game and is in an excellent humour. A young musician Richard enters the café. He is depressed because of an unhappy love affair. He wants to marry the beautiful Doris, daughter of the café proprietor Boudignot. The trouble is, that Boudignot only agrees to let Richard marry his daughter if he beats Philidor at chess. Of course, this is a good as a straight "No!" Hearing this, Philidor as a fellow-musician decides to help him and lose to him. He does not tell Doris, pretending that he is going to play seriously.

The game starts in front of a crowd of on-lookers. Richard, nervous, blunders terribly and Philidor has to be very careful not to win by accident. In the next room Doris is singing. Philidor recognizes the song as one of his own compositions, listens, forgets his plans in a mood of emotion — and wins.

What bad luck! All seems to be lost, but Phili-dor speaks bluntly to Boudignot, telling him that if he does not let the young lovers marry he will stop playing in his café and go to Boudignot's rival. Papa gives in and Doris finds happiness with Richard, who proves a better musician than chess player.

A little-known Polish play with a chess theme is one written by Karol Irzykowski in his youth and completely forgotten today, entitled "The Victory." He began it in 1897, but only finished it seven years later. It appeared in print in 1907 in a volume of collected poems and plays which is a rarity today. It abounds in irony, wit and humour, and for this reason a lot of it remains topical, although to the modern reader it is too overloaded with symbolism and too pretentious in its psychology and philosophy.

The first act starts in the tent of the great chief Sol who is discussing with the commanders of his army plans for a decisive battle next day. His most trusted commanders are called Blask

(Glare) and Płomień (Flame), and he, as "Sol," represents the sun and the day. Blask and Pło-mień cannot agree about tactics. Sol reacts to their quarrelling rather strangely: he disarms them and packs them away into a box. His strange behaviour is explained later.

Late that night, Queen Nox, "Patron of the Dark," appears in Sol's tent via an underground passage. She is the ruler of the town besieged by Sol's army. Nox tries to charm him with her beauty and persuades him to betray his comrades and his cause, promising him love and the sharing of her power. Sol refuses at first but his resistance begins to weaken under the influence of her charms. Passion turns him from a chief, master of his thoughts and desires, into a submis-sive slave of this despotic dark-eyed woman. Nox gains complete mastery over him and Sol becomes an obedient lamb who does everything the cunning queen of the dark asks him to. And now, the strangest chess themes begin to creep in:

"SOL: I will betray our plans to you. Or even better, I'll tell you how to win the battle. Here is the battlefield. Sit down. (He brings a chess-board and sets out the men.)

"NOX: Wait, it's a little too dark here. (She goes to the entrance of the tent, takes a few stars from the sky and hangs them on the candela-brum.)

"Sol gazes thoughtfully at the board.

"Nox sits down besides him, then sits on his knee, puts her arms round his neck and kisses him.

"SOL: Now look, my queen. The moves so far have been 1 P-K4 P-K4 2 N-KB3 N-QB3 3 B-N5 P-QR3 4 B-R4 N-B3 5 N-B3 P-Q3 6 P-Q4 B-Q2 7 BxN BxB 8 Q-K2 PxP 9 NxP B-Q2 10 Castles, B-K2 11 P-QN3 Castles 12 B-N2 P-QN4. Black' moves are not bad, he threatens 13...P-N5 or 13... P-B4.

"I now gave the order to make the thirteenth move, P-QR4, but over-hastily, for 13 P-K5 would certainly have been better.

Sofonisba Anguisciola: "A Game of Chess" (1555). The picture shows the painter's three sisters and their old servant. From the collection of the Poznań National Museum.

"NOX: So things aren't so bad for me as I thought?

"SOL: No, you are better off than I am for the moment. The battle has only just begun (he smiles). I like to give my enemy a little ground so as to work up my own fury.

"NOX: And what next?

"SOL: You play with my men and I'll play with yours. I move 13... P-N5, for instance.

"NOX: Then I could move the knight to Q1, for example.

"SOL: Excellent! There will be retreat all along the line now; see! 14... P-B4.

"NOX: Very well, 15 N-KB3.

"SOL: Now we place the bishop on B3. A further retreat is then essential, 6 N-Q2, after which, by advancing the queen's pawn, you'll eventually shut out my (white's) only bishop.

"NOX: Wait a minute, show me again, I was too busy kissing you to attend properly.

"SOL: ... You see, we can play against each other tomorrow more or less like this: I make this move, you make that, then I'll move this way — are you listening? Suppose we both advance our king's bishops' pawns to the fourth? I daren't make my moves too stupid...

"SOL: Your plan could be, for instance... K-KR1, R-KN1, your other rook to QR2, so that in due course, when you've advanced your pawn from KN2, you could bring your rook right across the board from QR2 to KR2. Can you remember all that?

"NOX: Yes, I've made dozens of attacks of that kind against a castled king. Leave the tactics to me; I'll play with you like a cat plays with a mouse and then smash you. My only request to you is, leave me an open file or two, I love open lines.

"SOL: Suppose White goes P-KR3? Then by... P-KN5 and... PxP you can get your open line?

"The Chess Players." Canvas by an unknown Venetian painter of 1590 (Berlin-Dahlem, Staatliches Museum).

"NOX: Yes, yes, I'll manage, it will be quite enough. I'll provide you with a shattering mate" (She nestles up to him.).

The first act then strays completely from chess to love. The second act scene is "the battlefield, a chessboard. On one side Sol's camp, on the other the camp of Night, behind which can be seen the town, built apparently of blocks of crystallized darkness. It is a rainy morning."

Preparations for battle begin in Sol's camp at dawn. To his comrades' surprise he demands not his sword but a mirror; calls for his hairdresser, has himself sprayed with scent. His disinclination for fight is further demonstrated by his saying a rusty sword will do and ordering a soldier to hold an umbrella over him during the battle. Meanwhile, in Queen Nox's camp, preparations are being made in grim earnest. The four commanders, bearing the names of NA, PO, LE, ON, are told the plan of attack in chess phraseology. The black queen orders ten thousand pairs of manacles to be prepared and a stake to be whittled for Sol, in revenge for the concessions she had made during the game of love. The battle begins, Sol conducting it in such a way that his subordinates begin to suspect him of wanting to lose. Could this be betrayal? Sol delivers orders with his eyes constantly straying towards the queen. From the 13th to the 28th move, the game swings steadily in Nox's favour.

His KN2 square is being bombarded with bombs and grapeshot.

"SOL: Look at that now: what an interesting way to be ruined! I seem to have seen those moves somewhere before. I'm afraid nothing can save us.

"PŁOMIEŃ: How can you be so calm! (He begins to weep.)

"SOL (With sympathy): What is this, tears in the eyes of a soldier? Keep calm, general. Have another cigarette. We'll manage somehow.

"Enters a herald.

"HERALD: My queen and mistress, Nox, the most glorious, most generous of all, calls upon

An engraving by Daniel Chodo-
wiecki from the second half of
the 18th century.

you, chief of the white spirits, to surrender, for your situation is hopeless, as you must see yourself if you know anything about the play of López and Philidor.

"SOL: Tell your queen that I have surrendered everything to her including myself but, for my pride to be completely broken, I am humbly awaiting a magnificent instructive checkmate, for in such a situation no true chess player surrenders.

"PŁOMIEŃ: What an answer!

"The herald takes the answer to the queen.

"NOX: Is he joking, or does he really mean it... But it doesn't matter anyway, I have him in my hands. If he's pretending, all the worse for him. Give the order to fire! (It gets darker and darker from the smoke of the cannonades.)

"SOL (shouts): You forget, my sweet queen, that I have been given the power to rend your night apart with lightning. (Flashes of lightning light up the battlefield.)

The position reached is as in the diagram.

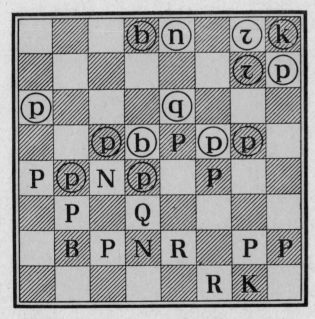

"SOL: Do not doubt, my queen, that I am yours, whether conquered or conqueror, but I'm not giving in yet. 29. P-KN3!

"NA: Sol is unable to reconcile himself to this unusual situation, he is putting up a despairing defence.

"NOX: All the better — nobody can blame me for what I am going to do.

29... PxP.

"NA: But, your Majesty, wouldn't it have been better to play 29... P-N5 so as not to open up the king's bishop's file for him?

"ON: Or, for instance 29... B-R1 and 29... Q-QB3...?

"NOX: Cowards! With your modernist daydreams! I am keeping to the classical traditions of the noble game and am playing for an open file myself. Do you realize what a noble sacrifice we might make on KN6? We must work out the combination later; it will be the crowning touch to the game we have played so well till now that it may one day be quoted as a text-book example in military academies.

"On the white side:

"SOL: That's interesting — give me a chair! The queen obviously hasn't realized what the situation will be when I take this pawn. Rook — bishop — the king in the corner. Ha! Now you can rest, gentlemen. Give me that chair. (He sits down.)

30 RxP R(N2)-N4

"SOL: Of course, we shall lose, gentlemen; that is inescapable. I told you it would be my wedding day today, there will be a great ball. But we might as well make a fight of this game. For instance, 31 BxP, PxB; 32 RxQP — ah! we threaten two bishops. But Black could reply 32 — BxN.

"For the moment, we'll just move 31 R (K2)-KB2 if you have nothing against it, gentlemen?

"I see a lot between the lines.

"For instance, if we were to be able to follow up with N-Q6, after exchanges on our Q6 and KB5, we might well begin to advance ourselves with P-KN4!

"NA: The lion has freed one paw from the trap. What will happen now?

"SOL (still thinking hard): But if I play N-Q6 I should leave my pawn on K5 unsupported — but Oh, that diagonal on to his king!! 31 ... N-N2

"NOX: Look, how obvious it all is, how logical, simple and powerful. For the time being the knight protects the pawn, and is going to KR4 either to gain the exchange or sacrifice on KN6. Do you see my plan, gentlemen?"

"SOL (thinking): now, by N-Q6 I could attack the pawn on my KB5 for the fourth time. But she could then capture my king's pawn; or she could go 32...N-R4... But by some strange chance I have a better defence than I expected.

I must think this over carefully. 32 Kt-Q6, Q×P; 33 N (Q2)-B4... No! 33 N×P, N-R4 34 N×P, N×P and my knight on Q4 moves — where? She could reply — Q×B. If only my bishop on QN2 were protected! (Shouts) What is my bishop doing?

"COMMANDERS (peering): He's asleep.

"SOL: Wake him up, in case I want him. No... that's no good... but maybe B×QP — or ah! — Rx QP — I may have a terrible double check at my disposal. True, that bishop remains unprotected... but double check! Where would my rook go? To Q3? No good! I thought I was beginning to see something, but now it has gone.

François Boucher: "A Game of Chess" (18th century).

M. Duboy: "The Chess Player" (19th century).

292

"NOX: Our enemy is thinking a long time. He's obviously wondering whether to surrender to at least avoid a shameful defeat. Let the herald go to him once more. Herald, go and tell the Chief of the Whites that death awaits him if he does not surrender! We won't stand on ceremony with him. Only immediate capitulation can save him."

The Herald calls upon Sol to surrender, but Sol, absorbed in the game, tells him "Go to the devil!" He suddenly gets an idea for a master stroke. Perhaps move the knight to Q6 yet. He analyses different versions of the move from all sides, muttering to himself. Finally:

"SOL:... Victory! What a triumphal march... what a miraculous vision!... Cross-fire!... Several positions won in one go... On that poor black Queen — so free but so powerless. What are the delights of love in comparison with the profound beauty of this combination! From what depths of my soul has this idea arisen? 32 N-Q6!

"HERALD (returning): He told me to go to the devil.

"NOX: ... I wanted to make peace, but now, I wash my hands of it all. I'll have him on his knees in a few moves.

32 ... Q x P

"He's like a wolf. He seems to be tame as lamb, but becomes fierce at the sight of blood...

"SOL: Oh, oh! I forgot about... N-K3, I only thought of the knight going to KR4.

"Well, it can't be helped, I'll play 33 N x P. If she now plays 33... N-K3 I could lose, for instance

34 R-R4, R x Pch! 35 P x R, B x R...

(To his commanders):

Make that move for me but hesitantly, conveying the impression that we are terrified.

33 N x P N-R4

"BLACK QUEEN'S STAFF: Bravo!

"NA: I should have preferred 33... N-K3.

"NOX (to the other generals, looking con-

temptuously at NA): He was a good chess player once, but he's getting old now. He's lost his youthful drive.

"SOL: I thought she'd do that. Blinded by the pretty picture of sacrificing on KN6, she doesn't see anything else.

34 R x P

"NOX (surprised): There is a flash of lightning. What... how dare he?

"NA: That is why you should have moved ... N-K3, your Majesty.

"NOX (furious, slaps his face): No insolence! Why are you all staring? What's the matter? you surely don't believe in his genius, do you? Block-heads! Don't you see it is mere desperation? We shall go through with our plan.

34...N x P. 35 N x N.

"NOX (contemptuously): Of course! What else could he do? He is playing into our hands!

35... R x Nch. 36 P x R R x Pch.

"SOL: Yes, all according to programme. I shall lose — but only because of beauty: I shall fail as a conqueror whilst gazing at a vision.

"NOX'S STAFF: Bravo, bravo! Our queen on K5 is serving us well.

"NOX: Telephone mother, tell her I've won! Put up posters announcing that Sol will be expected tomorrow! 37 K-B1. He's going on! It is time to put an end to this nonsense. We capture his helpless queen. Ho, there! I'm taking your queen, White Chief!

37...R x Q

"SOL: I'm beginning to wonder whether I ever really liked queens!

"NOX'S ARMY: Hooray!

H. Bielski: "A Game of Chess"
(19th century).

"NOX: And now we'll add some strong words to that strong blow!...

Nox tries to ensnare Sol with incantations. He seems to be falling under the spell of her hypnotic charm again but suddenly pulls himself together and with a great effort, tearing himself free from her ruinous fascination. "Here is my answer. Look at this, beast!"

38 R-KN4!!!

There is confusion in the black camp. Nox is so horrified that she cannot say a word, her army is dumbfounded. Black's pieces flee in all directions.

"NOX (finding her voice at last): You traitor! That game will be declared invalid at an international congress! He suggested those moves to me himself — he got me entangled in his net — what cunning, what treachery, how vile! Even history may take his side! Oh, what despair! Oh, my mother! (she flees.)."

Sol is triumphant. The walls of the town crumble. His men go in pursuit and reach Nox's retinue. Nox pleads for mercy, but Sol is relentless and strikes her down with his sword. The city of darkness is blown up... the blocks of darkness dissolve and the whole town is enveloped in the flame of sunbeams, and Sol drives off into the sun, followed by all those belonging to him.

The triumphal comedy comes to an end. Irzykowski added a long postscript:

"... In Act 1, the hero sacrifices everything for love; in Act II, this passion is countered by an intellectual passion which surges up in him to his own surprise, the zest for crystal-clear presentation of an artistic idea. Now Sol sacrifices everything to this.

"In spite of the play's whimsical framework, the basic idea is followed logically and in Act II it is taken to its limit. I wove a game of chess into the play because I could not be satisfied

Artur Markowicz: "A Game of Chess" (19th century). From the Cracow National Museum.

Wolff: "A Game of Chess," a 19th century lithograph.

with some cheap allegory to convey the intellectual passion I wanted to depict... I wanted to convey this passion with its specific atmosphere, to show the birth of the idea as a stroke of genius, coming like a flash of lightning from the blackness of the clouds... the material originally collected for this purpose was not suitable because I had practically no idea of war technique; so I substituted a game of chess, which can convey much of the atmosphere of warfare and of which I had a good theoretical and practical knowledge having played it for years. The game played is not my own invention, but one from the tournament at Hastings 1895 between Tarrasch and Waldbrodt, two of the most famous players of the day. That game seemed so strange and eloquent an awakening of the lion, that I could never have written 'The Victory' without it. Today, I cannot remember whether the idea for the play came to me through the influence of that game or whether the idea came first and then I associated it with the game as somehow kindred to my idea. But almost all the explanations of the game are my own, particularly where it is not a question of pragmatic evaluation of the moves, but of the psychology of creative thinking in chess; for it meant going to the root of a chess genius's ideas, reducing to words the equivalent of complicated and subtle processes of thought. Of course, only a true chess player can enter this magic circle in which sparks of fantasy by the thousand flash up and disappear unused before the right idea is born in a flash of genius. But I think that even he who is ignorant of chess will feel what I want to convey if only he does not throw aside 'The Victory' impatiently saying 'What's this? A chess textbook?'..."

It is because we agree with the author that we took the liberty of quoting such large excerpts from the play.

Other fields of art than literature have featured chess.

297

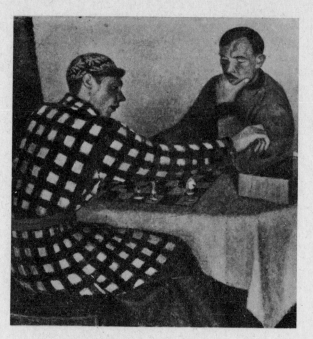

Stanisław Masłowski: "An Arab Coffee-House" (1912).

Marcin Samlicki: "A Game of Chess" (1934).

One very original composition is "The Chess Players" by the Dutch painter Lucas van Leyden, dated 1508. A woman is moving a black knight. The artist has depicted very finely the characteristically poised hand over the board. The faces of the players and spectators bear interestingly varied expressions; some absorbed, some allowing their attention to wander.

An unknown Venetian painter of 1590 depicted two players bent over the board, engrossed in the final moves of a game. The rich ornamentation of the walls, sumptuous splendour of their clothes, particularly the headwear, not to mention the presence of a small dog, made a lively contrast with the restraint and immobile calm of the players.

Paris Bordone (16th century) gave his picture a more stately character. Here the chessboard is only a pretext for posing two persons for a portrait. In the background there is a park, buildings, and a group of card players.

All three of these pictures are in the former Royal Gallery in Berlin.

Chess paintings are rare in galleries of Poland but in the National Museum at Poznań is a valuable one in oils by the well known Italian woman painter Sofonisba Anguisciola (1527–1623). It shows a group of women, the three sisters of the artist and their old maidservant, bent over a board. On the left is Lucia (another painter), on the right, Minerva, and behind the table, the youngest sister Eugenia. This picture, entitled "A Game of Chess" was purchased in Paris by Count A. Raczyński in 1824 from the collection left by L. Bonaparte. It is perhaps one of the most beautiful canvasses with a chess theme ever painted.

298

The annual national exhibitions constantly offer new drawings and paintings about chess; but those illustrating the game in really fresh and original ways either in subject or form, are rare. We usually find scenes in club-rooms or portrait studies of players and onlookers. Pictures from past centuries seem much more varied and inventive.

One painting in oils by the contemporary Polish artist Eugenia Różańska "Playing Chess," however, does have an unusual approach; the intellectual character of the game is contrasted with the clothing of the players, who are circus clowns. The whole picture radiates an atmosphere of serenity and contentment.

The outstanding French painter Ernest Meissonier exhibited his picture "A Game of Chess" in a Paris salon in 1836 where it aroused general interest in the hitherto unknown artist and was eventually sold for two thousand francs. Seven years later, his picture "Three Friends" brought the artist thirty thousand. So chess started him on a profitable path.

Finally, the cinema. Pride of place goes to a film made in 1925 by V. Pudovkin, in collaboration with N. Shpikovsky, called "Chess Fever."

Zygmunt Kowalewski: "Young Chess Players" (1954).

Danuta Rewkiewicz: "A Chess Problem" pen drawing (1940).

Eugenia Różańska: "A Game of Chess" (1957).

This was the first film-directing effort of Pudovkin's career. All Moscow was agog at the time over an international chess tournament there. The hero of the day was Capablanca, an immensely popular personality among the Muscovites. The tournament aroused wider interest than could have been expected, the games being followed attentively by chess players and laymen alike. People everywhere were talking about the games, in the streets, in the trams and in their homes.

This "Chess Fever" Pudovkin put on the screen was made at lightning speed. Shots were taken in the streets of Moscow, the roving camera catching the mood of the tournament fans as they analysed the games on pocket chess sets, discussing positions that had arisen. The camera penetrated to the very threshold of the tournament hall; its roving eye swept round the new Hotel Metropol, where the tournament was held. Capablanca took part in one of the episodes.

"Chess." A composition by Juan Gris.

301

Scenes from a two-act Soviet film comedy "Chess Fever" produced in 1925 by Vsevolod Rudovkin and N. Shpikovsky, a satire on mania for chess linked up with an international chess tournament taking place in Moscow at that time.

Scene from the German film "Illusion".

Scene from the French film "Beauty and the Beast".

Skillful montage mingled authentic shots with staged ones.

This short two-act film, to which Pudovkin did not attach any importance at first, treating it as a great joke, made him as a producer. It proved a very successful effort in a realistic comedy.

Kempelen's famous Chess Automaton became the subject of two feature films, as we have mentioned.

In a Czechoslovakian comedy film "Wedding with Obstacles" made in 1950 by Miroslaw Cikan, the main character is a young mechanical engineer played by Wladimir Raz, whose hobby is solving chess problems.

An unusual game of chess is the motif on which the Swedish film director Ingmar Bergman based his dramatic film "The Seventh Seal" in which a mediaeval "morality" touches on the philosophy of life.

A Swedish knight Antonius returns from the Crusades. A plague has swept over Europe spreading fear and uncertainty everywhere. Antonius, tortured by doubts about the very existence of God, and seeing all around him destruction and the injustices of fate, challenges Death to a game of chess. The stake is his life. If he wins, perhaps Death will reveal to him the secret of existence... By distracting Death's attention, he manages to save the family of a wandering actor from ruin... He perishes, without finding the answer to his question "Is some superhuman power directing the chaos of destruction and scourging mankind with the plague?" He saves others by sacrificing himself. He beats Death but loses himself.

The game is the film's main theme. Death appears as a mysterious wanderer clothed in a black cloak. The idea of the film came to Bergman from some old frescoes in a little rural church near Stockholm. An unknown mediaeval painter had depicted Death at a chessboard, in several scenes, culminating in the game with a Knight.

A beautiful, ingenious film about chess, the only one of its kind ever made, showing the game in progress without the players, was produced by a German amateur film-maker, Richard Groschop in 1936 "The King's Little Tragedy."

Scene from the Polish film "The Deserter."

Scene from the French-Italian film "The Volga Boatmen."

The chessmen moved about by themselves. The film won prizes and distinctions at international competitions (among others, at Lwów in 1938) and was subsequently shown throughout Europe.

It opens with a picture of an empty board. Out of the darkness, a white standard-bearer emerges. In the background we see the white army...

Then comes the black standard-bearer. We glimpse the black king. War has been declared. The white chessmen are standing ready to go into battle... An officer (a knight) inspects the ranks. Then the stone figures of the chess army begin to move forward over the vast chequered expanse.

There is a flash on the horizon. The battle begins. The infantry moves forward, the opposing sides clash with stubborn hand-to-hand fighting.

The black knight jumps towards the king and queen. He attacks the queen who is killed in trying to shield her consort. The knight carries the queen from the battlefield.

The black queen joins in the fray. She puts the king in check. The white king retreats. The lights go dim. The black bishop goes into attack. The white king dodges him, but another aggressor appears — the black knight.

It gets darker and darker. The white king is surrounded. He surrenders. The black men form

Two scenes from the Polish animated cartoon film "The Tournament," directed by Nehrebecki with décor and costumes by Jerzy Zitzman, 1959.

a lane along which the conquered king slowly walks off the battlefield. The white flag is lowered from its mast...

Then the lights go up. The little tragedy of the little king has been acted to the end. This film poem was brought to life by stone chessmen. We have seen a game of real "living chess," such as could never be acted by people dressed up for a masquerade; the entire spectacle was acted by the chessmen "in person," in a way that could be achieved only on film.

Hans Richter, the well known German producer of experimental films, in 1957 made a film called "8×8", in which he transposed chess elements by means of different associations of ideas and visual effects, linking a game of chess with eight episodes of a strange story. He gave sound a special artistic function in this film; for instance, in the scene where a pawn (Jean Cocteau) advances across the chequered battlefield to be promoted to a queen, instead of a musical background we hear a voice telling us how a pawn moves. The voice hurries or relaxes accordingly as the pawn speeds along or slows down. In another episode the director himself appears on the board playing against himself. He makes a mistake and finds himself in an awkward situation. The trumpet accompaniment to the action suddenly stills and begins to repeat itself like a cracked gramophone record. Finally he finds a way out of his troubles and the trumpet resumes its interrupted melody.

"... A huge chessboard hangs over the lawn, swinging on a massive tree. The only pieces on it are the white queen and Julien; they are painted on it.

"All the shots are taken through the leaves of the tree. Julien offers the queen a bow and arrows, but she does not want to take them and flinches away. He raises the bow and shoots.

"A close up: The arrow hits the white queen on the chessboard. The live queen shudders, for an identical arrow pierces her breast..."

The film continues with numerous associations

Scene from the American film "Casablanca" (1943).

Scene from the French film "The Condemned" (1948).

305

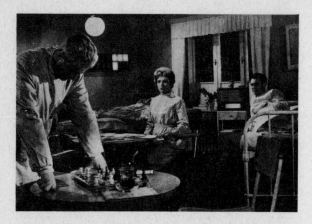

Scene from the Polish film "Signals" (1959).

In the Soviet film "The New Adventures of Puss-in-Boots" the decor and costumes are based on chess and playing card motifs.

A shot from Hans Richter's experimental film "8 × 8" (1957).

of a surrealist character and the chess motif typifies predestinations; man is moved about in space against his own will.

Carroll's story "Through the Looking-glass," is echoed in a Soviet fairy tale-film (1958) directed by A. Rou, "The New Adventures of Puss-in-Boots." A little girl Luba is to play the part of the Princess in the school play "Puss-in-Boots," but suddenly runs a temperature and falls ill. After taking her medicine she drops off to sleep. On her bed, near her, is a kitten, and, on the table, a dusty chessboard with chessmen scattered over it. The strangest things happen. We hear music in the distance and the chessmen come to life, turning into human figures. Luba becomes queen, her uncle the king. A lot of action takes place in the kingdom of chess. The castle and its rooms are decorated with chess motifs. Its courtyard is an enormous chessboard on which tournaments are held.

A Polish animated cartoon film "Tournament," produced by W. Nehrebecki after a project by J. Zitzman, had many original points.

The characters personify chessmen; grotesque happenings take place during a tournament between the armies of the white and black kings on the chequered courtyard of the castle. The battle is waged in violent tempo but strictly according to the laws of chess. The kings are constantly quarrelling over their rivalry for the hand of a certain lady, who prefers to lavish her favours on a little squire-pawn. After a stubborn battle, the kings make up their quarrel, but during the feast that follows it breaks out anew and the two hostile armies face each other once again on the black and white chequered courtyard.

We have come back to our starting point. The film puts amusing emphasis on the essence of chess: the repeated battles between the same two chess armies, repeatedly re-forming for a fresh conflict no matter how the last one has ended.

As chess goes on daily throughout the world, one thing is sure, that it will inspire many a writer, painter and producer yet.

In a Polish animated cartoon film "The Tournament" by Władysław Nehrebecki, the scene is a world of animated chessmen. The decor and costumes were designed by Jerzy Zitzman (1960).

Two scenes from "The Tournament": LEFT, the White Pawn, happy admirer of the beautiful Queen, for whose favours two suitors, the White and Black Kings, are competing (RIGHT).

XI. CHESS CURIOSITY BOX

A bas-relief showing a fox and wolf with a chessboard. An ornamental stove tile of Czech manufacture from the early 15th century.

310

BLINDFOLD CHESS

A strong chess player's powers of calculation and concentration have often been admired. Blindfold play has been regarded as quite phenomenal.

In "blindfold" chess the player does not see the board and the men but must rely on his memory of the various positions that arise. He is told his opponent's move in a recognized system of notation and, in reply, works out and announces his own. The moves of the game are made on a "control" chessboard. If both players are playing "blindfold" the referee or the two players' representatives sit at the board.

Anybody who knows the concentration called for in ordinary chess will realize what extraordinary demands are made by a game played in the memory. A good memory is, of course, an essential.

A good imagination is needed, also the ability to register the various chess positions in the mind as though they were being filmed. Great players have taken on not merely one, but dozens of opponents, blindfold at the same time. They must register the situation in each game separately in the mind and also envisage the possible further developments from each position in every game.

Leading chess players have often possessed excellent memories. Alekhine, for instance, after having played twenty-five or thirty simultaneous games, could re-enact the course of each game a few days later. Rubinstein could recall from memory thousands of the games he had played from the moment he started participating in such meetings. Botvinnik, former world champion, remembers several thousand games and a very large number of opening moves.

An expert's specialized memory may be much superior to his everyday memory.

In private life, apart from chess, Alekhine's memory was not remarkable; he was absent-minded, he was often to be seen searching in all his pockets for the spectacles he was always losing. Absorbed in solving the chess problems, he was reluctant to come down to everyday life.

During one of his simultaneous blindfold displays Alekhine, a big smoker, felt for and took out a cigarette but could not find a match box in any of his pockets.

"Could you lend me your matches," he asked a spectator, "I've left mine at home. Isn't it strange what a bad memory I've got?"

An anecdote is one thing, facts are another. With his "bad" memory Alekhine once played 32 opponents blindfold at once, establishing a new world record. The session lasted twelve hours, the then world champion winning 19 games, losing four, and drawing nine. This was at the Chicago world exhibition in 1933. One newspaper commentator wrote: "This record of his is surely the limit of the possibilities of the human mind and human memory in this field. Beyond this limit there can be nothing but chaos and madness begins."

This was certainly an extraordinary, and almost disturbing event. Simultaneous blindfold chess had been known for centuries, but never so many games at a time. The Saracen Buzecca played two blindfold games simultaneously in Florence in 1266 with a good result.

Blindfold chess in Ruthenia was mentioned by Łukasz Górnicki, a Polish writer of the 16th century, in his book "The Courtier." "Obviously in Moscow they do not pracise it much and yet they play chess very well, some of them even play from memory, during a journey."

Philidor's blindfold feats caused great astonishment. A description of the three blindfold games he played in London in 1788 has survived to our times. He gave odds of a move; his weakest opponent was given a pawn as well. He won the first game in 51 moves, the second in 47 and the third in 59.

Morphy once played eight games blindfold, winning seven. A detailed description has sur-

vived, supplemented by a drawing showing him in play against the eight best chess players of Paris. This was in the famous Paris Café de la Régence in 1858, the engagement lasting over ten hours. He sat in an armchair with his back to the room and did not stop playing for a moment, gazing at a blank wall all the time. After seven hours or so he took up the offensive on every board. One after another his adversaries resigned, only two managing to draw. An enraptured journalist wrote: "Morphy has proved himself superior to Caesar, in that, he came, he did not see, he conquered." But, as a result of overstrain, Morphy had to give up blindfold chess, which is detrimental to health, as we shall mention later. He died at the age of 47, the victim of delusions.

The Russian chess champion Tchigorin demonstrated simultaneous blindfold play more than once. In 1884 and 1885 he gave two sessions in St. Petersburg, the first time against eight adversaries (winning 7 games, drawing one), and the next against nine players (seven wins, one draw, and one lost). There is some interesting data showing how rapidly a chess player tires during such a display. Playing eight members of the St. Petersburg chess club blindfold in 1892, Tchigorin announced 58 moves in the first hour of play, 38 in the second hour, but only twenty to twenty five moves per hour after that; nevertheless his powers of concentration were demonstrated by the fact that after twenty moves he told one of his adversaries he would checkmate him in another five.

Emanuel Lasker, 26 years World Champion, also tried blindfold chess, taking on six opponents simultaneously about 1899 but he gave it up because of the nervous exhaustion it entailed.

The American Harry Nelson Pillsbury encountered sixteen opponents, among them a blind man and a good player named Montalvo, at Havana in 1900. Two years later in Hanover, he played 21 games, the demonstration lasting from 3 p.m. to two o'clock in the morning. Later in America he reached his maximum of 25. Once, making his 17th move, he announced a forced mate in eleven.

Janowsky, on his way to make a tour of America in 1898, played friendly games on board ship. The ship's logbook records that he played whist and blindfold chess simultaneously, winning at both.

Another kind of "blindfold" chess was demonstrated by two Berlin players Bordeleben and Cohn in 1909. They played, consulting with each other, against 21 opponents. To make their task more difficult they played, meanwhile, a blindfold game with each other.

A now forgotten Polish chess player of the second half of the last century, Maczuski, was a master of blindfold chess. Against a certain Mazzolani in Ferrara in 1876, on the 18th move he announced mate in eleven moves. He also won a match in Amiens without sight of board and men, against a group of players consulting together.

Another chess player of Polish origin, George Koltanowski, claimed to have established the world record in blindfold simultaneous chess in 1937. When in Edinburgh, he took on 34 opponents blindfold at once. He won 24 games, drew ten, the event lasting for almost 14 hours with three short breaks. He drank a lot of hot milk during the exhibition and smoked innumerable cigars. For beating Alekhine's record, which had been thought impossible, Koltanowski received £ 1,000 from a private patron. He admitted that only financial considerations had induced him to undergo such a mental and nervous strain.

After the exhibition he was asked by journalists how he could remember the course of 34 games, involving 1088 men moving on 2176 squares.

He answered: "I haven't got a good sight memory, but I can remember moves well. Before each move I reconstruct the course of the game in memory and make the next move mentally. I have worked out a mnemonic system of my own which helps me to remember each game separately. When I begin, I try to link whole groups of boards with the same opening moves; for instance, the first five of each ten chessboards. According to my opponents' replies, different opening variations arise, but the common point of departure helps me to trace back the course of the game."

In this way the various games played become imprinted in the memory like different variations of the same musical theme, so to speak. The player does not have to remember the situation on the board in a given moment, but he must be able to reproduce the "melodic line." Every infringement or deviation from the actual course of the game will "sound" as a false note. Stefan Zweig in his famous "Chess Story" com-

"And Daddy makes out that it's quite hard to play chess blindfold!" ("L'Echiquier de Paris").

"A difficult end-game." French gravure of the mid-19th century after Paul Gavarni's drawing.

pares the skill of "blindfold play" to the virtuosity of a composer or conductor who inwardly "hears" the music without an orchestra and can conduct without a score. An article was published in a French chess magazine where the author meditated on certain analogies between a piece of music and a game of chess, seeing a similarity in the fact that both develop in time. Only a person who has the gift of reproducing very short-lived particular situations can memorize melodies and chess games.

J. Mieses and Richard Réti were good blindfold players. The latter vied in this respect with Pillsbury, Alekhine and Najdorf, the acknowledged masters of it in their day. Mieczysław

Najdorf, a Pole by birth, Argentine by naturalization, broke the record of blindfold simultaneous play, which had remained unchallenged for many years when, in 1947, he gave a demonstration in São Paulo against 45 opponents which lasted nearly 24 hours. He won 39 games, drew four and lost two. It must be added, however, that the adversaries in this unique session were not on the same standard as, for instance, Alekhine's or Réti's in their greatest displays.

Najdorf's record was only beaten in 1961 when a young Hungarian, Janos Flesch, took on 52 first-class players in Budapest. He dictated the moves through a microphone, sitting with his back to the hall. After twelve hours of strained effort he won 31 games, drew 18 and lost 3.

J. Mieses published in 1918 a monograph on the history and psychology of blindfold chess. On the basis of his own observations, he maintained that this kind of play is detrimental to health, a mere show, and no true contribution to the art of chess at all.

Another interesting statement is that by the Russian master A. Petrov, who, as early as 1858, wrote: "It's easier to dive for pearls than to play chess like this. Chess thought gains nothing from it. If somebody can play well without seeing the board, he can certainly play better seeing it. So blindfold chess is more like a trick, for public entertainment. Chess is a noble art in itself; it does not need such tricks which, amazing as they may be, are not of any real value."

The French psychiatrist Alfred Binet conducted large-scale research into blindfold chess in 1894, collecting scientific data about it for the first time in chess history, based on measurements of the nervous reactions of players and answers to a questionnaire. The results proved without a doubt that the mental strain involved in several hours of concentrating of the mind and attention was almost pathological.

In the Soviet Union, the problem of "blindfold" chess playing was examined from the scientific point of view in the inter-war years. Players were

"I now move my bishop from KB5 to KR7 and you are mated."
Cartoon by Z. Lengren.

subjected to examination by psychiatrists. The researchers stated that master's blindfold chess memory would be explained by their special training as a kind of professional memory, based on a thorough knowledge of the subject, similar to that of musicians, philologists and even post office officials. The ability for exceptional concentration of attention, so greatly admired by the uninitiated, is no greater than the ability shown by many brain workers in other fields. In blindfold chess, however, the concentration is of excessively long duration and this is detrimental to health.

Blindfold chess was consequently officially forbidden in the Soviet Union in 1930. Alekhine himself expressed the opinion that it "had an adverse effect on one's play, distorted the line of thought and style of play considerably." Leading Soviet chess champions never indulged in it; they did not believe it had any training value,

Paris plays Vienna by telegraph, 1894: the scene at the Paris end (Café de la Régence). Engraving after an on-the-spot drawing by Motty. In the lower right-hand corner is Rosenthal with Tchigorin facing him.

acknowledging only its specific and spectacular character.

So much for blindfold chess, our first chess "curiosity."

Contrary to common belief, really blind chess players do not play "blind" in the way described above but finger chessmen to get the situation on the board. Their chessmen are pegged into a special slotted board, as in sets used for play whilst travelling, the white men differing from the black, e.g., by having little spikes which are easily discernible to the touch.

Blind chess players, however, have sometimes played from memory alone.

An interesting thing happened in France in 1865. A blind old man, who lived in the village of Ariège, was an excellent player, and never used any sort of men or board.

At the age of 60, his sight was restored. Now he could look at the board but he played better without. Seeing the position not only was no help but only disturbed him.

The so-called "chess blindness" often talked about among players is another thing altogether. It is a symptom of overstrain. Exhausted by nervous effort and concentration a player is blind to a threatened danger, does not see a chessman or takes it for another. Or chess blindness may make him analyse complicated lines of play, when the move he should make is obvious.

Or after thinking for a long time the victim hands his opponent a piece for nothing. Beware of overstrain yourself at chess, for the best optician in the world cannot cure you of chess blindness.

CHESS BY POST

Playing at a distance, that is sending moves by post or telegraph, first developed towards

In the Spanish film "Calabuig" (1956) the parson plays the lighthouse keeper by telephone.

the end of the last century. The increased speed of the mails and the invention in turn of the telegraph, telephone and wireless, gradually made it possible to play individual and collective chess games between more and more distant localities. As early as the 1830's, chess clubs in Berlin and Magdeburg conducted chess tournaments by correspondence. (Even earlier, Edinburgh and London had played a famous match by post — B. H. Wood.) Krupski, author of the first Polish textbook on chess wrote in the second edition of his "Chess Strategy," dated 1844, about a match played by correspondence between Berlin and Poznań. The first tournament contested by telephone was that between London and Liverpool in 1891. In the early years of this century, a series of cable matches between Britain and America aroused wide interest. After the second world war there were matches between the USSR and the USA, also Britain, France, Australia, Spain and the Argentine by wireless.

Some people regard correspondence chess as the ideal form of the game, eliminating as it does the distraction of the clock, which may ruin a good game; eliminating too the influence of nerves, indisposition, etc. Another advantage of playing by correspondence is the possibility of trying one's hand against strong adversaries one would perhaps never otherwise meet. Anybody can play with anybody! Distance ceases to be an obstacle.

Correspondence chess players form one big world-wide family. They are associated in an international federation. Periodicals have been devoted to correspondence play; e.g. "Fernschach," originally a supplement to "Kagans Neueste Schachnachrichten" but for many years since known as a publication in its own right, and "Mail Chess," published awhile in various languages from Yugoslavia, as the official organ of the International Federation of Mail Chess Players. One of the most enthusiastic propagators of mail chess was Dr. Eduard Dyckhoff, German chess club activist and an excellent player who died in 1949.

A giant Dyckhoff Memorial Tournament was organized, from 1954 to 1956 with 1,860 chess players from 33 countries. As many as 8,856 games were played in this one event.

An amusing episode based on playing chess at a distance occurs in the Spanish film "Calabuig" directed by Luis G. Berlanga. A lighthouse keeper is playing a curate by telephone. The clergyman uses a textbook to help him. The hero of the film, Professor Hamilton, suggests a better queen move to the lighthouse keeper. The keeper sends the better move and wins. The priest, very indignant, accuses his adversary of trickery and subsequently remarks that people who cheat at chess will not go to heaven.

In the Polish film "Gangsters and Philantropists" by Jerzy Hoffman and Edward Skórzewski, the first in a series of short stories — comical parodies of criminal and gangster films — presents

In the English film "Mandy" (1952), the grandfather of the little girl Mandy plays a lot of chess by post, getting moves every day.

318

the boss of a gang (starring Gustaw Holoubek), nicknamed "Professor" for his "scientific" methods in planning bank robberies. The gangster enjoys a frequent game of chess played through the phone with his regular opponent... an examining magistrate, who is not aware of the real identity of his opponent. When the "Professor" is away on managing a bank-car robbery a tape recorder ingeniously attached to his telephone answers the anticipated single move of the magistrate, thus providing for the champion-gangster an easy alibi which, as the future course of events shows, proves pointless.

References to matches played by correspondence by Venetians occur in old Italian books. Their opponents were in neighbouring towns but occasionally as far away as Dalmatia. The mails were so slow that games often went on for many years. In their last wills and testaments, fathers were known to instruct their sons to take over games

and with them the responsibility of pocketing or paying up the stakes, often no trifle.

But why look as far back as the Middle Ages? In the last century two Americans took no less than 25 years over one game! They began corresponding in 1850 and did not finish the game until 1875. We don't know how many letters were exchanged but the postage must have cost a lot.

Players have tried to save money by getting round the postal regulations. The simplest way was to write the move under the stamp. The card itself could then be sent as printed matter, the text being of no importance. A most involved system entailed sending the move in a code embodied in the name and address of the sender. Fictitious house, flat and telephone numbers were added to indicate the move in accordance with the code. Cryptograms virtually impossible to decipher consisted in slightly lowering or raising letters in the recipient's name and address.

The telegraph, in which each word has to be paid for, set harder problems. But the ingenuity of a dedicated chess player is amazing. At the end of the last century a London player named Anthony published a code in the form of a unique dictionary in which each word stood for a different move, 848 in all. Television opens up new prospects. A radio telephone, supplemented by a TV set, would allow two players hundreds of miles apart to play each other, almost as though they were sitting at the same board.

Conrad of Swabia and Frederick of Austria hear the death sentence whilst playing chess in prison. A late 18th century engraving by Daniel Chodowiecki.

Before this happens, the traditional telegraph-cum-telephone device will continue advantageously to serve in playing this game at a distance. To such a combination of telephone and teletype resorted the American champion Robert Fischer in order to be able to participate in the Capablanca Memorial Chess Tournament at Havana in the summer of 1965. Having been refused by his authorities a permission to go to revolutionary Cuba, Fischer resolved ostentatiously to take part in the contest by applying to the International Chess Federation with the request for their consent to his playing a correspondence game from a distance with the observance of all the specific rules prescribed for normal competitions. Thus he was prevented from consulting handbooks, obtaining advice, or taking his time at will.

He was seated in a small room at the Marshall Chess Club in New York where under the control of a referee he played a game with an opponent at Havana. As the players' moves were known at the other end of the line in about 10 seconds, the game proceeded at almost normal pace. His success in securing fourth place in a strong international tournament at a great distance from the playing venue aroused tremendous interest throughout the world.

It was the first time in the history of chess tournaments that a player situated outside the official scene of play directly took part.

IN PRISON AND PRISON CAMP

People deprived of freedom, those in exile, in prison or prisoners of war, have in every age found chess not only an entertainment and a way of taking their minds off painful reality, but a test of character and mental abilities, a way of helping them to bear and stand up to the stresses of life.

It is said that the inhabitants of the village of Stroebeck in Germany owe their passion for chess to the Slav duke Guncelin who was taken

Heinrich Wilhelm Tischbein: Conrad of Swabia and Frederick of Austria hear the death sentence while playing a game of chess in prison. Oil painting (1784) from the Gotha Schloss Museum.

prisoner by the Germans in 1068, and who was so passionately fond of chess that he persuaded his guards to play with him.

The situation of the Inca ruler of Peru, Prince Atahualpa, who was imprisoned by the Spanish conquistadors during the conquest of South America in the 16th century, was curiously different. Atahualpa learned chess by watching his guards play, and before long was beating them all. It is said that a certain Spanish captain hated him for this and had him murdered. Until chess was introduced to America by the Spanish conquerors, neither this game nor any game like it had been known to the Incas.

The Elector Johann Frederic, Duke of Saxony, a prisoner of the German Emperor Charles V, won fame for his calm acceptance of the death sentence, for he was playing a game of chess with his cell companion, Ernest of Brunswick, when the verdict was communicated to him, and he went on with the game as though nothing had happened. Another version has it that the story concerns Conrad of Swabia and Frederick of Austria. These scenes have been described in numerous literary works and have provided the subject for several paintings. Whilst a prisoner of the Turks, Charles XII, King of Sweden, spent almost the whole time playing chess. In exile on the Island of St. Helena, Napoleon would never sit down to dinner until he had played a game of chess. The memoirs of deportees and political prisoners of the Russian Tsars contain numerous references to the game.

Prisoners often had a problem to obtain boards and men. Their ingenuity has been unlimited. Sets have been made of bread, paper, straw, wood, and clay, the chessboard has been replaced by a blanket, a handkerchief, a chequer-

Scene in a prison cell from the German film "Die Schachnovelle" after Stefan Zweig's story "The Royal Game," directed by Gert Oswald.

ed floor, a sheet of paper, a table etc. In the Pawiak prison in Warsaw, for instance, chess was played during the Nazi occupation with men made of bread on a board marked out with ashes. If the guards came unexpectedly, the men could be eaten, the chessboard blown away.

After the failure of the Polish insurrection of 1863, the Polish patriot, artist and sculptress Helena Skirmunt was deported to Tambov. Parties of Polish deportees going to various parts of Siberia were continuously passing through Tambov, stopping there for several days on their way. The deportees, in chains, sitting in the squares and streets, passed the long hours of waiting playing chess with men either made of bread or primitively carved out of wood. Although not a chess player herself, Helena Skirmunt saw what chess meant to these unfortunate exiles and was persuaded by friends to design a set of chessmen that could be produced in large numbers by means of electrotyping and distributed among the deportees and which could even be sent to large concentrations of prisoners. Unfortunately the attempts to mass-produce the men failed, but she was still taken with the idea of designing a set and subsequently carved a set representing the relief of Vienna in 1683, the army of the Polish King Jan III Sobieski facing the Turks.

The well-known Russian writer Ivan Turgenev, banished by the Tsar for years under strict police supervision, spent most of this time playing chess. Pained by the limited abilities of his chance opponents, he spent a lot of time studying games in books and solving chess problems.

Chess was a favourite occupation among the Polish and Russian revolutionaries exiled to various distant parts of the Tsarist empire. Accustomed to an active life with little time for pleasure, they found chess an ideal outlet for their desire for action and struggle. When in 1898 Vladimir Lenin was exiled to the village of Shushenskoye, having nobody to play with there he played by correspondence with his friend Lepeshynsky in another part of Siberia. When he did find an opponent in the flesh, Lenin would play game after game. Whilst in exile he was known to engage against three opponents consulting and accomplished the rare feat for an amateur of conducting three games simultaneously blindfold. The Polish revolutionary Feliks Kon recalls that when in prison at Kara in Siberia, he participated in chess tournaments contested between various cells. These tournaments were a great event for the prisoners, absorbing their whole attention. Each participant contributed several lumps of sugar to the prize fund.

One of the Russian chess champions of the

Cartoon by Larry ("Münchner Illustrierte").

323

The Leningrad collector Vyacheslav Dombrovsky with some of his chessmen from various epochs.

older generation, Duz-Khotimirsky, writes in his memoirs about an event in the year 1905: "I was arrested during a meeting outside the municipal Duma and became acquainted with the prison in Kiev. The small room for the reception of arrested persons was so full that there was no place to sit or lie down. We were kept without fresh air and with no possibility of getting a little sleep. Finally we were put into different cells. There were twelve of us in cell number one. To take the prisoners' minds off their plight I began to teach them chess. We made chessmen from bread and organized a chess tournament for the title of champion of cell number one."

The possibilities of playing chess were much more limited in special prisons, citadels and fortresses, where the prisoners were kept in solitary confinement and strict rules forbade contacts between them. Yet all such obstacles have been overcome. In the memoirs of the Decembrists, imprisoned after the attempted assassination of the Tsar in 1825, chess is mentioned again and again. N. Basargin, for instance, who was imprisoned in the Petropavlovsk Fortress, describes how he played chess with his neighbour by tapping on the wall, using a previously established code to convey the moves. Another Decembrist, M. Ashenbrenner, imprisoned in the Shlisselburg Fortress, tells how chess tournaments were played between dozens of prisoners by tapping on cell walls in this way.

At first, only a few neighbouring prisoners played, but before long others were initiated and chess became the craze of the whole fortress. At first the chessmen were made of bread, but later, when the prisoners began to be employed in workshops, men turned in wood appeared. When the author left the fortress, two enthusiasts there had already played over ten thousand games.

In the novel "Un homme Langdon" by the French writer Georges Langelanne, the scene of which is set in modern times, two prisoners play chess, communicating with each other by an acoustic code. One of them plays with chessmen made of straw pulled out of his straw mattress and uses the chequered floor as a board. The other player keeps the position by writing on a piece of paper. Asked during an inspection what he was doing, he answered truthfully that he was playing chess with a prisoner on the floor below. His explanation was received sceptically. He suggested that the guards go downstairs to his opponent's cell and confirm that the position on his floor was the same as in his own diagram. Before the guards could reach the cell below, he had warned his opponent of their approach. So when they reached the cell, the other chess player told them he had been awaiting them and had already learnt the "authorities" were interested in the game. He moved his pieces to the same positions as upstairs, to his visitors' complete astonishment.

There is a dramatic scene in a short story "The Price of Cognac" by the Polish writer Roman Kogucki, telling of a man sentenced to death for collaboration with the Nazi occupying forces, whose last wish was to play chess the whole of the night preceding his execution. The story is told by one of the prosecutors.

"... As I said, he was a good player. He played chess in his cell. But I had to put him in solitary confinement before the sentence was carried out. He couldn't play with a prisoner and there were no chess players among the prison guards. Finally I found a good chess player, an investigation officer, who agreed to play with him.

The first game ended in a draw, the second too. Then, Ziołowski won one game after another. He played with his back to the chessboard without seeing it. He gave the odds of a piece, and even two, and still he won. The investigation officer told me later that he had never before seen anyone so absorbed in a game. I myself could not imagine how anyone could play like that whilst waiting to go to the gallows.

"At four o'clock in the morning I went to the cell. The prisoner stood to attention: 'Only the end game to be played, Sir, it shouldn't take longer than five minutes.'

"What was I to do? I broke all the rules and walked out of the cell into the corridor. Scarcely three minutes had passed when there was a knock on the door of the cell. We went in again. 'We've finished, I've been checkmated,' said the investigation officer. Twenty minutes later it was all over."

(A member of my Postal Chess Club died of cancer. After his death his sister wrote me: 'His postal games were a great solace to him to the very end.' — B. H. Wood).

Dombrovsky's flat was a veritable museum, filled with chess sets, paintings, drawings, sculptures, books and magazines, diplomas and documents on chess.

An extensive account of chess playing in the Nazi death camp of Buchenwald has been given by one of its inmates, the Soviet chess player J. Kheyfets. In March 1943, on the initiative of the Soviet underground movement operating in the camp, a simultaneous chess display by an expert player Bogdanov was organized. The aim was to demonstrate to everybody that persecutions, hard labour and hunger could not break the prisoners' spirit. The organization called for a terrific effort. Working in the workshops, prisoners secretly made chess sets under the very eyes of the S.S. men, then smuggled them into the barracks. Special observers were put on guard to give

The French collector Jean Maunoury collected original sets of chessmen, in a variety of materials, from nearly 60 countries.

the warning if S.S. men were seen approaching the barracks where the display was taking place. There were plenty of prisoners who wanted to play and even more who wanted to look on. Bogdanov scored a big success and news of the event and his prowess went round the camp like lightning. In the days that followed prisoners from other barracks came to Bogdanov bringing their own sets with them; Poles, Czechs, French-men and Germans all wanted to try their hand at beating the winner of the simultaneous display. But Bogdanov could not be beaten.

It was not long before making chessmen became a general occupation among the prisoners. Some were fine craftsmen who could make beautiful chessmen in the folk style of various nationalities, using primitive knives as their tools. The sets often went outside the camp to the town, where

327

The famous English collector and dealer Alexander Hammond who had a famous shop in the Burlington Arcade in London and later in Chelsea.

they were exchanged with the German population so that it all became not only an entertainment but also a means of bringing in extra food for the hungry prisoners.

STRICTLY CONFIDENTIAL

There is no knowing who first had the idea of using a chess score as a code for secret messages. A piece of paper with the written score of a game of chess is strange enough to qualify it for a place in any book on cryptography.

In the 1930's the Swiss press was full for awhile of the story of Adrienne Risa of the German intelligence service, who passed herself off as a cabaret singer in Zurich during the First World War. She sang in the evenings and in the daytime she liked to watch the chess players in a certain café; especially her favourite pair. When the French were preparing for an offensive, one of the chess players disappeared for a couple of days. When he returned he sat down to play chess as usual but played like a madman. The next day the cabaret singer disappeared. This attracted no attention; nobody associated it with the failure of the French offensive, which, it was rumoured, had been due to the fact that staff plans had been stolen by spies. Only years afterwards did it become known that the woman spy had deciphered the strange moves of the chessmen on the chessboard into the plans for the offensive. She had then passed on information about the positions of the French troops and details of the offensive to the Germans' intelligence service.

During the First World War an admirer of the well-known American collector John G. White sent him a rare and valuable book on chess from England to the United States. Unfortunately the book never reached its destination; it was confiscated by the military censors who suspected that this innocent book contained a message in code. There was nobody in the censors' office prepared to go to the trouble of confirming that it was all ordinary chess.

Chess had fallen under suspicion as a possible means of conveying secret information long before that. In the autumn of 1878, the Tsarist police in St. Petersburg, alarmed at the growth of revolutionary feeling in the country, stepped up the control of letters and parcels sent through the post. A postcard addressed to Tchigorin bearing a combination of figures and letters fell into the hands of a police informer. Worse, the laconic card said that if St. Petersburg did this, Moscow would to that, and if it did something different, then Moscow would act differently too. This postcard conveying chess moves and possible alternatives in a correspondence game between clubs in the two cities caused a veritable panic in the Third Department of the Police. Could this be a coded order to start an uprising? Another postcard with the words: "I am surprised at the inefficiency of our posts. I posted letters to you and Mr. Schmidt myself immediately after conferring with him," completed the effect. The postcards were sent to the chairman of the Council of Ministers, who recognized the symbols for what they were, laconically wrote the word "chess" on it and sent it back to the police. The postcards were never delivered, all the same. They were kept in the secret archives of the Third Department and were only recently discovered when the documents were being sorted at the history archives in Moscow.

CHESS COLLECTIONS

In 1856, a certain enthusiastic collector of chess books died in France, bequeathing his library, an impressive one for those times, numbering nearly four hundred volumes, to the municipal library of the town of Grenoble. An accompanying collection of drawings was not properly looked after; they became dispersed and disappeared altogether. A pity, for it was said that Frédéric Alliey, for that was the collector's name, had amassed some interesting material. His collection was divided into the following sections: theory of the game, manuscripts, knights' tours, automatons, unusual types of chess, various other games, translations from other languages, quotations about chess.

Note that there were no sections for problems and tournaments, two branches of chess which have provided many thousands of titles since. Alliey was working on an exhausting bibliography of books on chess, which was impatiently awaited by enthusiasts.

M. Dzieduszycki, Polish chess historian, wrote in 1856: "The mayor of Ardèche (Alliey) plans a new bibliography of works on chess, in which he deals extensively with 412 authors and quotes 326 more who refer to chess in other works but I do not know whether this immense and useful work has been completed."

It was not completed. When the above appeared in print, Alliey was no longer alive and his unfinished catalogue lay alongside his collection in the Grenoble library.

The most famous chess collection was John G. White's, the American chess expert and collector. He lived in Cleveland, Ohio. He died in 1928 at the age of 83. His immense collection, of which periodicals alone exceeded twelve thousand items, was left to the Public Library in Cleveland. A lawyer by profession, he spent all his money on his collection, travelling all over the world for specimens.

He grouped his collection under poetry, oriental chess, history manuscripts, chess in the theatre, chess congresses, correspondence chess, tournaments, monographs on chess players, games, problems, end-games, anecdotes, essays, articles from periodicals, mathematical chess, miscellaneous, living chess, chess automatons, drawings, documents, bibliography, periodicals, chess columns, pen portraits of chess players, chess in ancient times, etc.

White was an unselfish man. He readily gave access to his collections for research purposes and

Buckskin chessboard, chessmen carved in wood. Of modern Nigerian make.

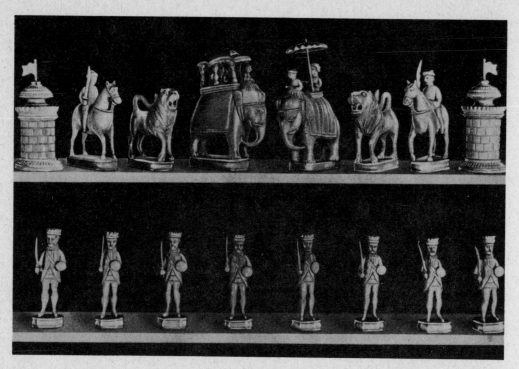

A half set of Indian chessmen from Hammond's collection, probably made in the Central Provinces in the late eighteenth century.

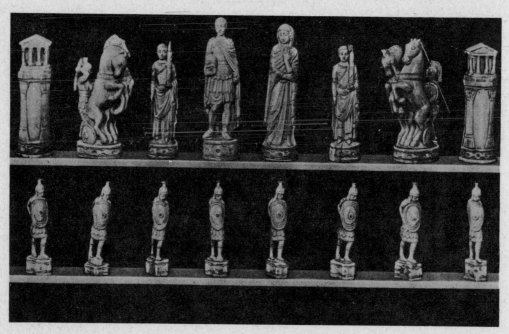

Another Hammond collection set: French, probably from the days of Louis XIV; Hannibal versus Scipio Africanus, with Roman chariots as knights (the Roman side only is given in this picture).

helped personally on primary source material, bibliographic lists and information of every kind. He had a big mailbag every day from all parts of the world from people seeking information.

An example of his passion for collecting literature on chess is the story of how he obtained a copy of a chess manuscript in the private library of the Sultan in Istanbul. It took him twenty years to get at this manuscript of which he dreamed, but knew very little about. The Sultan's library was only opened to the public once a year and it was prohibited under the threat of death to make any kind of notes. All attempts to get a copy, made year after year, were of no avail. The lack of this item in his collection was more than White could stand. He hired a special agent, who succeeded in bribing a member of the library staff to let him take the manuscript away from the library for a few hours. A photocopy was made at lightning speed. When this was examined, it was found that the manuscript was of no great value. But John White could now sleep in peace.

The collection of Dr. M. Niemeijer, Dutch chess problem composer and collector, comprised books, prints, press cuttings, autographs, portraits, caricatures, drawings, chessmen and other exhibits. Niemeijer presented his books to the Royal Library at the Hague, which thus increased its own collection to 6,500 titles, and deposited his other items at a chess club in The Hague.

The American collector M. Pfeiffer specialized in original sets of chessmen which he housed in beautiful show-cases matching their style. He presented his collection to the Metropolitan Museum in New York.

In France, the Parisian collector Jean Maunoury got together over 200 sets of chessmen of various lands and epochs. It took him many years to collect them, rummaging through antique shops all over France and employing agents in fifty-four countries. He bought many without seeing them, counting on finding among them enough rare specimens lying unnoticed in junk shops to justify the overall expenditure. He re-ceived so many Chinese sets with pieces on open-work globes made simply and rather mechanically for export, that he sent out photographs of this type of piece with a statement that he never wanted to see any more. Apart from European and Asian sets, he collected many of extraordinary interest from Oceania and South America. His oldest exhibit was a set dating back to the 14th century, from Cambodia. Then there was his jewelled Louis XIV set, of exquisite workmanship, in silver and crystal.

An English collector, Alex Hammond, presented photographs of many beautiful sets in his "Book of Chessmen."

An interesting and valuable collection of specimens and books on chess was made by a great lover of chess V. Dombrovsky of Leningrad. He spent nearly forty years of his life collecting books and sets, etc., including many very rare ones. His home became a veritable chess museum, freely visited by enthusiasts of chess from his own country and abroad. In his collection of books, numbering over one-and-a-half thousand volumes, there were rare items of world literature and almost every book on chess ever issued in Russia. On the walls hung drawings and pictures with a chess theme, and in a number of show-cases were Russian chessmen dating back to the 16th century, Indian chessmen over a century old; German, Dutch, English, Czech, Rumanian, Polish and Soviet sets, etc. There were historical sets and modern ones, men carved in ivory, wood and stone, some cast in metal, others of the most diverse materials. There were also chess curiosities: porcelain statuettes, sculptures, medals, souvenirs decorated with chess motifs, drawings and caricatures. V. Dombrovsky was not only a collector with a mania for getting hold of as many items as possible, but also a scholar engaged in the study of chess history. His collection fed his research, and he was always willing to supply information and primary source materials to any who approached him with the request for help or advice.

Ivory pieces from Central Europe with catafalques for bishops, about 200 years old (Hammond collection).

Etchings, drawings, reproductions of paintings, press cuttings, and advertisements with a chess motif have been collected by Julien Guisle, owner of a little chess bookshop in the Latin quarter of Paris. He has kindly supplied many illustrations for this book.

In Poland, at least two fine collections, those of the great player Przepiorka and Professor Kukulski's in Cracow (over two thousand volumes) were destroyed during the war.

After the war, the remains of a valuable chess collection were discovered in the castle at Osieczna, near Leszno. They were all that had survived of a large library compiled by the German chess historian and theoretician Tessilo von Heydebrand und der Lasa who died in 1899.

Apart from numerous manuscripts, original prints and rare publications, there were documents, correspondence and notes on games and tournaments of the last century. These were presented to the Library of the Polish Academy of Sciences in Poznań. (I have collected over 6,000 books on chess myself. I get the impression that production of chess books advances by about 50% each year — B. H. Wood).

ART, IN THE LARGE AND THE MINIATURE

Whereas many paintings, drawings and works of graphic art are connected in some way with chess, there are few sculptures.

There is a column at Winchester Cathedral, the capital of which is adorned with a figure of a man holding a chessboard. The cathedral was built in 1369. Information is lacking whether the board was supposed to be for chess, or for some other game (or for counting money?).

But in the palace at Bourges, France, there is a sculpture showing a man and woman completely absorbed in a game of chess. They are dressed in the fashion of the reign of King Charles VII, the beginning of the 15th century. The woman has a chessman in her hand and is just making a move.

A pillar in the 13th century cathedral at Naumburg, shows two monkeys playing chess with each other. It is difficult to guess what induced the sculptor to choose this subject for a church ornament. Was it meant to remind the faithful that the Church often placed chess on the list of prohibited entertainments?

In the French town of Villefranche-en-Beaujolais, near Lyon, the town hall has an interesting stained glass window dating back to the 15th century and showing, so it is said, Edward II de Beaujolais playing chess with Mlle de la Bessée. That a stained glass window presenting a lay

Half of a fine ivory set made in Dieppe soon after Napoleon's defeat. The opposing King is the Duke of Wellington. The bishops are the Dukes of Berthier and Massena, two of Napoleon's marshals (Hammond collection).

333

Czech chessmen from about 1790.

An Oriental set in ivory, of fairly recent date.

subject was a very rare thing at that time, makes it all the more pleasant for us to find chess as its subject.

In Peterhof, the splendid residence of Tsar Peter I on the Gulf of Finland near Leningrad,

one of the most spectacular cascades in the famous park surrounding the palace, was called "Shakhmatnaya Gora" (The Chess Mount). The water falls over three panels composed of black and white marble squares. Unfortunately the sculptures of the fountain are of mythological figures unconnected with chess, and the black and white squares are not like a chessboard, being arranged diagonally.

Since we are on the subject of parks, let us incidentally mention the Hover Gardens, in Kent, with a hedgerow shaped in imitation of chess pieces, according to the old English pattern from the Tudor period.

Some interesting artists' designs are to be found among the book-plates of chess book collectors. There is even an association of collectors of "ex libris" crests in France. These people collect private library book plates as others collect stamps. Dr. M. Niemeijer has adopted a beautiful book plate design derived from a 14th century miniature showing the Margrave Otto IV of Brandenburg at chess.

CHESS IN POSTAGE STAMPS

Philatelists at one time had little difficulty in collecting a complete set of postage stamps with a chess motif, because there were only a few specimens prior to the Second World War. Since then the post offices of various countries have issued more and more such chess stamps on the occasions of international chess events.

BULGARIA: one stamp (9 levs) issued on the occasion of the Balkan Games in 1947 and another, (80 stotinki) green, issued in 1958 to mark the Fifth Students' World Chess Team Championships contested in Varna. It shows a terrestrial globe presented in the form of a chessboard with a rook and a knight on it.

The Bulgarian Post Office issued a beautiful set of five stamps to mark the 15th Olympic

Chess Tournament contested at a seaside resort, Golden Sands, near Varna in the autumn of 1962. The issue comprised five stamps of different values (1, 2, 3, 13 and 20 stotinki) and colours, each stamp being distinguished by the fine modern design of the chessmen. There was a green stamp with a queen, an olive-green one with a rook, a crimson one with a king, a carmine one with a knight and a blue one with a bishop. The set appeared in two versions, perforated and imperforate. Apart from this, an ornamental cancellation was issued for the 20-stotinki stamp, with a special inscription to mark the occasion.

THE SOVIET UNION issued two stamps in 1948 (three values, 30, 40 and 50 kopecks) to mark the World Championship Match-tournament contested by Botvinnik, Keres, Smyslov, Euwe and Reshevsky. The stamp bearing a picture of a chessboard and a rook is more connected with chess than the stamp (issued in two values) with the picture of the Trade Unions Building in which Botvinnik won the game which brought him the World Championship in 1963. The U.S.S.R. issued three stamps to commemorate the match in Moscow for the world championship between Botvinnik and Petrosian. Again they are perforated and imperforate. The green, yellow and black stamp (4 kopecks) shows a king, a pawn and the world championship gold medal; the blue and crimson stamp (6 kopecks) shows a queen and a bishop, a chessboard and a terrestrial globe; the red-and-black stamp (16 kopecks) shows a rook, a knight and the building where the tournament was held.

In 1958, a stamp of 49 kopecks nominal value was issued with the portrait of Tchigorin, to commemorate the 50th anniversary of the death of this great Russian chess player. Under the portrait there is a ribbon bearing the dates 1850–1908 and two chessmen: a knight and a rook.

In 1966, a 6-kopeck stamp (brown-golden-black) was issued during the match between Petrosian and Spassky for the title of world champion. Against a background of the chessboard is a golden medal of world champion, laurels and two chess pieces: pawn and king; an inscription along one side: Moskva 1966. Moreover, in commemoration of Petrosian's triumph, a 10-kopeck stamp (white-silver-black) was included in the "World Championships 1966" block of four stamps: five chess pieces — pawn, queen, king, bishop and knight placed on a chessboard viewed

Typical men of Chinese make, carved for the European market.

Stylised Polish chessmen from about 1850.

sideways, with a world champion emblem as the background.

HUNGARY issued the first set of three stamps with the chess motif (60 fillér, one forint, 1,60 forints) in 1950 on the occasion of the World Championship Candidates Tournament in Budapest. The stamp showing two chess players deserves special mention.

YUGOSLAVIA issued in 1950 a set of five stamps, each of them with a different design (2, 3, 5, 10 and 20 dinars), to mark the Olympic Chess Tournament contested in Dubrovnik. The stamps are of fine artistic value; they were the most beautiful specimens of graphic art with chess motifs in philately for many years.

CUBA issued in 1951 a set of stamps of seven values and four designs, to mark the 30th anniversary of Capablanca's becoming world champion. Two stamps (orange, one centavo and brown, 25 centavos) show his portrait with a chess king in the upper left-hand corner. The next two (2 centavos and 8 centavos) show him bent over a chessboard meditating on a move. Another two stamps (blue, 5 centavos and red-and-brown, 10 centavos) show the chess club named after Capablanca in Havana, with two knights to the right. The last stamp (5 centavos), shows the position on the board in which his opponent resigned to make Capablanca World Champion. In 1962 a set of 36 stamps with sport motifs was issued, one of which (13 centavos, cream, red and black) showed a chess player bent over the board.

In 1966, a series of six stamps (value: 1, 2, 3, 9 and 13 centavos) was issued to honour the XVII Chess Olympiad held at Havana. The first four of these, vertical ones, feature, in turn, the following chess pieces: pawn (green background), rook (steel-grey), knight (coral-red), and bishop (olive-green), positioned on the stylised terrestrial globe with the chessboard-like ornamentation. The other two stamps, longitudinal in form, feature —

Chessmen of blue and white Meissen china in the shapes of various sea fauna on a board representing the bottom of the sea.

Postage stamps with chess motifs issued by Bulgaria, Finland, Yugoslavia, Cuba, German Democratic Republic, Poland, Hungary and the Soviet Union.

Modernistic chessmen shown at an exhibition of handicrafts at Weimar in 1924.

one of them, the chess queen and, next to it, diagram showing a "simultaneous giant game" (amaranthine), and the other — the king (blue background) and the Olympic emblem and inscription "Gens una sumus." The series is further complemented with a block containing a 30-centavos stamp (orange-white-azure blue) featuring the Olympic emblem and the concluding position in a 1914 game in Berlin in which Lasker had resigned to Capablanca.

FINLAND issued in 1952 one stamp (25 markkas) to commemorate the tenth Chess Olympiad contested in Helsinki.

POLAND issued two interesting stamps in 1956 to mark the First Individual World Championships of the Deaf, held in Zakopane in February that year. The stamps (red, 40 grosze and blue, 60 grosze) show two hands saying "chess" in the deaf-and-dumb language. A special postmark was used on this occasion showing the rook and bearing an inscription commemorating the event. Apart from this, envelopes with a chess inscription were sold during the championships.

GERMAN DEMOCRATIC REPUBLIC issued a set of three stamps in 1960 during the 14th Olympic Chess Games in Leipzig. The stamps show chessmen against the background of the Olympic emblem. All three chessmen that served the artist as models were displayed at the exhibition "Chess Through the Centuries" during the tournament. The 10-pfennig stamp (plus 5 pfennig surcharge) light green in colour, shows an ivory rook from an 18th century set now owned by a private collector. The 20-pfennig stamp (plus 5 pfennig surcharge), of a light carmine colour, shows a knight beautifully carved in wood from the Leipzig Museum of Artistic Handicrafts.

The third stamp, 25 pfennig (plus 10 pfennig surcharge), a most valuable philatelic specimen, was printed in blue. It reproduces a knight carved in walrus bone, dating back to the end of the 14th century. This specimen, now in the possession of the State Museum, Berlin, was saved, together with other collections, by the Soviet Army during the siege of Berlin and later returned to the German people.

A set of metal chessmen which, even when set out on the chessboard, can be held in a closed hand. The kings are 1 cm. high, the pawns no more than 2.5 millimetres. Made by an unknown German enthusiast, a fitter by profession.

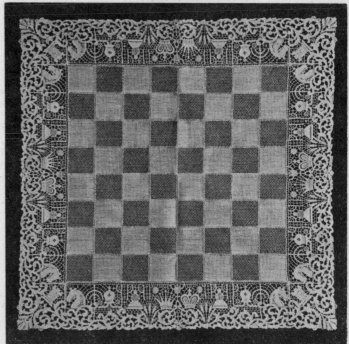

The biggest chess piece and the smallest set in A. Hammond's collection. A machine-made lace napkin with chess motifs from Plauen, German Democratic Republic, designed by S. Melnyk.

In 1968, the issue of a 15-pfennig commemorative stamp featured Emanuel Lasker's portrait to mark the centenary of the birth of this great player, world chess champion from 1884 to 1921.

DUTCH WEST INDIES published a set of stamps in 1962 (three values 10+5, 20+10, and 25+10 cents) each showing the terrestrial globe with a knight on the right side, the colours being green, red and blue. It was issued on the occasion of the Fifth International Tournament of Candidates contested on the island of Curaçao in May and June 1962.

PHILIPPINES — In 1963, the issue of a 6+4 centavos stamp (green-red) with a design of two men aboard playing chess. One of the men is Rizal, a known cultural worker of the Philippines, and his portrayal in medallion is in addition placed in the upper left corner.

ISRAEL — In 1964, the issue of two stamps of 0.12-pound (brown, featuring the knight) and 0.70-pound value (green, with the rook) to mark the XVI Chess Olympics held at Tel-Aviv. On both the stamps, against the background of the chessboard, five interwoven squares, a counterpart of the known Olympic emblem, are featured; on the plaques attached below, an emblem of the Olympiad and the inscription "Gens una sumus" (the International Chess Federation's motto).

SAN MARINO— In 1965, the issue of a 200-lire stamp (multicoloured) of a unique design, with chess not the principal theme but a symbol. Ten castles are seen arranged on the chessboard, each of different colour and, in consequence, unable to attack one another, which is symbolic of the peaceful coexistence of European states.

FRANCE — In 1966, the International Chess Tournament at le Havre was marked by the issue of a 60-centime stamp (azure blue-steel grey-sepia) featuring the knight, shown against the chessboard background, and emblems of two pieces: king and bishop, with an inscription above: "Jeu d'échecs" (game of chess).

RUMANIA — In 1966, the issue of a series of six stamps (multicoloured) publicising the Olympic Games Chess at Havana (Cuba): a 20-bani and a 1.60-lei stamps, identical in design, featuring a pawn shown against the chessboard and a stylised terrestrial globe with five Olympic circles; 40-bani and 3.25-lei values featuring the bishop and a facetious figure of a jester; and 55-bani and 1-lei stamps presenting the castle and a picture of a mounted knight in attack.

Jean Maunoury by showcases containing his exotic collection of chessmen.

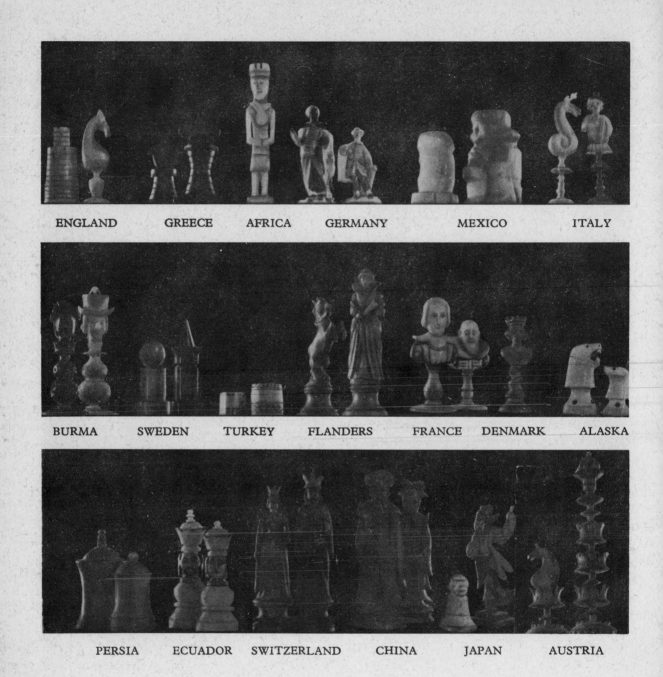

ENGLAND   GREECE   AFRICA   GERMANY   MEXICO   ITALY

BURMA   SWEDEN   TURKEY   FLANDERS   FRANCE   DENMARK   ALASKA

PERSIA   ECUADOR   SWITZERLAND   CHINA   JAPAN   AUSTRIA

Some museums have fine chess collections, donated or inherited from private collectors. The Calerbach Gallery, U.S.A. has many chess curios. Our photographs show chessmen from England, Greece, Africa, Germany, Mexico, Italy, Burma, Sweden, Turkey, Flanders, France, Denmark, Alaska, Iran, Ecuador, Switzerland, China, Japan and Austria.

A set of big chessmen carved in wood with a hint of the grotesque, and an unusual table with chess, card and domino motifs, in the chess shop in Prague run by Mr. Rosenblatt.

NICARAGUA — In 1963, in a series of sports stamps issued to commemorate the Tokyo Olympic Games of 1964, a 35-centavos stamp was included for chess: on an obliquely placed chessboard were two chessmen.

DOMINICAN REPUBLIC — In 1967, the issue of two stamps marking the V Chess Tournaments of Central America: a 10-centavos stamp (olive green) featuring the pawn and the bishop, and a 25-centavos value (blue-yellow-black) — the rook and the knight. These two stamps were also issued in a special block with an appropriate inscription.

MONACO — In 1967, the issue of a 60-centime stamp to celebrate the decision of renewing, after 53 years' break, the tradition of international chess tournaments in Monte Carlo. Alongside a drawing representing a game of chess, an inscription "Grand Prix International d'Echecs."

In 1968, another commemorative stamp was issued to mark the international chess tournaments at Monte Carlo.

SWITZERLAND — In 1968, the issue of a 30--rappen stamp to commemorate the XVIII Olympic Chess Games at Lugano: with a chess rook shown against a chessboard background and an appropriate inscription.

Philatelists also collect postmarks marking the occasion of important chess events, souvenir envelopes and all kinds of postcards, envelopes, etc. with postage stamps.

The Preparatory Committee for the 14th Olympic Chess Games in Leipzig issued labels similar to postage stamps and sold them to collect the funds necessary for the organization of the event. The labels were perforated and adhesive and bore diagrams of chess problems. Sets containing 15 labels each were on sale, the respective value of the labels being 20 pfennigs, 50 pfennigs, 1 mark and 2 marks, as well as sets of labels without printed value as a receipt for voluntary contributions. The first row of each set had problems to be solved in two moves; the second, problems to be solved in three moves, and the

A set of hand-made silver chessmen designed by Marta Obidzińska and produced by the ORNO Folk Art Industry Co-operative, Warsaw.

third, problems to be solved in four moves. Altogether there were 15 different problems in each set.

During the disastrous inflation, Germany, famous for its chess tradition, issued money-coupons with chess motifs (1921).

Playing cards with chess designs are a rarity. In 1508 Thomas Murner of Strasburg issued a book entitled "Cartiludum Logicae," illustrated with symbolic drawings of cards representing logical figures. One of them, the seven of diamonds, bore the picture of a chess player. In 1629, Tussanus du Bray printed playing cards in Paris using Murner's motifs, but introducing different designs. In his edition the chess player was a woman.

ZOOLOGICAL CURIOSITIES

Monkeys at chess is a theme not confined to the cathedral at Naumburg. Tales about intelligent monkeys giving checkmates may have been told with tongue in cheek like traditional fishing stories: so we must not be too critical...

In the "Arabian Nights" a story called "The Jealous Man and Jealousy" tells the very sad story of a certain young prince who was turned into a monkey by an envious dervish. After many adventures, the monkey prince gets into the court of the Sultan, where he entertains the courtiers with his tricks. Wishing to convince the Sultan that he is a man in the guise of an animal, he agrees to undergo various tests, among others, to play a game of chess with the ruler. The prince recounts this game as follows:

"...When the men and board were brought in, the Sultan made various signs to ask me if I knew how to play chess and if I would like to play a game with him. I bowed low to the ground and putting my paw on my head humbly agreed to this honour. I lost the first game, but won the second and third. I noticed that the Sultan wasn't at all pleased at this. To console him I composed a poem of four lines, which told of two

342

mighty armies fighting bravely all the day and making peace with each other in the evening."

In many anecdotes a monkey is just a monkey, with no spells and magic involved. It is said that Charles V, King of Spain, who reigned early in the 16th century, had a monkey who often won in games of chess with him and did not like to lose. Once, seeing that the game was lost, the monkey even threw the chessboard at the King's head. From that time on, when the King seemed to be gaining superiority on the chessboard, the monkey jumped down and ran away from the table so as not to let his feelings get the better of him.

We find quite another kind of game with a monkey in Łukasz Górnicki's book "The Courtier," written in 1566, which is a free translation of a work written by the Italian writer Balthasar Castiglione. "... A rather improbable story was once told by a certain Italian who swore it was true. He said he had seen a monkey, very different from the ones we knew, that had been brought from some newly discovered islands and played chess very well. One day, the monkey played chess with the nobleman who had bought it, in the presence of the King of Portugal. The monkey, having made several masterful moves which put the nobleman in a very difficult position, finished the game by checkmating him. And his good master, getting angry as sometimes happens when somebody is checkmated, took up his king (which was a big one, as chessmen are in Portugal) and hit the poor monkey on the head with it. The monkey jumped down from the table and began to scream as though appealing to the King for justice. Then the nobleman challenged the monkey to another game. The monkey could not be persuaded for a long time and made signs to indicate that it would rather not, but in the end allowed itself to be persuaded, and then played so well that, as before, the nobleman began to get angry. In the end, seeing that

Another set of hand-made silver plate chessmen in folk style designed by Marta Obidzińska and produced by the ORNO Folk Art Industry Co-operative in Warsaw.

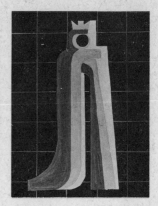

Chessmen: the king, bishop, knight and queen designed by the Warsaw plastic artist Adam Jabłoński, to be cast in silver.

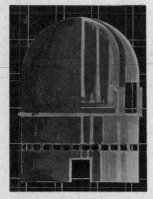

Adam Jabłoński's design for an "astronomical" set in silver. The rook is an observatory, the pawn a star, the king a space rocket, the queen a sputnik.

only one more move was needed to checkmate its opponent, the monkey cunningly protected itself from another possible blow: it slipped in under his master's elbow, who being delicate, was resting it on a cushion, and quickly snatched the cushion away; with its left hand, next, it made a checkmate move with a pawn and with its right hand, put the cushion on its head as a shield. Then it jumped about in front of the King to celebrate victory..."

The 18th century German poet Christian Fürchtegott Gellert included a chess playing monkey, with certain veiled allusions to human beings, in his poem "Der Affe." In the American film "Merry Andrew," starring Danny Kaye, Andrew plays chess with his elder brother, who leaves the room after some time. A trained monkey gets in through the window, bringing a message to Andrew from his girl friend who is a circus performer. The monkey sits down at the table, smokes a pipe and begins to move the chessmen about. Andrew's short-sighted father looks into the room and sees his son playing chess with somebody. Next day he asks who was the opponent. "Nobody was there," is the reply. "Then who was that little hairy chap smoking a pipe?" asks the father in surprise.

DEVIL'S WORK

In the early mediaeval literature of the West, in romances and ballads about the adventures of knights, we often find the motif of chess magic. Whoever sits down at an enchanted chessboard is bound to lose, and the stake may be one of life and death. So the heroes of these poems not only fought with sword, but also had to fight against the mysterious power of magic spells when playing chess. Often they succeeded, with unexpected consequences.

There is a well known Flemish legend, to be found in "Chronicle of Flanders" (1131) and elsewhere. A certain Castellan's daughter is persuaded by the Devil to kill her father because she was afraid he would reveal the secret of her low birth. For she was a changeling, a wet nurse having exchanged her for the real castellan's daughter. From that time on she was brought up as a princess. Her husband, on learning of the crime, hands her over to the Devil.

After several centuries, a certain monk comes to the castle and spends the night in the chamber where the murder was committed. At midnight the Devil appears with the Castellan's daughter and challenges the monk to a game of chess, the stake of which is the monk's life. The magic chessboard and chessmen were in a room prepared for the game. The monk, seeing no other course, sits down to play. Making a terrific effort, after many ups and downs, he succeeds at last in winning the game. The defeated Devil disappears. In the morning the monk finds the skeleton of a woman in the chamber with a dagger in her hand.

The Devil was again defeated in a game of chess in a fantastic story about the famous 16th century Italian chess player Paolo Boi, a man whose life abounded in all kinds of adventures.

As the legend has it, one morning Boi met a young woman of exquisite beauty by the door of the church in a little town in Calabria. Her eyes, mysterious and penetrating, shone with feverish excitement. They became acquainted, and their acquaintance soon ripened into friendship. The beautiful girl told him she liked playing chess. Paolo was surprised, and even more so when he found that she played very well indeed. He had to try harder and harder to win. The contest became keener and keener. At last Boi, sure he was going to win, announced checkmate in two moves. But as he looked, his white queen changed colour to black. The beautiful girl laughed and said, "No, Paolo, you can't win." "O Santa Maria!" cried Paolo, and stood up horrified. Then he suddenly saw that despite what had happened he could still mate her. The mysterious young woman saw this too, frowned and disappeared. It was then Paolo realized that he had been playing with the Devil.

A. Jabłoński's design for the queen and knight of a set in hand-forged silver plate, with Polish folk motifs.

The capital of a column in Naumburg cathedral with a sculpture of two monkeys playing chess; a unique specimen of sacral art by an unknown 13th century artist.

This story is illustrated with a description of the positions of the chessmen on the board at the culminating point of the game. Anybody who knows anything about chess can see that the white queen's changing sides does not save Black from checkmate.

So no tricks of the Devil will help in a game of chess against a good enough player??

Doctor Paul R., whose chess adventure is described by Edgar Allan Poe in the short story "Love Gambit," was one of these players. The story is fantastic and uncanny, typical of Poe.

Doctor Paul R. was a very keen chess player who had beaten the champion. Suddenly, however, he gave up chess altogether. He tells his friend why.

While travelling through Germany, he once found himself in the Rhineland, near the town of Bonn; there he heard a local legend telling of a certain Castellan's beautiful wife who had lived two hundred years before and whose ghost haunted a castle at night making people play chess with her. Any unfortunate man who happened to enter the castle and was beaten by her at chess was sent to the Devil.

Before the Castellan's wife formed this unpleasant habit, she had had a lively career. During the Thirty Years War, the Castellan left his castle, and to pass the time she began to play chess. One day a knight who was an excellent player came. The Castellan's wife sat at the chessboard with him for hours on end, which caused spiteful rumours. She began to lead a more and more loose life, invited many young men from the locality to the castle to play chess with her; and not only chess! — after which she had them murdered so that they would not reveal her double game. When her husband returned she had him murdered too, being afraid that he would get to know about her sins. People began to avoid her castle, passing it by at a distance. It was rumoured that the blood-thirsty Castellan's wife started to play chess with the Devil. Any men bold enough to visit the castle disappeared without trace...

It so happened that Dr. R. was caught in a sudden storm and sought refuge in the ruins of a nearby castle. In the night, the legendary Castellan's wife appeared and forced him to play chess with her. It is difficult to refuse a woman, even when she is a ghost, so the game began. The ghost was a very beautiful one, tried to seduce him, but in vain! Our Doctor R. refused to let her charms prevail and by a superhuman effort won the game. At that moment he came to his senses and realized that he had spent the night in the ruins of a castle, lying beside the skeleton of a woman.

One can understand him giving up chess after an experience like that.

We cannot omit from this little anthology of diabolical chess the fairy-tale film "Evening Guests" made in 1942 by the French film director Marcel Carné. The action is set towards the end of the 15th century. Lucifer sends two devils to earth on a secret mission. They take the forms of a young man and girl. Unfortunately, they do not do their job properly. One devil falls in love with the daughter of a prince to whose court he had come with his companion passing themselves off as wandering minstrels. Without going into the whole plot, we shall recount the chess episode.

Renaud, the princess's official fiancé, is playing chess with her father the Prince, watched by the beautiful Dominique, really the she-devil who is trying to seduce Renaud. Lucifer comes up to the table, having left hell in the guise of a jovial old man, to supervise the activities of his envoys on earth. Seeing Renaud looking troubled he asks: "Have I interrupted the game?" "Nothing can spoil my game... I was conquered from the start," replies Renaud, referring to Dominique. Lucifer picks up a piece and makes a move "Nothing of the kind! Look, you have won... it's so simple... in chess." Thus Lucifer humiliat-

A water cascade called "Shakhmat-naya Gora" (Chess Hill) in the park of the former Tsar's residence at Peterhof, Leningrad.

Two specimens of chess "ex libris" designs from the biggest in the world collection of a French historian L. Mandy; the first design by A. Herry, the second by M. Jamar.

An "ex libris" of the Dutch collector N. Niemeijer with drawing taken from a mediaeval miniature.

Two more "ex libris" of Dutch collectors of chess works, the first designed by V. Stuyvaent, the second by P. Mant. The third is that of the Polish collector W. Frantz, and was designed by J. Agopsowicz.

ed his disobedient envoy Dominique by showing that he could have made Renaud her master had he chosen.

Man's struggle with Satan for the human soul was the subject of an allegorical painting by the German artist Moritz Retzsch. The struggle takes place inside a tomb, the board being placed on the sarcophagus. The chessmen are symbols of positive and negative thought. The game, so far, is not going well for man. Satan is attacking and he has more chessmen. This painting became well known through anonymous copies and imitations, some entitled "Faust Plays Chess with Mephistopheles."

The outstanding Russian chess player Petrov was once told by his grandfather about a game of chess he had had with an African devil. One frosty winter's night, Ivan Sokolov, the grandfather, returned from a rousing party and couldn't sleep. He lit a candle and sat down at the chessboard, trying to solve a difficult problem by Stamma. But his head was spinning and, becoming impatient, he cried: "The devil himself could not solve this!" Suddenly he heard a voice: "I can help you..." and a strange figure appeared in the doorway, a man of giant proportions, flying hair, a black face with lumps on his forehead, dressed in some hairy garment. Ivan Sokolov started to call for help to the servants, but the strange guest told him not to be afraid, that he had come from Africa, he loved playing chess and that, having heard what a wonderful player his host was, wanted to see for himself if it were true. He suggested a match of three games, on condition that if he lost one game, then Sokolov would be recognized as the world champion; but if he won three times, Sokolov would have to stop playing chess for three years and keep the whole thing a secret for the next thirty. Grandfather, intrigued by the boasting of the intruder and wanting to know how African devils played chess, agreed to play the match. To exhibit his powers, the African solved Stamma's seven-move chess problem right off. The mysterious stranger did indeed prove himself to be a player of superhuman talent, or so grandfather said. He won the first game in fifteen moves, then the second, which he began with a gambit unknown to Sokolov, in twenty-five. The third game began in a very tense atmosphere. Sokolov, now very worried, concentrated every nerve on winning it. His situation did not look too bad, either; after forty moves, he still had a chance if not winning, at least of harassing his opponent or of prolonging the game till dawn, which was the limit they had agreed on for the match. So he went in for a desperate attack, and was very surprised indeed when his opponent announced that he could not escape losing in a further twenty moves. Truly enough, grandfather was mated exactly twenty moves later; being a man of honour he thereupon gave up the game as he had agreed.

LEFT: Another "ex libris" of Frantz's, by the same designer. CENTRE: the chess knight as an ornamental motif in the emblem of the German publishing firm "Springer Verlag." RIGHT: "ex libris" of the Soviet writer Leonid Borisov.

A playing card (the seven of diamonds) showing a chess player. The designer was Thomas Murner, Strasbourg (1508).

The truth was that one of the best chess players in Moscow had dressed himself up as a devil to play a practical joke on Sokolov, who was given to boasting. But grandfather was too proud to admit this and kept to his version of the story, to lessen the pain of his defeat. After all, what hope had an ordinary man against charms and spells?

But the best, the most infallible "magic chessmen" were shown in the Russian cartoon film "Magic Toys," made in 1953. A little boy dreams that he is in a shop where he can buy all sorts of miraculous things; a pen that does school exercises by itself, a box of paints that paint wonderful pictures and many other things making work or play pleasanter. There are also some magic chessmen for sale in the shop, chessmen that win every game for the owner. The manager of the shop, in the tall hat of a magician, personally demonstrates the way the chessmen work; when the signal is given, the box opens and the chessmen arrange themselves on the board. Another signal, and they begin to play the game. The chessmen move about the board at lightning speed, all by themselves. Every now and then, a black piece that has been captured jumps off the board and in a second or two the white forces parade in victorious array.

ENTER THE DETECTIVE

In quite a number of detective stories, chess has helped to catch the criminal. In "Checkmate in Three Moves" by the English writer M. Cumberland, a certain Dr. Robertson is shot in his garden by an unknown person while playing chess. The murdered man was holding a knight in his hand. His neighbour gave himself up to the police, saying he had been playing chess with the murdered man, and in the middle of the game, had got up, walked a little distance away and shot him. The detective, examining the position, established that it was a chess problem which would have been

Stamps issued for the 14th Chess Olympic Games Fund in Leipzig with diagrams of chess problems in four, two and three moves respectively.

solved by a move of the knight. So it became obvious that the doctor was not playing with anybody but was trying to solve a problem on his own. This disproved the neighbour's false confession and enabled the real culprit to be found.

The amateur detective in "The Black Queen," by the German writer Paul Hüssy, had a more complicated problem to solve.

A certain physician from Heidelberg, a keen chess player, receives an invitation to go to the United States to contest a match with the champion of America. Greatly honoured, he starts practising hard before leaving for the States. His fiancée's brother, whose hobby is criminology, is anxious about him; it so happened that three chess players who have previously participated in contests in the Chicago chess club (the U.S. Champion's Club) died shortly after returning home from causes the police could not establish. The deaths were ascribed to excessive exhaustion and nervous strain, but the chemist suspects that they were due to poisoning by curare, a strong Indian poison, and he thinks that the invitation sent to his sister's fiancé is somehow connected with these previous cases. So he follows the doctor to America to get to know the truth.

The most unexpected things start happening in Chicago and the story becomes a real thriller. The chemist's suspicions turn out to be justified. He gets on the trail of an organized gang working with great precision and murdering people who were "inconvenient" for them. The doctor from Heidelberg was to be the next victim. The "chess champion" was the head of the gang.

The doctor and the "champion" are playing the game which will decide the match. After some difficult play, a situation arises in which the doctor could improve his position by taking his opponent's chessman with his black queen. He took hold of the black queen and... then there was an unexpected interruption. Somebody knocked over the chessmen, stopping the game. It was the amateur detective. He picked up the black queen and examined it carefully. Inside it was the deadly

A special envelope with postage stamp and seal commemorating the 14th Chess Olympic Games in Leipzig, 1960.

Money coupons with chess motifs on both sides, issued at Ströbeck in Germany during the 1921 inflation.

curare, which would have been injected into the doctor's finger through a fine needle, a mechanism causing this to protrude the moment the black queen was placed on a certain square. The criminal was duly punished and all ended well.

In a thriller by the English writer Raymond Allen, "The Right Solution," an amateur detective had to know a great deal about chess to wreck the apparently cast-iron alibi of a person suspected of stealing a £1,000 banknote. The theft, carried out in the home of a certain lord, could only have occurred at a specific time which was narrowed down without a shadow of doubt to certain two minutes. All the evidence pointed towards one young girl whereas the real thief, the nobleman's secretary, had witnesses to swear that he had been in the drawing room where his master had been playing chess with a guest. The secretary, who was watching, had occasionally made suggestions during the game and, when the nobleman resigned, had showed how he could

have won it, proving his point by analysing the last few moves. The young girl's fiancé happened to be a very sharp fellow especially at chess. He gave a complicated demonstration to prove that the endgame was such that an excellent chess player, and the secretary was undoubtedly a master of the game, would have no difficulty in reconstructing the two moves made during the fatal two minutes. Moreover the secretary, during his explanations, had touched one or two of the pieces, on which stains appeared later. The amateur detective surmised that these stains had been made with invisible ink: the thief had taken the banknote out of one envelope and put it into another that he had ready, and had crossed out the original address, writing another, that of an accomplice, in invisible ink. The changing of the envelopes was discovered by accident, but the real thief's guilt was proved exclusively by way of analysing the situation on the chessboard. The story was based on a definite situation, giving

352

a diagram of the positions of the chessmen in the endgame, so that a reader who knew a bit of chess had an additional pleasure in going through the play.

INFANT PRODIGIES

Nobody has ever heard of a newborn baby being able to play chess, but children only a few years old have mastered the rules. Capablanca, later World Champion, could play at four, having learnt by watching his father play a Spanish officer. At eleven, he beat the champion of Cuba, the veteran Vadquez. Dr. Max Euwe also learnt to play at the age of four, by watching his parents at the board.

Then there was a wonder child, Milorad Bozic, the son of a Belgrade café proprietor. Little Milorad used to watch the chess players who frequented his father's café and at last tried playing himself. He was not yet seven when, to everybody's amazement, he beat them all. Invited to the local chess club, he beat many renowned players. Zweig probably had Bozic in mind when writing his "Chess Story" about the arch-champion Mirko Centovic.

Illustration by M. Orłowska-Gabryś to the Polish edition of the Arabian story about a prince turned into a monkey.

A monkey playing chess and draughts. French 17th century drawing.

353

"Is it a draw?" Czech children's post card.

Cartoon by Tetsu ("Noir et Blanc").

"You're dreaming again, and I'll win the banana." Cartoon by K. Schrader ("Eulenspiegel").

Cartoon by L. E. Karłowski ("Panorama Północy").

"I might as well admit I was a little afraid of you at first..." ("La Bataille").

354

After the First World War, we heard a lot about the Polish-born, later American, prodigy Samuel Reshevsky. At the age of six or seven, he toured Europe, then America, giving simultaneous displays against dozens of opponents.

"During the filming of "The Kid" Samuel Reshevsky, aged seven, the boy champion chess player of the world, visited the studio. He was to give an exhibition at the Athletic Club, playing chess with twenty men at the same time, among them Dr. Griffiths, the champion of California. He had a thin, pale, intense little face with large eyes that stared belligerently when he met people. I had been warned that he was temperamental and that he seldom shook hands with anybody.

After his manager introduced us and spoken a few words, the boy stood staring at me in silence. I went on with my cutting, looking at strips of film.

A moment later I turned to him. 'Do you like peaches?'

'Yes,' he answered.

'Well, we have a tree full of them in the garden; you can climb up and get some — at the same time get one for me.'

His face lit up. 'Ooh, good! Where's the tree?'

'Carl will show you,' I said, referring to my publicity man.

Fifteen minutes later he returned, elated, with several peaches. That was the beginning of our friendship.

'Can you play chess?' he asked.

I had to admit that I could not.

'I'll teach you. Come see me play tonight, I'm playing twenty men at the same time,' he said with braggadocio.

I promised and said I would take him to supper afterwards.

'Good, I'll get through early.'

It was not necessary to understand chess to appreciate the drama of that evening: twenty middle-aged men poring over their chessboards, thrown into a dilemma by an infant of seven who

"The devil plays a man for his soul." Reproduction of an allegorical painting by Moritz Retzsch, first half of the 19th century. Author unknown. (Museum of the History of Religion in Leningrad).

Scene from the French film "Evening Guests" (1942). Arletty plays the she-devil.

looked even less than his years. To watch him walking about in the centre of the table, going from one to another, was a drama in itself.

There was something surrealistic about the scene as an audience of three hundred or more sat in tiers on both sides of a hall, watching in silence a child pitting his brains against serious old

"... *The dead man was holding a knight in his hand...*" *Illustration by J. Flisak to a novel by M. Cumberland.*

men. Some looked condescending, studying with set Mona Lisa smiles.

The boy was amazing, yet he disturbed me, for I felt as I watched that concentrated face flushing red, then draining white, that he was paying a price with his health.

'Here!' a player would call, and the child would walk over, study the board a few seconds, then abruptly make a move or call 'Checkmate!' And a murmur of laughter would go through the audience. I saw him checkmate eight players in rapid succession, which evoked laughter and applause.

And now he was studying the board of Dr Griffiths. The audience were silent. Suddenly he made a move, then turned away and saw me. His face lit up and he waved, indicating that he would not be long.

After checkmating several other players, he returned to Dr Griffiths, who was still deeply concentrating. 'Haven't you moved yet?' said the boy impatiently.

The Doctor shook his head.

'Oh, come on, hurry up.'

Griffiths smiled.

The boy looked at him fiercely. 'You can't beat me! If you move here, I'll move there! And if you move this, I'll move that!' He named in rapid succession seven or eight moves ahead. 'We'll be here all night, so let's call it a draw.'

The Doctor acquiesced."

He grew up to be one of the leading chess players of the United States. Sceptics have observed that he and other child prodigies at chess often win through being under-estimated by their opponents. The youthful chess player has nothing to lose and everything to gain. As at music, however, there are talented young people with "absolute chess pitch." A child like this may not know much theory but has an instinctive feeling for the strategy and tactics of the game. The routine player may fail to adapt his knowledge to his young opponent's unusual moves.

In 1958 a sensation was caused in the Soviet Union by a five-year-old boy from Tashkent, Ernest Kim, who played wonderful chess. He even beat players of the second category and qualified as a third category player according to the rigid standards in the USSR. When asked why he had made this or that move, he would reply: "I couldn't do otherwise, I should have lost if I had." The little boy did not know how to analyse positions, but he could generally make a very good evaluation of the situation. With all his amazing mastery of chess, he was never anything but a little child, even for a moment. He was as excited about winning as another child would be about receiving a new toy and cried bitterly wh n he lost. Which reminds me, Reshevsky toonwept bitterly when as a child he lost to the grand master Rubinstein.

In Mikhail Botvinnik's opinion, a child prodigy at chess should not be allowed to play until at least eight to ten years old. If he is exceptionally talented his talent will develop in later years anyway. On the other hand, premature and excessively intensive mental effort by a child can have serious consequences on his physical and mental health.

The chess champion Dr. Tarrasch gave his views on the ability of a child to master the secrets of chess in a charming and ironical anecdote based on an authentic happening. He tells us about an eighteen-month-old toddler who showed him a decisive move in an adjourned game. It was in the Monte Carlo tournament of 1903. He was staying in the outskirts of the town with a family who had a little child. One day, playing with chess champion Marshall, he interrupted the game in a difficult position. He was a pawn to the good but might only draw, and then he would miss first prize. He sat down and began to examine the position, but he could not find a satisfactory move. His efforts had been watched with great interest by a toddler. When, finally, he gave up and started to put the pieces back in the box, the child sudden-

In the U.S.A. "He had the impertinence to take the white queen with a black pawn." Cartoon by Z. Lengren in "Przekrój."

ly cried "Aa-Aa!" It's mother came and took her pet away. Of course she did not know what the child was trying to say; but Tarrasch (or so he claims) understood it at once; he was being told to move a pawn one square further than he had intended. It was a flash of genius. The move led to victory.

Tarrasch was a fair-minded man. Players ought not to be assisted by outside persons. So at the prize-giving he openly admitted his "guilt."

THE CHESS VILLAGE

Not far from the town of Halberstadt, in the western part of the German Democratic Republic, lies the village of Ströbeck. There is nothing in its outward appearance to show that chess has become an inherent part of its traditions and local customs.

A glance at any of the official village documents reveals a big seal with a chessboard on it. On the top of the church belfry there is a chessboard instead of weathercock to indicate the direction of the wind. Young scouts in Ströbeck wear chess badges.

Chess has been a school subject there for over a century. Pupils are obliged to pass a theoretical and practical examination in chess. A young man wooing a girl used to have to beat the village bailiff at chess or pay a big fee, otherwise the wedding would not take place. When the Ströbeck bailiff was a good player, the village had a permanent income from it. This interesting custom is dying out nowadays.

How and when did chess find its way to this exceptional village?

J. Bots: "A Lost Game." An engraving dating back to the end of the 19th century.

Elaine Saunders, now Mrs. D. B. Pritchard, at eleven, when she was already a most promising player.

A Soviet cartoon of 1948: The World champion Botvinnik makes his opponents look like children ("Krokodil").

Long, long ago in the year 1068, Duke Guncelin, a Slav nobleman of the Wendic tribe, was taken prisoner of war and kept in the stone tower of Ströbeck. To kill time, he played chess, a game taught him by guards recruited from the local peasantry. Chess was gradually winning more and more popularity in the village and, as time went on, it became the passion of the population. Travellers passing through Ströbeck could easily get a game there. The fame of the village spread; kings and bishops exempted the village from certain taxes in return for its inhabitants' constant readiness to play chess. There had to be a chess set and board in every farm, so that a game could always be arranged without delay. At coronation ceremonies, young people from Ströbeck used to give a performance of "living chess," the pageant being repeated in its traditional form to this very day.

Regrettably, the old passion for playing chess has been gradually weakening of late. Yet it was still very much alive up to a few years ago;

"Dad's lost again!" (*"Münchner Illustrierte"*).

"We wanted to play chess just like daddy and uncle do."
(*"Ludas Matyi"*).

"We'll never finish this game, you must do your homework now." Cartoon by Z. Lengren ("Świat").

ignorance of the game was regarded as a kind of illiteracy. Young people are looking for other kinds of entertainment, and there are fewer and fewer old chess players. The chess village of Ströbeck is becoming more and more of a myth, a historical exhibit, and not a living beautiful example of chess being bound up with everyday work and entertainment. It would be an irreparable loss should chess in Ströbeck become nothing more but an attraction for tourists and a bait for visitors, a folk custom preserved like a museum exibit.

Chess is peculiarly popular in advertising.

Shop window displays frequently involve various commodities placed on a chessboard, the commodities can range from kitchenware to hats. Sometimes chess comes in as mere decoration, but sometimes there is a real chess significance.

For instance, a giant fly in the corner of a chessboard has been "checkmated" by other pieces representing insecticides.

I have seen chess motifs used in advertisements for underwear, optical products, drugs, food articles, machines, cigarettes, lottery tickets and innumerable other articles of everyday and not so everyday use. Slogans accompany such as "Heat waves are in check if you wear the airy shirt produced by X;" or "The best move you can make is to choose ball-bearings produced by Y; or "Z syrup checkmates influenza" and so on.

On the cover of an issue of the French magazine "Connaissance des Arts," which contained an article about the famous chess collection of Jean Maunoury, was a beautiful composition of a few pieces from the collection with an ingenious pedestal of light and dark blocks in the background. A Polish film poster advertising the Franco-Italian film "Helen and Men," conveyed the essence of the plot through chess symbols. The poster showed Helen in the background, a chessboard with her admirers as cardboard pawns — indicating their role as her playthings in the game of life.

THE CHESS FAN, UNKNOWN STRANGER

The spectator at chess is a notorious figure. He appears in many an old drawing. Without the spectator, matches and tournaments would lose much of their appeal and excitement. In this, chess has much in common with other games. But as a Soviet journalist once put it:

"... Even the most enthusiastic and temperamental football fan would never dare to think of appearing on the 'Dynamo' football pitch, with the ball at his feet, just opposite the goalkeeper. He only admires other people doing it. The boxing fan would be very embarrassed if you suggested he go into the ring to tackle the champion.

"In chess it is completely different. The spectator is bold, aggressive, and ready to fight. An onlooker will criticise almost every move, convinced the players are wrong; it is not Smyslov but the unknown talented stranger, undiscovered till now, who should be competing with the world champion.

"The reason for this is that a chess enthusiast enjoys an enviable privilege: he can play against champions. What a pleasure to take part in a simultaneous exhibition game given by a chess master! There is nothing to be lost, it is no dishonour to lose the game if one plays against a master! (I am not joking!) And if, by chance, one succeeds in winning! Oh, my goodness! Quivering with emotion and wondering how it could have happened, one gets up from one's chair seemingly complete master of oneself, gives one's name to the referee as if by accident, walks slowly to the door listening to the whispers about you.

"And this is not the end of it. After some time, when quite by chance one is talking to a group of one's friends about the defeated champion, one may say in an offhand way: 'Who? Oh, you are speaking about X? I beat him the other day.' You absent mindedly forget to mention that he

The "chess tower" in the German village of Ströbeck. Legend has it that long ago the Slav prince Guncelin, whilst imprisoned there, taught his guards how to play chess.

Members of the Pioneer youth organization at Ströbeck wear a chessboard badge.

361

Children from the "chess village" of Ströbeck going to school with their chessboards.

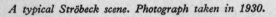

A typical Ströbeck scene. Photograph taken in 1930.

was confronting thirty-nine other people at the same time."

Open tournaments, for which anybody may enter, are not very common. Denied an adequate outlet for his ability a man may become an obtrusive spectator.

An ill-bred onlooker can be the bugbear of a club.

Such spectators are called "Kibitzers" among the Jews. They were described in an issue of Chess Weekly in 1898.

"It would be difficult to enumerate all the inconveniences suffered by chess players.

"The most painful are the Kibitzers. A disrespectful and badly behaved onlooker can be a real plague. He criticizes every move, or questions it; he blows tobacco smoke over the board or into the players' faces... he rattles his walking stick or the captured pieces; he crowds in on the players, leans on them..."

There is no remedy for chess fans. Although... a remedy was found once.

Two keen chess players were having a friendly game in their club, when two equally keen chess enthusiasts sat down beside them. Soon the air was thick with critical remarks about every move. The game became torture to the players. Requests and persuasion had no effect. Then one of the players turned round to his "fan" and said, "You know a lot about this game?" "I certainly do," replied the fan. "That's fine," said the player, "perhaps you will be so kind as to take my place for a moment?" "With pleasure." The spectator replaced the player, who left the room. A few minutes later the other player asked the other fan the same question and made the same proposal. Having been assured that his fan's abilities were superior to those of the other, the player "agreed" to give him his place for awhile.

The game did not seem to be so interesting now. Being an onlooker seemed to have suited both of them more than playing. After some time of waiting for the real players to come back, they peeped

into the next room. The traitors! The players they had so kindly replaced were quietly finishing their game on their own.

But sometimes the chess fan triumphs. The French actor Jacques Tati once recalled an amusing scene from a comedy starring the American comedian W. C. Fields.

Two men were playing chess in a café run by Fields. They had been sitting there for hours and had only drunk one glass of fruit juice each. Mr. Field's wife became annoyed. Fields went

"You've heaps of time, the next news photographer won't be here for ten minutes." Modern cartoon on Ströbeck by K. Klamann ("Eulenspiegel").

363

A Polish poster designed by Liliana Baczewska advertising the French film
"Elène et les hommes."

A Polish pre-war paper factory advertisement showing an 18th century
chess knight.

A poster by Scarolet advertising the
14th Chess Olympiad in Leipzig in
autumn 1960.

Cover of the French magazine "Connaissance des Arts" (1958) showing
a set from Maunoury's collections.

An advertisement of an American agricultural machines producer incorpora-
ting a chess king.

An advertisement for anti-flu medica-
ments by the well known Swiss firm
CIBA

up to them and, just as one of the players was
about to move a pawn, nudged him with his
elbow as a sign to delay his move. The player
made as if to move another pawn and, again, was
held back by a light kick on the shin.

The third time, however, Fields winked to the
player in approval. The move was a blunder which
lost the game at once. Fields brought them their
hats and bowed them out politely and shut up for
the night. Outside in the street they look at

364

A 13th century miniature which reminds us that the inter-fering bystander has always existed.

Women have not only played chess from olden days but liked to watch it. Miniature from the manuscript of Alfonso the Wise.

each other, one not knowing quite how he had won, the other how he had lost.

Once a spectator butted into a friendly blindfold game played by two American champions without a chessboard; the moves being conveyed vocally, the spectator shouted out a better move than the one announced. It really was a better move. The moral of which is, I suppose, that it is advisable on the whole to go about with your eyes open.

Chess players and spectators in a workers' district in London. Photo 1934.

In the Cracow "Planty" gardens you can't see the players for the onlookers.

The "silent spectator" is certainly an awkward person here. A French 18th century engraving.

An interfering onlooker has wrecked the game. A mid-19th century French lithograph.

In a London café. Drawing by L. Roberts ("Chess Pie").

The incorrigible onlooker gagged ("Panorama").

366

The onlooker-consultant ("Shakhmaty," U.S.S.R.).

A typical scene on the Vistula embankment, Cracow. Drawing by J. Bruchnalski ("Świat").

The Onlookers. Drawing by J. Skarżyński.

Charles Dullin as Kempelen, constructor of an automatic chess player, in the French film "The Chess Player" (1926).

ILLUSTRATIONS BY:

J. Agopsowicz: 348f, 349a
S. Anguisciola: 287
L. Baczewska: 364a
K. Baraniecki: 92e, 96b
M. Berezowska: 249, 251, colour
H. Bidstrup: 127
H. Bielski: 295b
L.-L. de Boilly: 80b
P. Bordone: 289
J. Bots: 358
F. Boucher: 292a
J. Bruchnalski: 367b
B. Cepleha: 159
Chaval: 116b
M. Cheremnych: 164d
Y. Cherepanov: 118
H. Chmielewski: 268, 271
D. Chodowiecki: 185, 290, 320
H. Daumier: 80a, 294
E. Delacroix: 29
G. Demetriades: 171
Desprez: 163a
N. Duboy: 292b
F. Dietrich: 219
J. Flisak: 105, 356
A. François: 96f
P. Gavarni: 314
I. Gench: 119c
I. Grinstein: 115b
J. Gris: 301
Z. and L. Haar: 157b
J. Hegen: 92f, 96e, 125c
A. Herry: 348a
J. Heyden: 25
J. E. Hummel: 295a
A. Jabłoński: 344ab, 345
M. Jamar: 348b
A. Johannet: 184
B. Jurgielewicz: 224, colour
A. Jurkiewicz: 238
L. E. Karłowski: 354d
W. Kashchenko: 145a

K. Klamann: 96g, 123abc, 363
S. Kobyliński: 93, 128a, 164b
J. Kosieradzki: 96d, 125a
Z. Kowalewski: 299a
Kovarsky: 121a
Kruger: 28
Larry: 323
Z. Lengren: 119a, 147, 181, 216b, 315, 357, 360c
E. Lipiński: 92c
Lucas van Leyden: 66
S. Łuckiewicz: 9, 49, 65, 95, 111, 131, 153, 189, 205, 237, 309
M. Majewski: 70
C. de Man: 183
P. Mant: 348e
A. Marczyński: 178, 263
A. Markowicz: 296
S. Masłowski: 298a
H. Matisse: 84
E. Meissonier: 293
L. Mendez: 165
G. Miklaszewski: 98a, 126abc
D. Milty: 146
L. Mintycz: 100
A. Mor: 210
Moreau le Jeune: 215
L. Morin: 112
M. Motty: 316
D. Mróz: 252, 255, 256
Müller: 128b
T. Murner: 350a
J. Noël: 38ab
T. Ociepka: 167
A. Orlov: 278
M. Orłowska-Gabryś: 353a
H. Parschau: 143a
J. Petry-Przybylska: colour
A. Pictor: 160
M. Pokora: 98b
J. Pop: 158b
T. Popiel: 225a

G. Rechowicz: 272, 273
M. Retzsch: 355a
D. Rewkiewicz: 299b
L. Roberts: 366c
F. Roybet: 37
E. Różańska: 300
M. Rulewicz: 16a
G. de Saint-Aubin: 218b
M. Samlicki: 298b
Scarolet: 364c
K. Schrader: 354c
I. Semyenov: 119b
S. Siennicki: 78a
E. Shcheglov: 120
J. Skarżyński: 36, 282, 285, 288, 367c, colour
W. E. Spradbery: 162b
A. Stańczyk: 71a, 74, 75, 86, 87, 88a, 89, 99, 101ab, 102ab, 107, 108, 291
V. Stuyvaent: 348d
J. M. Szancer: 196ab, 246
B. Tabey: 121b
J. Tenniel: 274, 276ab, 277
Tetsu: 119d, 354b
F. Themerson: 122a
L. Tinayre: 41
H. W. Tischbein: 321
A. Uniechowski: 264, 267, colour
O. Vereysky: 234
V. Voyevodin: 145b
E. Vuillard: 83
P. Vasilyev: 222
L. Werner: 92d
Wolff: 297
B. Yefimov: 46
J. Zaruba: 158a, 164a, colour
J. Zen: 103
J. Zitzman: 307abc, colour
J. Zubov: 96c
J. Żuławski: 156

PHOTOGRAPHERS:

T. Biernacki: 235b
A. de Blieck: 106ab
J. Borkowski: 17a, 241, 338c
H. Braun-Chotard: 115a
K. Broniewski: 27c
Constantin: 141
L. Fogiel: 228b
W. H. Fox-Talbot: 39a
S. Frey: 361ab
A. Giraudon: 15
Glogar: 172

K. Gorazdowska: 176b
A. Gros: 337
H. Hermanowicz: 27b, 168a, 229a, 335b, 365d
Kostka and Mulert: 174
S. Kragujewič: 223
C. Lukas: 230
Z. Maksymowicz: 226a
F. Nowicki: 281
Ostermayr: 31
M. Ozerskiy: 232a

L. Perz and F. Maćkowiak: 287
B. Rose: 245
L. Sempoliński: 225b, 226b
P. Skingley: 151
O. Staněk: 310, 334a
J. Świderski: 299a
W. Wolny: 300
J. Zen: 347
S. Zieliński: 342, 343
F. Zwierzchowski: 76a, 222, 295a, 298ab, 301, 310
L. Żukowski: 167

Note: Photographic reproduction of illustrations from various publications and periodicals by: Centralna Agencja Fotograficzna, I. Małek-Jarosińska, J. Zen, F. Zwierzchowski and W. Żdarski.

SOURCES OF ILLUSTRATIONS

Abenteuer des Prinzen Achmed — German film, 1926: 32

Alfonso el Sabio, *Libros de acedrex, dados e tablas*, Geneve 1941: 20, 21, 73, 208c, 365ab

H. R. d'Allemagne, *Récréations et Passe-Temps*, Paris (s.a.): 22, 23ab, 69, 71b, 79, 81, 162a, 163ab, 168ab, 192, 206, 208ab, 215, 218a, 292a, 293, 353b, 366a

Atlantic-Photo, Berlin: 134ab, 135, 195, 338b

La Bataille, Paris: 354e

Berlin National Gallery: 66, 289

M. Bessy, *Les Truquages au cinéma*, Paris 1951: 140, 216a

L. Borisov collection: 349c

J. Boyer, *Nouveaux jeux d'échecs non orthodoxes*, Paris 1951: 86, 87, 88a, 89

The British Museum: 68

Budapest Art Gallery: 183

Campo Mamula — Yugoslavian film, 1959: 319

Carelbach Gallery: 340

La Caricature, Paris: 163ab

L. Carroll, *Alice in Wonderland and Through the Looking--glass*, London 1947: 274ab., 276ab, 277

Celtic Cinéma: 370

Centrala Wynajmu Filmów: 317

Le Charivari: 80a

Chess Fever — Soviet film: 302

Chess Pie, London 1922, 1927: 40, 43b, 162b, 366c

China Reconstructs, Pekin 1956: 85ab

Chopin's Youth — Polish film: 34, 82

Cinémathèque Française, Paris: 217

Connaissance des Arts, Paris 1958: 342, 364d

M. Cumberland, *Mat w trzech ruchach*: 356

Cyrulik Warszawski, Warszawa 1931: 164a

DEFA, Berlin: 30

The Deserter — Polish film 1958: 304a

Dikobraz, Praha 1958: 158b, 159

Dookoła Świata, Warszawa 1954: 127

L'Échiquier de France, Paris 1956: 160

L'Échiquier de Paris, Paris 1949, 1950, 1951: 122b, 124a, 313, 348de

Échecs nouvellement moralisés (MS): 22

L'Écran Française, Paris 1945: 182

8 × 8 — film by Hans Richter 1957: 202a, 306c

Eremitage: 84

Express Wieczorny, Warszawa 1954: 126a-c, 233b

Eulenspiegel, Berlin 1954, 1956: 96g, 123a-c, 143a, 354c, 363

Evening Guests — French film, 1942: 355b

Frischer Wind, Berlin 1954: 92bf, 96e, 125b

Garmont, Paris: 303b

Die Geschichte vom kleinen Muck — German film: 30

The Ghost in the Palace — Polish puppet film, 1960: 149

J. Giżycki collection: 43a, 47, 48b, 91, 114, 176a, 324, 325, 347, 350b, 351ab, 354a, 364b, 366b

Goskinofond, Moskva: 302a-f

Gotha Schloss Museum: 210, 321

A. Górny collection: 338c

H. R. Grätz collection: 72

A Guide to the Mediaeval Antiquities and Objects of Later Date, British Museum Catalogue, London 1924: 18a

C. Hálova-Jahodova, *Vergessene Handwerkskunst*, Praha 1955: 310, 334a

A. Hammond, *The Book of Chessmen*, London 1950: 14, 169, 170, 330ab, 332, 333

Hussite Trilogy — Czechoslovak film; 211

W. Hausenstein, *Rococo*, München 1918: 218b

H. Havard, *Dictionaire de l'ameublement et de la décoration*, Paris: 180, 209

F. H. Hoffmann, *Das Porzellan*, Berlin 1932: 27a, 177

C. Hüther, *Schnell Mat!* München 1913: 288, 289

I. Ilf and E. Petrov, *Dwanaście krzeseł*: 268, 271

Illusion — German film, 1941: 303a

Illustrated, London 1947: 198a-d

L'Illustration Journal Universel, Paris 1951: 38ab

Ilustrowany Kurier Codzienny, Kraków 1932: 200

Institute of Art, PAN (Polish Academy of Sciences), Warszawa: 27c, 167

K. Irzykowski, *Pałuba*, Warszawa 1948: 228a

Istoria kultury drevniei Rusi, Moskva 1948: 16b

Ivan the Terrible — film by S. Eisenstein, 1945: 203, 214

Izogiz, Moskva 1956: 48a

M. Jastrun, *Poeta i dworzanin*, Warszawa 1954: 224

S. Jeleński, *Lilavati*, Warszawa 1954: 101

M. Jókai, *Szachy*: 263

A. Jurkiewicz, *Podręcznik metody grafiki artystycznej*, Kraków 1938: 254

Kalendarz Rodzinny, Kraków 1956: 367c

Karuzela, Łódź 1959: 96ab

Keystone, Paris-London: 44, 194ab, 362ab

Printed in England